The Commedia Dell'Arte: A Study in Italian Popular Comedy

Winifred Smith

BIBLIOLIFE

J. Callot.

SCAPPINO.

THE COMMEDIA DELL'ARTE

A STUDY IN ITALIAN
POPULAR COMEDY

BY

WINIFRED SMITH, Ph.D.

New York
THE COLUMBIA UNIVERSITY PRESS
1912

PREFACE.

A small Pennsylvania town turned itself out one breathless summer day not long ago to watch an entertainment given in a large airy barn by a family of wandering geniuses, not gypsies or minstrels, certainly not "agents" as the term is generally understood, but hard-headed Yankee originals with something of their own to sell and apparently a novel way of their own of selling it. The something was a certain soap, guaranteed of the purest; the method of advertisement was to take it as the theme of a simple farce, a theme varied by all manner of songs in its praises and allusions to its perfections, brought as by accident into the pauses of a banal dialog.

In the brief play each member of the band had a part. The leader represented himself as a fashionable doctor, the rush of whose city practice had driven him to the country for leisure and fresh air; his brother figured as a wealthy friend of the physician, a millionaire off for a holiday; the doctor's two young sons flirted madly with the millionaire's pretty daughter and quarreled with each other about her behind their parents' backs; the smaller children in the rôles of errand-boy, page and petted little housemaid saw to it that the audience was kept smiling at their tricks, their blunders and their comical songs. The plot, such as it was, centered only incidentally around the young people's love affairs, essentially on the doctor's scientific pursuits, the object of the

vii

latter being of course the discovery of a formula for
an absolutely peerless soap, one which would make
the dingiest complexion bloom with health and that
after one application. The lovers vied with each
other in helping their father to the discovery, for the
millionaire, some of whose capital was sunk in the
experiment, had promised his daughter and his fortune to the lucky man. When the elder son proved
the efficacy of his particular recipe by washing
away the yellowness from his father's wrinkled
cheeks and leaving them firmly and evenly ruddy,
when he was rewarded as he deserved by a parcel of
bonds and a bride,—a climax greeted by whoops,
songs and hand-springs from the younger members
of the company,—is it any wonder that the audience
flocked up to the stage to buy pounds of so magical a
cosmetic?

The lively spectacle, quivering in the dusty heat
of an American July, induced in the mind of one
spectator instead of the practical judgment of the
majority of the audience a mood of reflective reminiscence. Here was a scene in all its essentials
similar to others enacted hundreds of times in sixteenth century Italy by traveling charlatans who
chose just such a miscellaneous farcical vaudeville
performance for advertising their vilely compounded nostrums, and yet so different were the
details, the local color, the character of the audience
and of the setting, that the modern situation demanded no small effort of imagination to relate it to
those older farces, with which of course it could
have had not the slightest direct connection. Such

connection as exists lies merely in the fact that this rural seller of soap and his professional ancestors in the sixteenth century, like the actors of vaudeville on Broadway at present, for mercenary purposes of their own take advantage in similar fashion of the ordinary man's need for purely recreative amusement, by consulting his thoughtless prejudices in the expression of commonplace social satire and by provoking him to uproarious laughter as he follows a simple intrigue or a series of rough jokes. The likeness therefore between the characteristics of ancient and modern farces should, I feel sure, be attributed much more to their like function—just this response to an ever-present demand for carefree recreation—than to any hypothetical line of evolution drawn through the centuries from the old to the recent, from the Roman mime to the comic opera, for instance, by way of Italian *commedia dell'arte* and French pantomime.

The following study in popular comedy has resulted from an effort to find material for testing the hypothesis that I have just stated and further—at first by the way—from an attempt to open up to English students of the drama a byway in their field little known to them. The *commedia dell'arte,* interesting and for comparative purposes important as it is, has received many tributes of passing mention and inexact allusion from our scholars and critics, but except for the two brilliant and vivid essays of John Addington Symonds and Vernon Lee, no study worthy the name; even these two treatments are inadequate, centered as both are on eigh-

teenth century developments and taking little account of earlier days and their complex problems.
It seemed accordingly time to bring together in English some of the widely scattered facts and theories
about the improvised plays and to point out their
significance for our own literature.

Materials for such a synthesis are not lacking.
The Italian professional actors, who in the Renaissance evolved these extempore farces, have left no
no scanty or uncertain memorials behind them; there
abound letters telling of their struggles and successes, books of their poetical compositions for the
adornment of bare plots, collections and scattered
leaves of the plots themselves, and in various
archives records from which we can reconstruct
imaginatively some of the actual performances.
Moreover Italian and French scholars have turned
over and expounded and related so great a mass of
these dusty documents as to smooth and make plain
the way to any foreign student who may wish to
investigate the subject. My indebtedness to the
work of these men, particularly to that of Adolfo
Bartoli, Alessandro d'Ancona, Michele Scherillo,
Benedetto Croce and Armand Baschet, is naturally
even greater than I can acknowledge in bibliography
and footnotes. In the field of the foreign relationships of the *commedia dell'arte* there remains much
to do; France has been pretty thoroughly searched
especially for the period of Molière; on Italian
comedy in Spain little that is satisfactory is as yet
published; as to Elizabethan and Jacobean England
I feel fairly sure that if more definite traces and

names of Italian actors in London at that period are
unearthed, there will be no difficulty in adding to the
suggestions I have brought together, some further
proof of the existence and the influence of the *commedia dell'arte* in England.

It is not only to foreign scholars that I realize my
indebtedness as I look back over the progress of this
little book. Professor John W. Cunliffe, Associate
Director of the School of Journalism, Columbia University, who almost alone of American scholars is
investigating the interrelations of Elizabethan and
Italian drama, has taken a very helpful interest in
my work. To many of my friends and to several of
my fellow-students at Columbia University, to my
colleagues in the Department of English at Vassar
College, most of all to several members of the Division of Modern Languages at Columbia, I am under
heavy obligations. Professor Arthur A. Livingston
has made a number of suggestions on matters of
detail. Professor Ashley H. Thorndike has been
especially kind, not only in reading the manuscript
twice but in offering much valuable criticism. To
Professor Jefferson B. Fletcher, who first suggested
the *commedia dell'arte* to me as a subject worth investigating, and who has been unwearied in his interest and helpfulness throughout my study, I owe
not only particular thanks on many scores, but much
gratitude for very far-reaching illuminations of the
wider meanings of scholarship. Finally the study I
have done with Professor John Dewey has been of
vital importance in helping to formulate my point of
view. My friend, Mrs. J. S. P. Tatlock, and two

others, who from personal interest have read the manuscript entire, must accept this bare acknowledgment as a mere symbol of deeper feeling; these last two are my brother, Dr. Preserved Smith, of Amherst College, in constant and close touch with my work and never unfruitfully, and Professor Laura J. Wylie, of Vassar College, from my undergraduate days my most stimulating critic and always an untiringly generous friend.

TABLE OF CONTENTS.

ARLECCHINO.

CHAPTER I.

"Contemplo nella commedia dell'arte un pregio dell'Italia."
(*Carlo Gozzi.*)

Many people who have never heard of the *commedia dell'arte* have enjoyed *Le Mariage de Figaro* or *Don Giovanni*, or have seen Watteau's and Lancret's pictures of Italian comedians—Gilles and Pierrot—or have smiled at a Christmas pantomime, gay with bespangled Colombines and Harlequins. Again they may possibly have laughed at a Punch and Judy show, or have watched some Mardi-Gras carnival in which black-masked and patchwork-costumed clowns tickle with wooden daggers a kilted soubrette or a long-robed, spectacled Pantaloon. Or if they are practical folk, unused to such holiday gaieties, they may still characterize an enemy as a "miserable zany" or a campaign speech as "a mere harlequinade." Such and even more diverse, are the traces left by "Italy's pride" on the surface of our modern life; when we dig deeper we find roots that spread far and are interlaced with many a foreign growth.

Disengaging the original stem from others as nearly as may be, we can follow it back quite clearly to about the middle of the sixteenth century when it begins to have a life of its own. The Italian stage in the Cinquecento was richer than that of any other country, rich in popular farces and moralities, rich

2   1

in academic pieces imitated from the classics; they crowd upon each other most confusingly, as we try hopelessly to separate the May dance from the *bruscello*, the *farsa* from comedy or from allegorical morality. Yet among them all the *commedia dell'arte* is one of the few kinds of entertainment that may be loosely defined even by those who despair of arriving at any satisfactory classification of literary genres. Here the definition is not to be made on the basis of subject-matter, for that is most various, but by a peculiarity of form. A *commedia dell'arte* was always in part the transitory creation of the individual actors who played it; the plot was known to each member of the troupe, so well-known, indeed, that an entrance or an exit was never missed, but the dialog was chiefly left to be struck out by the suggestion of the moment. Hence the name,—*commedia dell'arte all'improvviso*, professional improvised comedy, for only the actor profession or gild, *arte*, could be sure enough of itself and sufficiently at home on the stage to play without being tied to lines. Dilettanti noblemen and academicians did, to be sure, try their skill occasionally in this difficult art, as in the first recorded performance of the kind, that at the Bavarian court in 1568;[1] yet such gentle-

---

[1] Cf. V de Amicis, *Com. pop. latina*, etc., 13; he says the name was "inventato appunto in quel tempo (i. e., the sixteenth century) per distinguere queste specie di rappresentazioni, fatte da gente mercenaria, da commedianti di mestiere, che facevano *un'arte* a fino di lucro, da quelle di commedie erudite, scritte secondo le norme degli autori classici, che si facevano da letterati, accademici, o dilettanti nelle corti, nelle sale di palazzi principeschi ed in private accademie."

Other amateur performances of improvised plays are recorded by Bartoli, *Scen. inediti*, cl, note 6; one dates from 1686, the other from 1753.

men usually confined their histrionic efforts to the easier "sustained" or "learned" written drama and left the improvised to professionals.

This simple definition of our comedy by form alone is really the only workable one. Any attempt to limit its content results in a confusion like that of the traveling players in *Hamlet:* "Tragedy, comedy, history, pastoral, pastoral-comical, historical-pastoral, tragical-comical - historical - pastoral," — the Italians played them all, both in free improvised, and in formal written versions. Should we adopt the usual English synonym, the Comedy of Masks, we should again be inexact; the Masks, as certain of the characters were called from the grotesque visards they wore to heighten their comic effect, were after all not very different from the persons of written plays; even with the special *commedia dell'arte* names and costumes they often appear in regular comedies, particularly in those of late date, and therefore they ought not to be made a distinguishing mark of the improvised pieces.[2] A third test has sometimes been applied, the *lazzi,* or comic business, with which these plays were so overloaded,[3] yet what lively stage is without such ap-

[2] Allacci, *Dramaturgia, passim,* gives a number of titles of written plays in which the Masks figure, as *Il Pantalone innamorato,* by G. Briccio (Viterbo, 1629); *Il Pantalone impazzito,* by F. Rigelli (Viterbo, 1609).

[3] *Lazzi* is defined by Riccoboni, *Hist. du théâtre italien,* 65: "Nous appellons lazzi ce que Arlequin ou les autres Acteurs masqués font au milieu d'une Scène qu'ils interrompent par des épouvantes, ou par des badineries étrangères au sujet de la matière que l'on traite, et à laquelle on est pourtant obligé de revenir: or ce sont ces inutilités qui ne consistent que dans le jeu que l'acteur invente suivant son génie."

Lazzi, according to a doubtful etymology, comes from the Tuscan

peals to a primitive sense of fun? The devil in the Mysteries chased sinners off to Hell-mouth with blows as resounding as those inflicted by Arlecchino on his master's rivals, and Shakespeare's Fools play practical jokes on each other nearly as often as do the Italian Zanni.

Whenever even the loosest definition is laid down it must of course immediately be qualified. If improvisation is to be the test for marking off the *commedia dell'arte*, it must at once be stated that the improvisation was never more than partial. Not only was the scenario[4] or plot outline written in some detail, with entrances and exits noted, but each player possessed a book which he filled with compositions either original or borrowed, suitable to his rôle.[5] One actor rarely took more than one kind of part, whether he learned or improvised it; if he were young, handsome and sentimental, he was cast

word *lacci*, bonds, because these tricks bound the action together. Cf. Re's discussion, Gior. Stor., LV, 329.

[4] The word *scenario* for the plot outline does not seem to have been used before the beginning of the nineteenth century; *soggetto* was the earlier word, or simply *comedia.* Cf. Brouwer, *Ancora una Raccolta,* etc., 393, note 4.

[5] N. Barbieri, himself an actor and playwright, bears witness to this practice in *La Supplica,* Chap. VIII: "The actors study to adorn their memories with a great provision of things such as sententious remarks, figures of speech, love discourses, rebukes, desperations and ravings, in order to have them ready at need; and their studies are appropriate to the kind of part they represent."

Perucci, *Dell'arte rappresentativa,* 364 f., lists and gives examples of "primuscite, disperazioni, dialoghi, rimproveri, saluti, paralelli." Cf. Croce, Gior. Stor., XXXI, 458 f., a description of a MS. collection dated 1734, of a "wealth of rags and literary scraps" in the form of prologs, sketches for plots, *lazzi,* poems, monologs for the Doctor's rôle, etc.

for first or second lover and memorized Petrarchan laments and rhapsodies: if his skill lay in counterfeiting the "childish treble of old age," he played the pedant Doctor Gratiano, or the

> . . . lean and slipper'd Pantaloon,
> With spectacles on nose and pouch on side,

and made up long paragraphs of nonsensical, would-be-wise saws and "counsels to youth" on the order of Polonius' farewell to Laertes; if he preferred "Ercles" vein, a tyrant's vein, or "a part to tear a cat in, to make all split," he figured as the Capitano Spavento, or Rodomontade, or Slay-the-Moors, and composed tirades full of the wildest exaggerations and the most impossible feats; if he were merely a comical fellow, he studied out *lazzi* suited to the clown's part and appeared all his life as a Zanni,— Pedrolino, Arlecchino, Pulcinella, as the case might be. The actresses too had their aids to eloquence, though for the women the choice of parts was narrower; the *prima donna* was naturally the most poetical and lackadaisical, and drew for inspiration largely on the sonneteers; the *seconda donna* was her paler shadow; the *servetta*—Franceschina or Colombina—kept closer to earth, had always a ready and none too squeamish word for everyone, and in love speeches to her adorers parodied ludicrously enough her mistress's romantic flights; the old woman, who sometimes though rarely appeared, had often an unsympathetic rôle and got through it with the plainest words possible and few of them.[6] All

---

[6] The Masks were neither so few nor so simple as this general classification might lead one to think; a broadly inclusive list is how-

these "conceits" are very similar to the speeches of corresponding characters in the fully written comedies and are not unlike the language of the more affected of our Elizabethans, Nathaniel Field for instance. Even the dialects, supposed to mark off the Masks of the *commedia dell'arte*, are to be found in the learned plays as well, often in great variety.[7] Again English drama offers a parallel, for from certain early moralities and interludes to *Henry V* and the *Merry Wives of Windsor*, dialects were freely and successfully used to give comic tone. Even in our own day the vaudeville stage makes capital of Irish Paddies and French barons and English dukes.

Although the Masks resemble the personages of written plays who are partly responsible for their existence, they had also distinctions of their own. In the first place they were almost entirely the creatures of whatever actors happened to be interpreting a given scenario,—they were not poetically realized characters but pawns in the plot,—and secondly each one tended to assume a stereotyped habit and name, more significant, really, than anything he might do. When Pantalone de'Bisognosi came on in the long black robe and scarlet hose of a Magnifico of Venice, the audience knew at once that according

ever easy to make because only the outlines of characters remain in the scenarios, all their life and variety came from the genius of the actor who filled in the outlines. Cf. a list of some twenty-five minor Masks in G. Petrai's *Lo spirito delle maschere*, and cf. Bartoli, *Scen. ined.*, clxi f., for the names of the principal actors in different rôles.

[7] Cf. below, chapter II, on Beolco and Calmo. V. Verucci's *Li diversi linguaggi* (Venetia, 1609) contains French and the dialects of Venice, Bergamo, Bologna, Rome, Naples, Perugia and Florence. Such a mixture was in no way peculiar to Verucci's style.

to convention he would speak Venetian patois, would
be stupid, avaricious and amorous and the dupe of
the young people in the intrigue.[8] His old crony,
Gratiano, or Doctor Gratiano as he is called in the
more ancient scenarios, was oftenest from Bologna,
and wore the gown and hood of that university, with
in addition a mask blotched by wine stains to contra-
dict slyly his dignified garb. His rôle varies; like
Pantalone he is sometimes the husband, sometimes
the father of one of the heroines of the piece, and is
generally in love with another young woman. In
pursuit of their ends these two old fools are willing
to condescend to any disguise and are therefore
unmercifully baited by the hero and his servant.
Gratiano figures in early scenarios now as a charlatan, now as a pedagog, sometimes a councillor,
again—shade of Malvolio!—a majordomo, most
often a legal authority or a doctor of medicine.[9]

[8] Pantalone's name has given a good deal of trouble to students;
he was quite certainly not christened after St. Pantaleone, nor does
he seem to have been named because he represents a Magnifico who
planted the lion of Venice in the Levant. A modern derivation from
the Greek, *pantos-elemon*, seems still less likely; cf. Piangiani,
Vocabolario etimologico, and J. A. Symonds' discussion, *Mem. of
Count C. Gozzi*, I, 44. The name Pantalone was semi-proverbial by
1568 whatever its derivation.

[9] Bartoli, *Scen. inediti*, xviii f. and 1 f., studies some of the variations of this Mask. A modern rather superficial analysis of the
Doctor in his later developments is Sarti's *Teatro dialettale bolognese;* the author shows how Gratiano persisted on the popular stage
in dialect farces, well on into the nineteenth century; cf. especially,
131 f.

The origin of Gratiano's name is no clearer than that of Pantalone's.
The creator of the Mask, according to the older scholars, was Luzio
Burchiello who subscribed himself *Lus Burchiello Gratià* and who
imitated an old barber, Gratiano delle Celtiche; cf. Quadrio, *Storia*

Whatever his station in life and his relation to the other characters, his manners and morals are much the same, his speech alternately maccaronic Latin nonsense and Bolognese riddles or gnomic sayings of evident folk ancestry, often indecent in their double meaning.

The old men's almost invariable enemy, a butt who had seldom a friend in the play, was the Captain, a Spaniard usually, copied from life after the hated foreign mercenaries who crowded sixteenth century Italy. Each actor impersonating him gave a slightly different turn to his countenance, wore his hat and his moustache cocked at a different angle and changed the color of his cape and the size of his sword, but one and all followed the general outlines laid down by the Thrasos and bravos of written plays and by the first famous Captain of the *commedia dell'arte,* created by Francesco Andreini.[10] A boastful, cowardly bully, always in love and always unsuccessful, he took small part in the plot except as an object for the wit of others to prey upon,—in that

e ragione, etc., V, 219. Ancona, commenting on this (*Origini,* II, 446, note I) prefers to agree with the derivation of the Doctor from the "canonist Graziano." If Gratian were indeed the learned original of all the foolish clowns who caricatured under his name pretentious scholars, until "a Gratiano" became a synonym for fool, the distortion would be no more curious than that of Duns Scotus' unfortunate first name into our English dunce, or that of great-souled Hector into a verb meaning to bully. However Gratiano is not an uncommon Italian name and may have been adopted simply for its humorous suggestion of grace and favor, so ill-assorted to the character.

[10] Benigaglia, *Cap. Spavento,* is the best single study of this Mask. Cf. also Scherillo, *Commedia dell'arte in Italia,* Chap. IV, and Rasi, *Comici italiani,* under Andreini, F.

capacity he seems to have been unfailingly delightful to his audiences. As he was one of the first figures to appear in the improvised plays—there is a "Spanish desperado" in the oldest known scenario—so he is one of the longest lived; under various names he trod the boards all through the seventeenth century, indeed his ghost still walks and talks in the Neapolitan marionette theater as Rogantino or Guappo. And everyone I suppose, knows Gautier's *Capitaine Fracasse,* a sympathetic attempt to clothe an old idea with flesh.[11]

Of the tiresomely monotonous lovers around whom all the other personages circle, there is no need to say more than a word here. They were never Masks, that is, they played with uncovered faces and spoke the most polished Tuscan instead of some provincial dialect; they were in short in the *commedia dell'arte* just about what the academicians had made them in written comedies, centers of the plot and mouthpieces for love speeches. The Zanni, however, was a Mask, or rather an infinite variety of Masks. Always of humble station, usually the servant and confidant of a principal character,[12] sometimes a rascal, sometimes a dunce, oftenest a complex mixture of the two, almost always the chief plotweaver,—his main function was to rouse laughter,

[11] It is odd that Gautier named his Gascon Fracasse, for Fracasso was at first a good-for-nothing more like Pulcinella than like the Capitano. The earliest Captains, those pictured in Callot's *Balli di Sfessania* ("little dancers"), are called Cardino, Zerbino, Cerimonia, etc.

[12] Scala's Burattino is, however, occasionally an inn-keeper, a bailiff or a majordomo, and Pulcinella, as Croce points out, was a whole collection of persons in himself. Cf. Croce, *Pulcinella,* passim.

to entertain at all costs.[13] One of the means he took to this end was the use of some patois, generally Bergamask, not infrequently Neapolitan; another was his curious costume and mask; the most effective of all were his actions, his surprisingly dexterous gymnastic feats, his multifarious disguises and his absurd songs and *lazzi*. Popular horseplay of this sort is invariably made up of very old traditional jokes, so it is not extraordinary to find that some of Zanni's names point back to a remote antiquity.

Arlecchino's origin has by some adventurous souls been traced to that fearful spirit of the night, Hellequin, who with his *mesnie* rode the air in the wildest medieval imaginations,[14] hence, they say, his more than human agility and careless deviltry. Pulcinella, it appears from the latest investigations,

[13] Riccoboni, *Hist. du théâtre italien*, Chap. II. All the characters in the improvised plays of course aimed chiefly to rouse laughter, but Zanni tried harder and succeeded better than the others.

[14] For the French Hellequin cf. Raynaud, in *Etudes romanes dédiées à Gaston Paris*, 51 f., and O. Driessen, *Ursprung des Harlekin*. Dante mentions Alichino among his grimly comic devils, *Inferno*, XXI, line 118, and XXII, 112 f. Cf. Wesselofsky, *Alichino e Aredodesa*, Gior. Stor., XI, 325 f.

Renier, *Arlecchino*, Fanfulla della domenica, Anno XXVI, no. 12, gives a sensible summary of the problem, showing that the tradition of the diabolical Charivari existed in Italy as well as in France, and admitting that the "transition from the devil-clown to the Zanni-Arlecchino" is very hard to trace. All that we know is that Arlecchino appeared on the stage at least as early as 1574 when Ganassa played the part in Spain, and that he figures prominently among Scala's Zanni, before 1611. Whether the protection accorded to Zanni in Paris by Achille de Harley affected the name of the Italian clown as some have thought, seems exceedingly doubtful; cf. Sand, *Masques et Bouffons*, I, 73, and Bartoli's criticism, *Scen. inediti*, clxxiv.

has an ancestor at least as illustrious as Arlecchino, preferable perhaps as being historical instead of mythical; his name at least, whether or not any conclusions may be drawn therefrom as to character resemblances, is the same as that of a restless and grotesque patriot of thirteenth century Verona, Pulcinella dalle Carceri.[15] It may be a stretch of imagination to see a popular memory of this adventurer preserved in the Pulcinelli of carnival songs, whether of the fourteenth century or of Sicily to-day; the facts are that such Pulcinelli are mentioned as long ago as 1363 and that it was probably from them Silvio Fiorillo took the name and idea for the Mask he created in the early seventeenth century. From that time on Pulcinella takes his part in numerous scenarios and written plays; Scala does not use him, but he appears in other plots, now as peasant, now as merchant, or as painter, soldier, thief or bandit, always as the successful lover of Colombina.[16] In G. B. della Porta's outline, *La Trapolaria,* he is a silly old burgess, who among other performances disguises himself as a Turkish slave-girl.

[15] Fainelli, in Gior. Stor., LIV, 59 f., makes the connection between Pulcinella dalle Carceri and the Pulcinelli of carnival songs. The best study of this Zanni in comedy is Croce's *Pulcinella,* etc. The name may possibly mean little cock, as some have thought from the birdlike mask worn by Pulcinella. Or there may have been an actor who gave his name to his creation long before Fiorillo: Croce has discovered a Joan Polcinella in 1484 (cf. his *Teatri di Napoli,* 689) and Scherillo records a Lucio Pulcinella who flourished about 1572. (*Comm. dell'arte,* 57–8 and 68–9.)

Cf. Rasi, *Comici italiani,* I, 921 f., and for the modern carnival figure, Pitrè, *Studi di poesia popolare,* 58 f.

[16] Cf. the description of Passante's scenarios by Croce, Gior. Stor., XXIX, 211 f. For Porta's scenario, cf. Scherillo, *Comm. dell'arte,* Chap. VI.

With Arlecchino and Pulcinella are to be grouped
Brighella, Pedrolino, Mezzetino, Cola, Trappolino,
and innumerable other Zanni, hard to classify because they vary with every actor of the rôle. None
of them wears so bizarre a suit as Arlecchino, whose
many colored patches are reminiscent of his original
rags, yet they all have some ludicrous peculiarity of
dress and they are all as adroit as Arlecchino in
their use of comic tricks and gestures. Ability to
move quickly was the first requisite for the clown;
on this he had to depend for the effectiveness of his
instantaneous maskings and unmaskings, and the
appearances and disappearances that so mystified
slow-witted old Pantalone and Gratiano and propor-
tionately delighted the audience. Brains, too, had
to move as quickly as muscles if Zanni were to fulfil
his function of embroiling as much as possible his
master's rivals and even, with pretended stupidity,
his master himself and the heroine. Sometimes he
did this by disguising two lovers of the same lady in
the same style and sending them to meet under her
window where a fight was sure to ensue; frequently,
by ventriloquism in the manner of Ariel,[17] he imitated different voices and led on his impatient dupes
to their own confounding; again he would dress himself as a ghost or a lunatic or in a gown exactly like
that of the heroine or her maid, and so cause either
terror or confusion;[18] still more remarkable he was
able in his own person to play several parts, even on

[17] Cf. scenario published by Toldo, Gior. Stor., XLVI, 128, and that
published by Martucci, Nuova Antologia, Ser. II, No. LI, 223 f.

[18] The ghost motif is found most often in the early plays; cf.
Scala's Gior. I, Act I, Gior. VII, Act I, and elsewhere in his book.

occasion simultaneously.[19] The ancient repertory
of practical jokes was drawn upon again and again,
—blows, trips, stumbles, starts of causeless fright,
pretence of stupidity, misinterpretation of orders
with laughable results, puns and satiric repartee, all
these ways of rousing mirth, ways still thriving on
our vaudeville stage, were the chief stock in trade
of the *commedia dell'arte*.[20]

Just when the tricks came to be conventionalized
and listed for the benefit of their performers is not
very certain; Scala's book contains few evidences
that the *lazzi* had become by 1611 as stereotyped as
the "conceits," whereas Perucci about a century
later draws up a long table of apparently well-known

[19] Cf. *Arlequin lingère du Palais*, Gherardi, *Théâtre*, etc., I, 61 f.;
Arlequin dressed half as a man and half as a woman, bobs in and
out of two adjoining booths, alternately offering Pascariel linen and
lemonade, and in his double rôle, abusing himself and even aiming
blows at himself in the most ridiculous way. Similar double parts are
still to be seen to-day in the popular theatres of Italy and Spain and
are not unknown in city vaudevilles. The device is, I suppose, merely
a kind of objectification of a mock-serious debate with oneself, of
the sort that Shakespeare often used in the comic soliloquies of his
clowns; Launcelot Gobbo's remarks, *Merchant of Venice*, II, 2, offer
an excellent chance for a dramatisation of the two disputing elements
in the boy's own mind.

[20] Old jokes constantly reappear in the scenarios. For example the
central incident of Scala's *Cavadenti* is the same as that introduced
in a minor part of Boccaccio's ninth novella (*Decameron*, Gior. VIII)
which in turn goes back to the medieval *Comoedia Lydiae*; of Francia,
Gior. Stor., XLIX, 201 f., especially 224. In one of the later eighteenth century scenarios (cf. *Dict. des théâtres de Paris*, VI, 195 f.)
Gratiano and Pantalone are hung in two baskets at an equal distance
from the ground because they had confided in the promise of a servant
to introduce them to her mistress through the window. The same joke
was played on Virgil and Hippocrates according to a medieval tale.
Cf. Comparetti, *Virgilio nel medio evo*, II, 109.

jokes, as the "*lazzo* of fear," "of weeping and laughing," "of knocking at the door," "of the slipper,"
and "of crying loudly."[21]   The process of recognizing, labeling and classifying the *lazzi* must have
begun in the Cinquecento, for in Porta's scenario
just mentioned, there are noted the "trick of going
back to knock" and "of hiding" and "the I-don't-
know-you dodge," all as though familiar to the
actor. Presumably they made the basis of a book
of reference like those of the set speeches for the
other players. Zanni had also, however, written
compositions of his own; he often spoke the prolog
or epilog to the comedy, and in the course of his love
affairs with the *servetta* he had need of "com-
plaints" (for beatings as well as for slighted love)
"passions," serenades and sonnets.[22]   No one firmly
defined character is behind these speeches of course;
they merely express incoherently enough, sentiments
and opinions appropriate to the cleverest, the most
plain-spoken, the most satirical and the most cynical
of the Italian Masks, for whom the insensate rap-
tures of a lover are only food for mirth.[23]

[21] For other *lazzi* cf. Croce, Gior. Stor., XXXI, 459 f.

[22] Bocchini, *Corona Maccheronica*, I, 6 f., preserves a number of
speeches for the servants' rôles, for "Zagna" as well as for Zagno;
cf. II, 28 f., for a typical Petrarchan cursing sonnet, burlesqued, to
be used as a clown's serenade.

For the *servetta* cf. Scherillo, *Comm. dell'arte*, Chap. II, and
Guillemot, Revue Contemporaine, 15 mai, 1886, 97 f.

[23] One Zanni thus expresses the unromantic view of love to his
master: "This love has made you timid, from a brave man it has
turned you into a coward, from a wise man into a fool, from sensible
to silly, from a Spanish charger it has changed you to a mule, for
from the hour you fell in love you have made nothing but trouble,
singing your sonnet nonsense through the streets, your Petrarch in

Yet a love intrigue, usually doubled and even tripled, is the life of the Italian plays as of the Elizabethan.[24] In every case the *commedia dell'arte* tends to be more lively, more exaggerated, more disheveled than her formal sister, but allowing for the difference in their dress, the resemblance between them is striking. It is the style of drama familiar to us in the *Comedy of Errors,* the *Two Gentlemen of Verona,* some of Chapman's, Middleton's and Jonson's comedies, in short the less serious plays of our great age which combine material from the novellas with borrowings from Plautus and Terence. Only, be it remembered, the English imagination is colder even in the sixteenth century than the Italian, English taste more hesitant to report or to enlarge upon immoral complications and to jest with ribaldry. If the *Decameron* is truly the fount of all Italian comedy as it certainly is of many single plays, it is the *Decameron* unexpurgated, unsoftened, not refined as Shakespeare refined it in *All's Well.* In the improvised farces especially, a popular amusement above all things and at least in its beginnings an amusement for men alone, the unsavoriness of the fable was intensified by acting and by jokes far more impudent than the English stage knew in its most unregenerate days.[25]

your fist." (*Gl' amorosi inganni,* by V. Belando, Paris, 1609, Act I, sc. 13.)
[24] The complication of plot as a characteristic of Renaissance drama is well illustrated by a comparison of Cecchi's *Rivali* to the *Casina* of Plautus, Gior. Stor., XXII, 417 f.
[25] The better Italian actors were constantly having to apologize for

Not that there was not always an underlying theme
of at least apparent dignity! Those commonplaces
of fashionable Renaissance discussion, the opposition of love to fortune or to friendship or to duty,
were worked out in the academic plays under the
guise of a rivalry between father and son or between
a pair of youths for the favor of one mistress; or
in the story of a father's recovery of his long lost
children, or in the winning back of a faithless lover
by a constant maiden. The *commedia dell'arte* took
these themes and twisted them to suit its purpose of
merrymaking; shameless old men and still more
shameless young people attempt to get their wills
through a series of outlandish maskings and tricks,
and disguises like those of Viola in *Twelfth Night*
and Imogen in *Cymbeline* occasion mistakes quite
other than those permitted by Shakespeare's sympathy for his heroines. In all these intrigues it is
the subplot group of characters, the servingmen and
maids, who set the tone for the piece as well as plan
most of its complications; endowed with more wit

their profession. Cf. N. Barbieri's *Supplica* and P. M. Cecchini's
Moderne commedie, passim.

Baschet, *Comédiens italiens*, etc., gives an account of the difficulties the Italians had with the authorities in Paris, because of the
immorality of their plays. Priests, like the Jesuit Ottonelli, launched
execrations at the abandoned character of their country's theater and
urged in vain a more decent comedy. Ottonelli says the most harmful
plays are those given indoors, but this is only because robbery and
other ill deeds could more easily be committed in a hall than on the
piazza; cf. *Della christiana moderatione*, 457. The priest further
accuses the *commedia dell'arte* in particular (p. 29), "I Zanni,
Covielli, Pantaloni . . . e simili . . . voglion cavare il Ridicolo dall'-
oscenità."

Cf. also Bartoli, *Scen. inediti*, xiv.

than sentiment they go about to attain their ends
with a fertility and a straightforwardness of bold
invention that often plunges them and their betters
into most embarrassing situations. Therefore, while
among the pairs betrothed at the end of the play
there is always at least one couple from below stairs
"coming toward the ark," their concession to matri-
mony does not mean that a romantic tone predomi-
nates at the climax, it rather intensifies the effect of
the whole as a piece of parody.

Improvisation, with the Masks and all the farcical
quips accompanying them, was by no means confined to "right comedies." To the scandalizing of
critical theorists in the academies, the Italian actors
lightened their serious plays by bits of quite as lively
clowning as any in their farces. Laughter, yet more
laughter, was the end and aim of the professional
entertainers, and they cared only enough for the
sacred critical canons to make a few such concessions
to decorum as would bring them popularity among
well-educated audiences. So they generally passed
off *lazzi* in tragedies as acts of madness, not unlike
Hamlet's freakish doings and like them when first
presented, undoubtedly highly amusing to the
house.[26] Scala's *Mad Princess* was evidently very
popular and successful for he has preserved larger
extracts from her ravings and a fuller account of
her wild deeds than of those of most of his heroines.[27] A hundred years later several madmen

---

[26] Corbin, *The Elizabethan Hamlet*. There were comic mad scenes
in Marlowe's *Dr. Faustus* and *Tamburlaine* as first acted, scenes
omitted in the printing. Cf. A. H. Thorndike, *Tragedy*, 90.

[27] Scala, Gior. XLI; cf. Gior. XXXVIII, *La passia d'Isabella*,

3

make a scenario in which they figure extravagant enough for the comic opera stage.[26] If lunatics were made to bear the burden of ridiculous *lazzi* in tragedies and tragicomedies, peasants and magicians had to perform a major share of them in pastorals and extravaganzas imitated from the Spanish, for only by seeing the horse-play assigned to such inferior characters could a possible objector with his Horace in his pocket, be persuaded that the actors knew their rules as to the observance of dramatic propriety.

No definition of the *commedia dell'arte* however summary would be complete without at least a glance at one of the fundamental perplexities connected with it: why, it will occur to everyone to ask, did Italian players alone develop a peculiar kind of comedy out of all the elements of farcical amusement found singly or in partial combination on the stages of other countries? Improvisation, masked fools, acrobatic tricks, intrigue plots, satire and music are widespread in the sixteenth century theater, but only the Italians combined them all on outlines roughly resembling regular plays. The phenomenon has been variously accounted for, most often by ascribing to the Italian race superlative mimetic excellence. But such a would-be explanation begs the question and falsifies the facts; surely

summarised below, chap. IV. The *pazzie* device was used in written plays as in improvised, cf. Porta's *La furiosa*.

[*] *Un pazzo guarisce l'altro*, Wiener. Sitzungsberichte, phil.-hist. Klasse, CXLIII, part 16. The play is of Spanish inspiration,—Don Quixote figures in it,—and it is closely allied to a written comedy of the same name by G. Gigli ·(pr. 1704).

it takes much greater mimetic power to represent adequately Othello or Alceste than to play Pantalone or Gratiano.

More truly, I think, the materials making up the *commedia dell'arte* should be recognized as nothing but the contents of a kind of general property-box, tricks of the trade demanding not so much great as superficial readiness of technic. Just why the Italians were able to use these professional tools more freely and effectively than their foreign rivals is ultimately perhaps inexplicable. Yet one reason for the fact is pretty certainly that dramatists of great talent were rarer in Italy than elsewhere and that such men as did write for the stage were entirely aristocratic and academic in training and sympathies; consequently a large proportion of literary plays are narrow in their appeal and imitative and unconvincing in their art. Another and even weightier cause for the formation of the improvised pieces is to be found in the position of professional actors; these bands were attached to noble patrons longer than in other countries, owing to the relatively late establishment of public theaters in Italy, and since educated Italians very early had become persuaded of the value of the drama and the importance of its presenters, all the players had been allowed great liberty in the matter of repertory. Naturally such willingness on the part of their public to take what was offered it at the theater would in the long run lower the average of the art by bringing to the surface the mediocre resources of merely mercenary troupes and individuals, and therefore the habits of improvising dialog, of using masked characters and old jokes, would be formed and set. In so confused a situation no one reason for the origin of the *commedia dell'arte* can be singled out as decisive, though it is perfectly easy to see that its peculiarities sprang from tenacious and by no means unique folk customs and that under academic supervision they were pruned and trained by the skilful hands of the professional actors who later spread them broadcast over Europe.

CHAPTER II.

Not a little nonsense has been written about the "evolution" of the *commedia dell'arte*. Of the three main theories that attempt to account for our farces the hoariest and most outgrown is that concerning their putative Roman father, surely a ghost that by now ought to be permanently laid; next in respectability as in age is the hypothesis that makes the Masks direct descendants of comic personages in the mystery plays; finally a modern student[1] takes pains to trace back what he considers *commedia dell'arte* motifs and figures into the folk literature of the middle ages and from this material to deduce a medieval profane comedy which he asserts must have existed perhaps for centuries, side by side with the sacred representations, until it flowered into the sixteenth century professional plays we know. On the whole dispassionate criticism is tending to abandon or radically to modify these theories in such a way as to make the actor class itself and in the very Cinquecento, responsible for its peculiar product. Exactly what this responsibility was and how it caused the formation of improvised plays, I shall, complex though the process be, try to explain in this chapter and the next, after showing briefly why the older hypotheses have become untenable.

The theory concerning the derivation of the

[1] Stoppato, in *La commedia popolare in Italia* (1887).

Italian masked plays from the Atellanae took its rise among the classicists of the Renaissance, admirers of antiquity so enthusiastic that they traced every element in their own experience back to a Latin prototype. Such irregular performances as the improvised farces, no matter how amusing, were naturally regarded askance by the sticklers for dramatic propriety until the suggestion that the Romans had enjoyed something similar put an end to embarrassment by giving a reason for admiring and encouraging these pieces. Niccolò Rossi in 1589 reluctantly admits the apology: "I would never call those things *comedies* which are carried about by wretched mercenary creatures, — containing Gianni of Bergamo, Francatrippa, Pantalone and such like buffoons,—if we could not compare them to the mimes, the Atellanae and the planipedes of the ancients,"[2] and Minturno still earlier likens carnival farces of Cava which he had seen, to the "Comedie Atelane" that made hearers in old days "laugh themselves lame."[3]

For about a hundred and fifty years such statements continued to be made without much attempt at proof, until lucky accident stimulated and fortified the theorists. A grotesque statuette representing a beak-nosed, hunch-backed individual, was unearthed at Herculaneum in 1727, which by a slight stretch of imagination could be identified with Maccus, supposed a type character in the Atellanae and often compared to one of the masked clowns on the Italian

[2] *Discorsi sulla commedia*, 34.
[3] *Arte poetica* (1563), II, 214.

stage.[4] Riccoboni, encouraged by this find, very soon published a fairly elaborate argument for the Roman connection, supporting his assertions by references to the classics, calling Arlecchino for instance a survival of one of the "Mimi centunculi," and tracing the Zanni to the Sannio mentioned by Cicero.[5] A little later Du Bos definitely reads back the *commedia dell'arte* into the Atellanae, a proceeding that underlay Riccoboni's line of thought, though evidently it was with him unconscious: "The Atellana (says Du Bos) was a kind of piece very like the common Italian comedies; that is those whose dialogs are not written. The actor therefore of the Atellanae performed his part just as he pleased and flourished it as his fancy directed."[6]

With A. W. Schlegel the theory which had begun as nothing more than an apologetic analogy and had developed into an apparently proved hypothesis,

[4] Cf. Dieterich, *Pulcinella*, and Collier's *Punch and Judy*, amusing and inaccurate. The identification of the statuette with a figure in the Mimes or even with a stage character at all is very uncertain, nor is it safe to press its resemblance to the English Punch; there is no doubt that it looks like Punch but this, I think, is best explained by the fame of the figure at the time of its discovery and by the influence of its peculiarities on the face and figure of the English villain-clown.

[5] *Hist. du théâtre ital.*, Chap. I; Riccoboni, in the pride of scholarship, ridicules the derivation of Zanni from the Bergamask abbreviation for Giovanni, a common-sense suggestion that had been made even before his time and that is now generally accepted. The passage from Cicero is "Quid enim potest tam ridiculum quam Sannio est? Qui ore, vultu, imitandis motibus, voce, denique corpore ridetur ipso." (*De oratione*, lib. II, parag. 61.) The allusion seems to be quite as probably to a particular actor as to a masked character type in a certain kind of farce.

[6] *Critical Reflections* (1748), I, 136.

entered on a third stage,—the two forms of art were
explained as similar expressions of similar race
characteristics: "Of the many talents for art and
literature displayed by the Italians, the dramatic is
by no means preeminent, and this defect they seem
to have inherited from the Romans, in the same
manner as their great talent for mimicry and
buffoonery goes back to the most ancient times.
The extemporary compositions called Fabulae Atellanae, the only original and national form of the
Roman drama, in respect of form were not perhaps
more perfect than the so-called *commedia dell'arte,*
in which the parts being fixed and invariable, the
dialog is extemporized by masked actors.'"[7]
Modern students[8] have in general combined the point
of view here suggested with attempts to trace the
"evolution of the genre" from Roman days to the
Cinquecento and beyond, often with a weight of
classical quotation that is quite appalling. Maccus,
Pappus, Dorsennus, assumed to be masked personages in the Atellanae, are respectively compared to
one or other of the Italian Masks with an industry
that fails to convince only because it does not suc-

[7] *Lectures on Dram. Art and Lit.,* Lecture II, 35. As usual Schlegel
is inaccurate in details, he evidently had little knowledge of the
commedia dell'arte at first-hand.

[8] V. de Amicis, *La commedia popolare latina,* etc., makes the most
serious effort to enlarge on Riccoboni's thesis and to prove his statements more scientifically; the best modern view of this "tempting"
but "uncritical proceeding," as Symonds calls it (*Mem. of Count C.
Gozzi,* I, 36–7), is clearly stated in a review of Amicis' book, Gior.
Stor., XLII, 219.

C. G. Grysar, *Der römische Mimus,* is a study of the facts about
the Roman Mime, so unprejudiced and thorough as to be still authori-
tative, though dated 1854.

ceed in proving that the mimes have been fairly approached; in every case the Latin allusions have been interpreted in the light of the improvised comedy.

The facts disinterestedly probed seem to be pitifully meager. The fancy pictures of Maccus, drawn so sharply from the ancient statuette, and of Pappus, Bucco and Dorsennus, generalized so readily from imaginary etymologies of their names, disappear in the haze of uncertainty which surrounds the names themselves. Was Maccus, who figures in so many surviving titles as *exul* or *miles* or *virgo*, a type character taking the chief rôle in a little drama, or was he not more probably a favorite actor or reciter who satirized well-known individuals or some unpopular class in society?[9] Were the Atellanae farces or realistic monologs and dialogs on everyday life, like those of the Sicilian Herodas?[10] What part, if any, did masks, improvisation and gymnastic feats play in the mimes? No example of an "Atellanan farce" has lived to answer these questions definitely and as I have said most studies in this field have been vitiated by deductive reasoning based on the *commedia dell'arte* itself. The weight of impartial opinion now inclines to regard the Mimes not as farcical intrigues but as dramatic character satire, for that reason if for no other widely different from their supposed offspring.

Even admitting the unproved hypothesis that the

[9] Scherillo suggests that Maccus may have been an actor, *La Comm. dell'arte*, 57.

[10] Sharpley, *A Realist of the Aegean*, a translation of Herodas. Cf. P. S. Allen, Mod. Philology, Jan., 1910, 320 f.

Atellanae were farces marked by improvisation and masked personages, it would be impossible to establish between them and the Italian extempore plays a connection worthy the name. Riccoboni to be sure with his comfortable eighteenth century dogmatism, assumed that the *commedie dell'arte* of his day were literally linked to the Mimes by an unbroken chain of similar comedies extending back through the middle ages; he went so far indeed as to assert that scenarios of Dante's time were in existence. It is this meager statement that has been seized upon by a different school of students, those who are primarily interested in proving the continuity of profane comedy through the middle ages rather than in finding its origin in ancient Rome. Of these scholars Stoppato is the most serious but with all his erudition he has not succeeded in making his argument convincing; his examples of farces, *contrasti* and the like, however analogous some of their features may be to some of the elements of the professional plays, are still quite distinct kinds of dramatic performances. As Mr. Allen has recently and forcibly said, "If we make one thing the literary source of another . . . then we mean the first thing is the direct and ascertainable source of the second thing. We do not mean that vaguely and despite our utter lack of proof the first thing is in a general sort of way perhaps in its age what the second thing is in its later time."[11] And no amount of good will can make the shadowy Roman Mime or the still more insubstantial medieval profane comedy take the definite form of the perfectly familiar *commedia dell'arte*.

[11] *The Medieval Mimus*, 339, note 2.

Neither is it possible to trace the Masks as some have endeavored, to certain dramatic figures in the Mystery plays, for instance to the boasting captain, the pedantic or magicianlike astrologer with his Latin lingo, and the clownish devil and his imps. These personages may offer some analogy to those of later Renaissance comedy but merely because they represent quite universal kinds of people, the soldier, the old scholar, the rustic, and fools and knaves of various stripes. If the sacred representations had any real influence it was not through their characters so much as through the tradition of stage technic learned and handed on by the actors in these earliest regularly organized and regularly performed dramas. Strolling professional players apparently first brought into the Mysteries in the burlesque roles of devils, next took over the parts susceptible of comic color and in the late fifteenth century became not only the chief actors but the managers of these spectacles, by that time gorgeously presented.[12]

Instead then of ancestor-hunting in imperial Rome or in the middle ages, the *commedia dell'arte* might better try to account for itself by looking about in the sixteenth century where it first comes to consciousness. There, overflowing with life, alternately shouting and tumbling with vulgar strength and

[12] For texts of the *Sacre Rappresentasioni* cf. Torraca, *Teatro Italiano*, and Giudici, *Storia*, etc. The best work on the early Italian theater is of course Ancona's *Origini*, etc. For the part taken by the professional actors in the sacred plays, cf. Ciampi, *Rappresentasioni sacre nella parte comica*, 30 f.; Quadrio, *Storia*, etc., V, 207; Ancona, *op. cit.*, I, 55 and 77.

posturing and singing with exquisite grace, the genius of the people expressed itself through the drama as freely and variously as did the English spirit under Elizabeth fifty years later. Carnival dances, folk plays, courtly mythological spectacles, moral allegories and sacred legends all satisfied some of the general demands for amusement, and each in turn contributed something toward the education of those wandering entertainers who became more important with every increase in their repertory. Gradually the players formed themselves into gilds whose prerogative was acting; gradually, by a combination of effrontery and merit, they made their way into the presence of nobles powerful enough to protect them and to give them position; finally through their attachment to great families they became firmly enough established to venture on their own initiative something bolder than the mere representation of the texts given them. It is in this last moment of their successful social climbing that they seem to have thought of creating extempore plays, yet not until they went at least one step farther and began to emancipate themselves from aristocratic patronage by looking to a larger public for approval could they have dared to bring from the streets and squares, farcical themes and masked clowns of popular origin and to introduce them often and systematically into plays of semi-literary appeal; thus only after the middle of the sixteenth century do *commedie dell'arte* as we know them,—outline plots filled in by extempore dialog,— begin to be recorded. So tangled a situation is naturally impossible to sketch very clearly except as it is bound up with the history of the men and women who worked it out in their daily rehearsals, after they had painfully forced their way into legitimate drama.

If then the actors themselves are to explain the *commedia dell'arte* it is the least respectable of this despised class who are most important for the purpose, since it is they, fluent improvisatori, active gymnasts and shameless wits, who gave their creation its peculiar stamp by keeping alive on public squares the themes and language and grotesque figures of popular festival, and by beginning in the late fifteenth century, to bring their tricks into the pastimes of the great.[18] *Cantimbanchi, saltimbanchi,* mountebanks, charlatans, jugglers,—so they were called, men, women and children together, wandering gypsylike from country fair to city carnival, setting up their temporary stages wherever they might hope for a few pennies from the crowd, free for half an hour from the interference of civil or ecclesiastical officers. They were compelled to lurk in corners partly because they sold quack medicines of doubtful composition, "counterpoisons" more apt to kill than cure,[14] partly because they practiced

[18] Bartoli, *Scen. inediti,* ix-x, says of improvised comedy: "questa commedia che probabilmente si recita per tutto il Medioevo degli istrioni più volgari, mezzi commedianti e mezzi saltimbanchi, salì in grande onore verso la fine del secolo XVI."

[14] Picot, *Le monolog dramatique,* Romania, XVI, 492 f., published a monolog by Rutebeuf, *Li dis de l'erberie* (Paris, c. 1250), which proves the antiquity of the charlatans' practice of selling their wares in public with commendatory speeches. Picot draws an analogy between these early mountebanks and those of the fifteenth century.

sleight of hand and magic, still more because their
songs and dances and jests were judged unwhole-
some for the public morals.[15] Probably the early
street performances varied little from those so gaily
painted by Garzoni and Coryat a century later,
although by 1600 official intolerance was somewhat
less marked than it had been.

Coryat, an open-minded English traveler who saw
Venice in 1608, begins his description: "I hope it
will not be esteemed for an impertencee to my discourse, if I next speake of the Mountebanks of
Venice, seeing that amongst other thinges that doe
much famouse this Citie, these two sorts of people,
namely the Cortezans and the Mountebanks, are not
the least: for although there are Mountebanks also in
other Cities of Italy: yet because there is a greater
concurse of them in Venice then else where, and that
of the better sort and the most eloquent fellowes; and
also for that there is a larger tolleration of them
here then in other Cities (for in Rome, &c., they are
restrained from certain matters as I haue heard
which are here allowed them) therefore they vse to
name a Venetian Mountebank . . . for the cory-
phaeus and principall Mountebank of all Italy;
neither doe I much doubt but that this treatise of
them will be acceptable to some readers as being a
meere nouelty neuer before heard of (I thinke) by
thousands of our English Gallants . . . when I was
in Venice they oftentimes ministered infinite pleasure vnto me. I will first beginne with the etymologie

[15] Cf. Chambers, *Medieval Stage*, Bk. I, for a description of the
medieval strollers and their art.
[16] *Coryat's Crudities*, reprinted from the edition of 1611, II, 50-4.

of their name: the word Mountebank (being in the
Italian tongue *Monta'in banco*) is compounded of
two Italian words, *Montare*, which signifieth to
ascend or goe vp to a place, and *banco*, a bench, because these fellowes doe act their part vpon a stage,
which is compacted of benches or fourmes, though I
haue seene some fewe of them also stand vpon the
ground when they tell their tales, which are such as
are commonly called *Ciarlatanoe's* or *Ciarlatans*, in
Latin they are called *Circulatores* and *Agyrtae*,
which is derived from the Greeke worde ἀγείρειυ
which signifieth to gather or draw a company of
people together. . . . The principall place where
they acte, is the first part of Saint *Marks* street that
reacheth betwixt the West front of S. *Marks* Church,
and the opposite front of Saint *Geminians* Church.
In which, twice a day, that is in the morning and in
the afternoone, you may see fiue or sixe seuerall
stages erected for them: those that acte vpon the
ground, euen the foresaid *Ciarlatans* being of the
poorer sorte of them, stand most commonly in the
second part of S. *Marks*, not far from the gate of the
Duks Palace. These Mountebanks at one end of
their stage place their truncke, which is replenished
with a world of new fangled trumperies. After the
whole rabble of them is gotten vp to the stage, wherof
some weare visards being disguised like fooles in
a play, some that are women (for there are diuers
also amongst them) are attyred with habits according to that person that they sustaine; after (I say)
they are all vpon the stage, the musicke begins.
Sometimes vocall, sometimes instrumentall, and

sometimes both together. This musicke is a preamble and introduction to the ensuing matter: in the meane time while the musicke playes, the principall Mountebank which is the Captaine and ringleader of all the rest, opens his truncke and sets abroach his wares; after the musicke hath ceased, he maketh an oration to the audience of halfe an houre long, or almost an houre. Wherein he doth most hyperbolically extoll the vertue of his drugs and confections:

Laudat venales qui vult extrudere merces.

Though many of them are very counterfeit and false. Truely I often wondred at many of these naturall Orators. For they would tell their tales with such admirable volubility and plausible grace, euen *extempore,* and seasoned with that singular variety of elegant jests and witty conceits, that they did often strike admiration into strangers that neuer heard them before: and by how much the more eloquent these Naturalists are by so much the greater audience they draw vnto them, and the more ware they sell. After the chiefest Mountebanks first speech is ended, he deliuereth out his commodities by little and little, the iester still playing his part, and the musitians singing and playing vpon their instruments. The principall thinges that they sell are oyles, soueraigne waters, amorous songs printed, Apothecary drugs, and a Commonweale of other trifles. The head Mountebank at euery time that he deliuereth out anything, maketh an extemporall speech, which he doth eftsoones intermingle with such sauory iests (but spiced now and then with

singular scurrility) that they minister passing mirth
and laughter to the whole company, which perhaps
may consist of a thousand people that flock together
about one of the stages. . . . I haue obserued mar-
ueilous strange matters done by some of these
Mountebanks. For I saw one of them holde a viper
in his hand, and play with his sting a quarter of an
houre together, and yet receiue no hurt; though another man should haue beene presently stung to
death with it. He made vs all beleeue that the same
viper was linealy descended from the generation of
that viper that kept out of the fire vpon *S. Pauls*
hand, in the Island of Melita, now called Malta, and
did him no hurt; and told vs moreouer that it would
sting some and not others. Also I haue seene a
Mountebanke hackle and gash his naked arme with
a knife most pitifully to beholde, so that the blood
hath streamed out in great abundance, and by and
by after he hath applied a certaine oyle vnto it,
wherewith he hath incontinent both stanched the
blood and so throughly healed the woundes and
gashes, that when he hath afterward shewed vs his
arme againe, we could not possibly perceiue the least
token of a gash. Besides there was another black
gowned Mountebanke that gaue most excellent contentment to the company that frequented his stage.
This fellow was borne blinde, and so continued to
that day: he hath neuer missed Saint *Markes* place
twise a day for sixe weekes together: he was noted
to be a singular fellow for singing extemporall
songes, and for a pretty kinde of musicke that he
made with two bones betwixt his fingers. Moreouer

4

I haue seene some of them doe such strange iugling trickes as would be almost incredible to be reported. Also I haue obserued this in them, that after they haue extolled their wares to the skies, hauing set the price of tenne crownes vpon some of their commodities, they haue at last descended so low that they haue taken for it foure gazets, which is something less than a groat. These merry fellowes doe most commonly continue two good howres vpon the stage, and at last when they haue fedde the audience with such passing variety of sport that they are euen cloyed with the superfluity of their conceits, and haue sold as much ware as they can, they remoue their trinkets and stage till the next meeting. Thus much concerning Mountebankes.''

Garzoni throws more light on the bizarre creatures, the masked, bedizened tricksters, male ·and female, who clustered around the chief charlatan.[17] "Here (he says) is Zan della Vigna with his performing monkey; there Catullo and his guitar; in another corner the Mantuan merry-andrew, dressed like a zany, Zottino . . . and a pretty Sicilian ropedancer. Tamburino spins eggs on a stick, the Neapolitan capers about with brimming bowls of water on his pate; and Maestro Paolo da Arezzo makes his solemn entry with a waving banner, on which we see St. Paul . . . his great ancestor.'' Again "in one corner of the square you see our gallant Fortunio with Fritata . . . entertaining the company every evening from ten to twelve, spinning

---

[17] Garzoni, *Piazza universale*, 738 f. I quote the first selection in Symonds' translation (*Mem. of Count C. Gozzi*, I, 78), the others in my own.

yarns, inventing tales, composing dialogs . . . singing extempore, getting angry with each other, making up, dying of laughter, changing countenance again, falling on the stage, quarreling anew and at last pulling out their purses and coming to the point, the cash for which they have fished with all this polished chatter." "In the background Burattino staggers along with a sack on his back like a peasant porter; elsewhere snake-charmers and dog-trainers attract a portion of the crowd, while the gymnasts too have their admirers." Fabio, an actor "of great worth," holds his audience spellbound by "his grace and fair discourse" as well as by his accomplishment of turning from red to pale and back again.[18] The agility of several members of the band is shown by an appallingly various list of jumps which they exhibited, "somersault, standing jump, . . . backward jump with feet crossed, . . . out of the window, . . . on to the table, . . . the cat's leap into the chair," and among numerous others, the one for which Gabriele da Bologna was noted, "the back somersault with hands on hips."[19]

The central figure in every group of charlatans, the quack doctor, half astrologer, half magician, nimbused by a certain mysterious terror, traded on the superstitions of his audience in his long-winded nonsensical speeches about the more than natural

[18] The same feat was a chief acquirement of the Spanish actress Marie de Riqueline (Fl. c. 1625). Cf. Rennert, *Spanish Stage*, 163. Fabio like several, perhaps all of the strollers mentioned by Garzoni was a real person who made his name c. 1580. Cf. Rasi, *Comici italiani*, I, 854.

[19] Garzoni, *Piazza universale*, 197.

powers of his drugs.[20] He made a specialty of
riddling couplets, gnomic sayings and burlesque prescriptions—ancient conceits that undoubtedly influenced the Doctor of the *commedia dell'arte*. Lodovico de'Bianchi, the famous Gratiano of the Gelosi,
himself sometime a mountebank, published in 1585
a book of wise observations, "conceits" for his role
in the improvised plays, that probably represents
very fairly a portion of the charlatan's stock
speeches. The author introduces himself thus:

> A poet well-known from afar
> And near as an unexcelled star,
> A doctor who cures all the healthy,
> Fortune-teller, helps all to be wealthy,
> Magician who surely will find
> The things you've forgot from your mind.[21]

After such claims we might be justified in expecting
something more stimulating than the actual platitudes he presents us; in fact it is hard to understand
the popularity of such remarks on the stage, for to
most of us it would be a little wearisome to be told
often that, "The man who walks is not dead," "The
ship on the high seas is not in port," "A hungry

[20] The problems of the relation of the charlatan to the doctor of
folk-plays and of the latter to the primitive medicine-man are too
complicated to go into here. Some curious facts on the medical superstitions of the Italian peasantry are collected in Zanetti, *Medicina
delle nostre donne*. For the universality of the quack-doctor in folk-
plays cf. Chambers, *Med. Stage*, Bk. II, and Ordish, *Folk Drama*, Folk
Lore, II, 331.

[21] I translate the doggerel somewhat freely from the introduction
to *Le cento e dodici conclusioni in ottava Rima del Plusquamperfetto
Dottor Gratiano, Partesana da Francolino, comico geloso . . .*, pub.
c. 1585.

K. Dujardin.

THE QUAILAND

person has great appetite," "A gentleman is not a peasant," "One who does not hear may be called deaf," "He who does not speak might be considered dumb," etc. Probably the Bolognese dialect of these rimes and the weight of gravity with which they were uttered at various inapropos moments in the comedy accounts for their unfailing comic appeal. In kind they are not unlike the ever green platitudes of folk poetry, statements of analogy self-evident to sophisticated minds but always delightfully fresh to the simple.[22]

The quack doctor beside selling his wares sometimes took part in one of the crude farces or *contrasti* given on the street stages. Perhaps the oldest theme in which he found his place is the struggle between winter and summer, personified in the *Contrasto between Master Carnival and Lady Lent;* each of the leading characters appropriately dressed salutes the other in foully abusive language till both

---

[22] Ancona, *La poesia popolare*, 94, gives an example of *Contrarj* from a MS. of the Quattrocento that is very similar in tone to these rimes of Gratiano. For instance

> La salsiccia non è carne,
> Ne la carne non è salsiccia;
> Ne bu non è torriccia,
> Ne la torriccia non è bu.
> Ne le tre non son du
> Ne le du non son tre . . . etc., etc.

The rimed couplets or quatrains closing a speech or scene in some *commedie dell'arte* may perhaps be a relic of another folk tradition; many Italian folk tales end with a rime, sometimes a little charm or blessing, sometimes a challenge to another story-teller to "do it better." Cf. Neri in Gior. Stor., I, 78, Bartoli, *Scen. ined.* lxxix, for the *chiusette*, as the couplets were called in the improvised plays; and Crane, *Ital. Pop. Tales*, xvi–xvii, and Pitrè, *Fiabe*, etc., I, 196, for the rimes in folk tales.

fall to blows to decide their contest. Carnival must
die of course but not until he has called in doctors
and magicians, heard and even attempted their
burlesque prescriptions, and made a ridiculous will,
leaving to his sisters his "credits never acquired,"
to his wife "property not yet bought" and to others
still less desirable gifts; then amidst howls of grief
from members of the family, Lent summons her
enemy's soul,[23]—a piece of unadulterated folk humor,
with all its outrageous flyting, its fisticuffs, its in-
decencies and its parody of serious subjects in the
mock testament, death and lamenting. In a little
Frottola di Carnasciale printed in 1554 there is more
evidence of "cultured" interest; the themes are the
same but there is inserted a conversation between
two councillors who try to explain a dream Carnival
has had, in a coarse and senseless Latin.[24]

Realistic farces of common life like those of medieval France were also given by the mountebanks.
The doctor frequently took part in them, always in
a grotesque manner, and the comic consultations
and the extravagant remedies of Gratiano were inherited from these popular pieces.[25]   Cola's advice

[23] A. Lumine, *Farse di carnevale*, etc., 67. Others are given in the
same collection. For a modern example cf. Gior. Stor., XXXI, 178.

[24] Ancona, *Origini*, I, 538. Cf. the *Tragicomedia di Squaquadrante
Carnevale et di Madonna Quaresima* (Brescia, 1544), described in
Manzoni's *Libro di carnevale*, etc.

There is a strong influence surviving from such *contrasti* to be
found in scenarios; cf. that published by Toldo, Gior. Stor., XLVI,
128 f., where one of the main episodes is a dispute and fight between
two peasant merchants who finally appeal to a judge for settlement.

[25] In the *farse* of P. A. Caracciolo, early Cinquecento, the doctor
takes a prominent part; cf. the *Farsa in persona di un Malato e di
tre Medici*, cited Ancona, *Origini*, I, 578 f.

to the Zanni in *Il Medico Volante* on a cure for toothache is quite absurd enough for the charlatan's
repertory: "Hold a ripe apple in your mouth (he
says) and put your head in the oven; before the
apple is cooked your toothache will be gone."[26] In
another scenario a doctor tells Arlequin that there is
no hopeless insanity, "upon which he speaks a
tirade, enumerating ridiculously various madnesses
of men, adding thereto remedies just as ridiculous
for curing them."[27]

It is not of course Gratiano alone who preserves
bits of the charlatan's repertory in the *commedia
dell'arte*. Many of the *lazzi* of the Zanni were
simply the mountebank's tricks introduced into the
improvised plays as episodic farce, furnishing a
means for the clown to exhibit his characteristic nim-
bleness. Scala's scenarios indicate that the Pedrolino, Burattino and Arlecchino of his company could
leap on and off the stage with disconcerting rapidity,
sometimes from a dark corner of the street, sometimes through a window; that they slipped into a
disguise and dropped it again in the winking of an
eye; that they were equally expert in whatever required manual deftness, whether fencing or picking
pockets; in short that they were accomplished in all
those "singeries très-agréables" which Gherardi
tells us have always been proper to the Italian
plays.[28]

[26] Bartoli, *Scen. inediti*, 104 f., Act II, sc. 3.

[27] *Un passo guarisce l'altro*, Wiener Sitzungsberichte, CXLIII,
part 16.

[28] Gherardi, *Théâtre italien*, IV, 21, *L'opéra de campagne*, Act I,
"Cette scène est une des plus plaisantes de toute la comédie, mais

The mock fights that so often mark the close of a scene or an act in the scenarios are among the most important of the agreeable monkey tricks inherited from the charlatan's bench by the actors of *commedia dell'arte*. The more extravagant these fights the more the brawlers were clapped; when Scaramuccia at the age of eighty-three was still able to administer a box on the ear with his foot, he was considered the marvel of the Italian stage, "the completest, the most famous Italian artist of the seventeenth century."[29] That trick to be sure was only one of his large collection yet it is fairly representative; not many jokes in the improvised farces got beyond the low level of horse-play set by the mountebanks' exhibitions. Sometimes however there was a slight seasoning of wit to disguise the flatness of the jest, as in a deceit practiced on the Doctor in Scala's fifteenth piece. The old miser enters with a plate of seven delicate little fritters "received from one of his clients," and begins to count them, saying,

" 'Three for me, two for my guest and two for my son'; then saying that the maid would be offended if she didn't eat some, he made a new division, saying, 'three for me, two for my guest, one for my son and the other for the maid.' Then he decided that this

c'est une de celles qui ne se peuvent exprimer . . . c'est ce qu'on appelle scène italienne, scène jouée sur le champ, sans rien apprendre par coeur et qui dépend entièrement du génie et de l'esprit de l'acteur." Ib., Act II, sc. 2, p. 39, "La scène . . . est encore très-plaisante, par le jeu que Arlequin y fait, en donnant au bailli tantôt un coup de pied, tantôt un coup de bâton, et par d'autres singeries très-agréables. . . ."

[29] Rasi, *Comici italiani*, I, 888 f.

was not a good thought, to make the maid equal to his son. Arlecchino signals the Captain to get behind the Doctor, then Arlecchino kneeling, begs alms, saying he had been driven out of his home. The Doctor asks the history of his misfortune and Arlecchino begins: 'Signor mio, your lordship should know that my father had a stranger to break-fast with him one morning; when they had finished eating many dishes a platter was brought in with seven little fritters on it; I seeing it and delighting in such fodder, cast my eye on them and saw how they swam in their batter, and were all a golden color, wrapped up in honey; then the guest stretched out his hand, took one and ate it' (here the Captain from behind the Doctor, reached over, taking a fritter and eating it at a mouthful), and so as Arlecchino numbered the fritters they were taken and eaten by the Captain, Arlecchino remarking, 'I had to watch the greediness of this gluttonous stranger.' Finally, seeing that he had got to the last . . . he drew his sword and giving him (*i. e.*, Gratiano) a blow said 'Much good may they do you!' and then left with the Captain.'' From the context it is clear that Arlecchino's rage is directed against the Doctor for his miserliness which is here rewarded as it deserves. The incident is a kind of interlude in the comedy and is exactly the type of trick that the miscellaneous performances on street corners were likely to develop and actors coming from them into more regular plays, to utilize as they could.

Most of the absurdest *lazzi* in the improvised farces fell to the rôle of the servant-clown, the

Zanni. Like the grotesque lad, the Tommy, of English folk plays, the Zanni shows signs of being a traditional relic of immemorial ceremonies; his mask, either a black animal face or a birdlike beak, the rabbit scut in his cap, his suit of many-colored rags, his wooden dagger, all point back to the rustic agricultural festivals whose spirit the carnival license and the mountebanks' exhibitions preserve.[30] Perhaps, as has been suggested, this primitive figure was early associated in some parts of the country with satire of the Bergamask peasant facchino who haunted Venetian squares; certainly from the middle of the sixteenth century the Zanni of comedy tended to speak the patois of Bergamo and to be paired off in dialogs with the rich old Venetian merchant, Pantalone.[31] This ancient sage, at first only one among several clowns in the charlatan's band, by about 1550 had definitely put on the long gown and beard of the Magnifico and had begun to illustrate the proverb,[32] "Vecchio innamorato è il saracino

[30] Chambers, *Medieval Stage*, I, 192, and Bk. II passim.
The derivation of Zanni's name from the Bergamask abbreviation of Giovanni is now generally accepted. Cf. Tiraboschi, *Vocabolario*, etc., and Panigiani, *op. cit.*, under Zanni.

[31] Merlini, *La satira contro il villano*, 139 f. The suggested connection of the Zanni with the Bergamask facchino is apt only in Venice where the peasant porters were unpopular; it does not apply to south Italian types.

[32] Mr. Livingstone tells me that the reference in the proverb is to a "saracen" or block of wood tilted at in a game something like the Elizabethan quintain. One example of the popularity of this judgment gives the gist of many *stornelli*:

> Sentì questo stornel, com'è curioso,
> Un vecchio di sessant'anni vuole un bacio!

Canti pop. della montagna lucchese, ed. Giannini, 85.

della piazza," "an old man in love is the butt of
the *piazza*."

As early as 1518/9 Pontano describes an entertainment played outdoors by masked actors,[33] but
whether or not Zanni and Pantalone were among
them he does not say. From that time on however
Zan, or Zanni, or Zoan, "Bergamask servant,"
begins to appear in written plays, "ludi zanneschi"
to be mentioned vaguely among courtly amusements
and Zanni with various companions to be noted in
accounts of carnival merry-makings.[34] At the
Roman Mardi-gras of 1555/6 Joachim du Bellay saw
Marc'Antonio and Zanni "bouffoner avec un Magnifique à la Venitienne"[35] and to 1559 belongs the
much-quoted carnival song of Anton-Francesco
Grazzini, supposed to be sung by this pair of fools.
This *Canto di Zanni e Magnifichi* is one of several
madrigals seemingly written by Grazzini for professional strollers to sing;[36] there is a *Song for
Buffoons and Parasites*,[37] "cheerful, happy folk,"

[33] J. J. Pontani, Opera (Venetia, 1518/9) II, 91 f. Quoted by
Croce, *Teatri di Napoli*, Chap. I.

[34] Merlini, *Satira contro il villano*, 144 f., says that the various
kinds of rustic plays containing satire of the peasant,—*frottole*,
contrasti, etc.—are called indifferently "vilaneschi," "alla bergamasca" and "alla facchinesca." Like the entertainment given by
Beolco, referred to below, these simple little pieces were often recited
at banquets, probably with some of their jokes improvised at the
moment. Cf. Ancona, *Origini*, I, 414–5.

Solerti, *Ferrara, etc.*, lxxxix–xc, says: "In una lettera del 18 gen-
naio, 1585, cominciano ad apparire gli Zanni, ma non sappiamo quali
e quanti fossero," etc. This seems to refer to a particular company
which took its name from its chief actor.

[35] Cited by Flamini, *Il Cinquecento*, 314.

[36] *Tutti i Trionfi*, etc., Grazzini's songs are in volume II. He is best
known by his nickname of *Il Lasca*.

[37] Ib., II, 468–9.

they call themselves, though they go on to complain
of the discouraging number of clowns in Florence;
there is a song of *Youths impoverished by Courtesans,*[38] which except for its verse form might serve
as one of the lover's laments in an improvised play;
there is also a description by the "surgeon-doctors"
of their cures for human ailments, doggerel quite
possibly droned by some mountebank in the street.
The most interesting of these pieces is the first, the
duet, or perhaps the two part chorus, of Zanni and
Magnifichi which has frequently been called the first
satisfactory evidence of the *commedia dell'arte.*[39]

> Playing the Bergamask and the Venetian,
> Traveling in every part,
> And acting comedies our famous art, . . .
> All Zanni we,
> Actors fine as you may see.
>
> The other chosen players,
> Hermits saying burlesque prayers,
> Lovers, women, braggart captains,
> At the hall are guarding treasure. . . .
> When you our brand new farces hear and see
> You'll laugh beyond all measure,
> At their quips and jests so free.
>
> The comedy well ended
> Gorgeous ballets are appended,
> Whose fresh and varied jokes cannot be mended.
> But since in this old town

[38] Ib., II, 471–3. There is a *Canto de'medici fisichi*, I, 48.

[39] This song may have been written as early as 1540 though not
printed till 1559; the piece is so important that I attempt a rough
translation of the more significant parts, though they have often been
noted before.

Ladies, you are not allowed to come
To see us at our hall,
We 'll visit you in your own home,
To show you at least some
Of the sweet and lively pleasure of our art,
As lucky men in public see each part.

Pray hear awhile what jolly clatter
Among themselves these witty Zanni chatter ! . . .
See from the scabbard
How daggers fly, and staves, and do such acts
As force wise men with folly to make pacts.

Moreover we will show you there
A painted scene well-made and fair,—
There where Cantinella acts
And Zanni offers you such mirth and gaiety.
So if you wish to be
Diverted for a time,
And laugh more than your fill,
To-morrow seek our playhouse on the hill.[40]

[40] I append the original with apologies for the freedoms I have taken
with it, especially with the final couplet.

> Facendo il Bergamasco, e 'l Veneziano,
> N 'andiamo in ogni parte,
> E 'l recitar commedie è la nostra arte. . . .
> E Zanni tutti siamo
> Recitatori eccelenti, e perfetti:
>
> Gli altri Strioni eletti
> Amanti, Donne, Romiti e soldati
> Alla stanza per guardia son restati. . . .
> Commedie nuove abbiam composto in guisa
> Che quando recitar le sentirete
> Morrete della risa
> Tanto son belle, giocose e facete;
>
> E dopo ancor vedrete
> Una danza ballar sopra la scena
>   Di varj e nuovi giuochi tutta piena.

The whole poem reads like an advertisement for an approaching performance of a highly amusing kind. The repertory of this troupe can be inferred or rather guessed from the list of characters, to be composed of realistic farces popular in theme and origin, for May-plays and other rustic comedies loved to ridicule the hermit of unrighteous life and pretention to holiness, and they were quite as severe on the chicken-livered braggart who in Italy as elsewhere took a prominent part in folk merriments.[41] The soldier of these city street shows, however, was

> Ma perche'n questa terra (i. e. Florence)
> Donne, che voi non potete venire
> A vederci alla stanza
> Dove facciamo ognun lieto gioire:
> Se ci volete aprire
> Verremo in casa a far gustarvi in parte,
> La dolcezza, e'l piacer della nostra arte.
>
> Di grazia udite un po', che ciarleria
> Insieme fanno que valenti Zanni. . . .
> Vedete fuor de'panni
> Uscir pugnali, stocchi, e far certi atti
> Da far crepar di rider savj e matti.
>
> Alfin vogliamvi una ben fatta e bella
> Prospettiva di nuovo far vedere,
> La dove il Cantinella
> E Zanni vi daran spasso e piacere.
> Or se volete avere
> Buon tempo un pezzo
> E rider fuor d'usanza
> Doman venite a trovarci alla stanza.

Ancona, *Origini*, II, 405, says *stanza* is the term for a private room where professional actors played, *sala* for a hall in a palace where private performances were given.

⁴¹ Mazzi, *Congrega dei Rozzi*, II, passim, gives many examples of rustic comedies in which the hermit's ill-living and pious professions are satirised. Cf. Stoppato, *Comm. pop.*, 107 f.

more than a reminiscence of the boasting peasant fools; he was a merciless parody on the well-hated foreign bravos and military mercenaries, French and Spanish, who overran the country at this time.[42] It was just because he was made to express the general loathing of these tyrannical aliens that in Italy his figure is especially definite and ubiquitous. Numerous farces survive which though late in date give a fair idea of this grotesque soldier among the mountebanks and prove it to have been alive with vulgar force and homely wit.

Like the quack doctor the hero has to have someone to talk to and chooses Zanni as his confidant, just as in the speeches for the Captain's part published later by Andreini, it is to his squire that the vain-glorious one looks for an audience,[43] unfortunately without finding the sympathy and support he might wish. In one dialog Zanni comments, verse about with his master, on the exaggerated statements of the latter: "He is the king of cowards, this fellow, in all his acts and doings."[44] The Captain answers, "If you knew how many this hand has slain, . . . " and so on in his usual style, till Zanni

[42] Senigaglia, *Cap. Spavento*, introductory pages, and Rasi, *Comici italiani*, I, 82.

[43] Ancona, *Origini*, II, 59 f., notes some resemblances between popular types in folk tales and in the *Sacre Rappresentazioni*. Cf. Stoppato, *Com. pop.*, 193 f., for an analysis of a *Farsa satira morale* by V. Venturini (pr. before 1521) in which a certain Spampana takes a large part, "dimostrandosi . . . bravissimo bravo."

[44] *The tremendous force and bold deeds of Cap. Heads-off-and-Spit-Dart, an honest and laughable trifle*, is the title of one of these rimed conversations, pr. Bologna, 1606; cited entire with others of the same sort by Rasi, *Comici italiani*, I, 67 f.

brings him down with "I know well enough that hand has slain a quantity of lice."[45] It is hardly necessary to quote more to show that in his way the Captain was as much of a charlatan as the quack doctor; both dealt with words rather than deeds and both were fair game for the satire of the plain man whom Zanni always represents.

The "Donne" of the company whom Grazzini's clown mentions as preparing at the Hall for a performance, were probably really women, not boys dressed for female rôles. Their characters as well as their repertory, can be inferred from the remark here that honest women did not attend public spectacles, at least in Florence.[46] There was always a great deal of license on the Italian stage and what it must have been in the lower class of entertainment, certain scenes of the *commedia dell'arte* remain to witness.[47] The heroine's maid exhibits all the traditional agility of a mountebank by dances and "feats of activity" like those of a wandering Signora

---

[45] Rasi, *op. cit.*, I, 71–2, *Contrasto alla Napolitano ridicoloso.*

[46] Montaigne, *Voyage en Italie* (1581), 253–4, says of Italian women, "ou elles se laissent voir en public, soit en coche, en feste, ou en théâtre elles sont à part des homes." The same custom was observed in the Spanish theatres, cf. Rennert, *Spanish Stage*, 118 f. As to the character of the women who went to the public plays generally in Italy, cf. Coryat's account of the Venetian playhouses, cited below.

Ademollo, *Teatri di Roma*, xxii–iii, states that he has found records of boys occasionally taking the part of "Franceschina in comedy," even in public performances in the latter half of the Cinquecento; this would have been more usual in Rome however than elsewhere.

[47] The written plays immoral though they are in tone and plot, probably could not have been presented with as much brazenness of action as the freer improvised comedies. Cf. Bartoli, *Scen. ined.*, xii f.

Angela "who jumps so well" commended by the Duke of Mantua's secretary in 1567.[48] Moreover the most outspoken in effrontery among the Masks was always the maid, and in her boldness she was quite true to her antecedents; when Franceschina advises her mistress to put on a masculine habit and volunteers to teach her how to wear it, she reminds us of the girl in the mountebank's troupe who, dressed as a man, marched at the head of the company, announcing a coming performance.[49] So Garzoni pictures her in his satirical account of an indoor play by a traveling band of the very sort Grazzini's carnival song advertises:

"When they (the actors) enter a city, a drum immediately lets everyone know their arrival; the woman dressed as a man goes ahead, sword in hand, to make the announcement and invite the populace to a comedy or a tragedy in a palace or at the Pilgrim Inn, where the mob, eager for novelty and curious by nature, flock to occupy the Stanza, passing into the room by means of a groat; there they find an imitation stage, a scene painted with charcoal; they hear an introductory concert of donkeys . . . ; a prolog by a charlatan, an awkward thing like that of Fra Stoppino; the action is as stupid as misfortune; the *intermedj* as bad; a Magnifico not worth a penny; a Zanni who is a goose; a Gratiano who spits out his words; a silly idiotic bawd; a lover who lames everyone's arms when he talks; a Spaniard who can say nothing but *Mi vida* and *Mi*

[48] Ancona, *Origini*, I, 449.
[49] Garzoni, *Piazza universale*, 320–1.

corazon; a pedant who goes off on Tuscan words all
the time; a Burattino who knows no gesture but that
of putting his cap on his head; a Signora who is a
monster in her speaking, dead in her talking, asleep
when she gesticulates, who is at war with the Graces
and has had an important difference with Beauty.
So that the crowd comes away scandalized and ill-
satisfied with them, carrying off the memory of the
villanous speeches recited, resolved not to spend a
penny the next day to hear again such nonsense.
. . . Thus by the wretched doings of such people
good actors come to be despised and suffer affronts
not at all suitable to their merits.''

Although Garzoni is pleased to be very sarcastic
over the "wretched doings" of these humble players
it is in exactly such a school as the one here portrayed that the good actors he commends were
trained. By his time—the mid-sixteenth century—
differences between fine and poor players were
easier to note than they would have been fifty years
before the formation of regular companies and their
alliance with aristocratic patrons. When the older
records are searched for traces of the steps in the
actors' upward progress, the earliest are found to
be a few tantalizingly scant and unsatisfactory
notices, scattered chiefly in accounts of carnival
gaieties[50] and for the most part mere allusions in the
letters of princes to some buffoon whom they have
taken from his companions and established as court

---

[50] Passages in the *commedie dell'arte* recall this association of its
actors with the carnival; Cf. Scala, *Teatro*, Gior., XXI, where Graziano
excuses himself for being drunk by saying it is carnival season, *Il
finto negromante*, Act II.

fool.[51] Such was "our Fritellino" described in a note from Giovanni Gonzaga to Isabella d'Este,[52] as leading a dance with all the grotesque motions "which he knows how to do," a juggler rather than an actor. More dramatic were the powers of a certain Strasino who at the Roman carnival of 1518 recited a farce "all by himself,"[53] and a "comedia bufona" performed by Fra Mariano, a clerical clown in the protection of Leo X.[54] Another jester under the same papal patronage, Francesco de'Nobili, fled from Rome in 1527 and became popular in Venice in a kind of farcical comedy which has often been confused with the improvised plays of fifty years later.[55]

Of Zan Polo, still another Venetian buffoon, there is recorded a success that throws more light on the court performances given by these men; between

[51] It seems probable that in the Quattrocento as in the following century there was a good deal of interaction between *piazza* and palace, less differentiation than in earlier days between court fool and strolling player. Cf. G. Bonifacio, *Giullari e uomini di corte nel Dugento* (Napoli, 1907), for the early history of court entertainments.

[52] Dated Jan. 25, 1495, cited Ancona, *Origini*, II, 366-7.

Whether Fritellino were the real name of this clown or the nickname of a Mask, is not known; as will appear below Fritellino was the stage title of the famous actor-manager P. M. Cecchini, about a century after this. Cf. Ademollo, *Una famiglia di comici italiani*, ix-x.

[53] Ademollo, *Alessandro VI, Giuliano II e Leone X*, 78-9.

[54] Graf, *Attraverso il Cinquecento*, 369 f., brings together the extant information about this curious person, once a priest. Cf. Rasi, *Comici italiani*, I, Giov. Ammonio, for the account of another actor-friar of the period. Also Bartoli, *Buffoni di corte*, Fanfulla della domenica, 1882, number II.

[55] F. de'Nobili (called Il Cherea or sometimes Terenziano), on the authority of Klein, *Gesch. des Dramas*, IV, 903, has been credited with the "invention" of the *commedia dell'arte*,—quite mistakenly, as is proved by Bartoli, *Scen. ined.*, x, note I, and Rossi, *Lettere di M. Andrea Calmo*, xviii.

the acts of Plautus' Miles Gloriosus, played by dilettanti (February 16, 1515), Zan Polo acted, evidently
with helpers, a "new comedy, feigning that he was
a necromancer and that he went to Hell, and showed
a Hell with Furies and Devils; then he represented
the God of Love and was carried to Hell . . . there
was a dance, then music of nymphs in a triumphal
car who sang a song. . . . "⁵⁶   Zan Polo here was
the victim of his environment; he was obliged to
consult the tastes of the academicians, choose a semi-
classical fable and keep to the stage usual in aristocratic entertainments, the open, three-story arrangement of the Mysteries.⁵⁷   With the exception of the
lazzi of the devils and necromancer there is nothing
here to suggest the peculiar art of the street mountebanks nor to point the way toward the perfection of
"professional comedy."

Yet it was in Venice that an actor took the first
long stride toward self-asserting independence and
there that he worked out a form of art of his own,
in some ways prophetic of the *commedia dell'arte*.
Angelo Beolco, a Paduan associated with Zan Polo
in Venetian records of 1520 and after, is certainly
one of the first of those actor-manager-dramatists
who were responsible for the evolution of the im-

⁵⁶ The play was given before the Accademici Immortali at San
Beneto near Pesaro and was described by a witness, cited Rasi,
Comici ital., II, 748. Cf. ibid., II, 600–1 for more discussion of Zan
Polo.

⁵⁷ The stage of the Mysteries was used for allegorical performances
after it had been discarded for the presentation of the classical
comedies so fashionable at the end of the Quattrocento. Cf. Ancona,
Origini, II, 2 f., for a description of the first version of Poliziano's
Orfeo, played in 1471, "not at all different" in form from a Mystery.

provised plays. An illegitimate son of a noble house, a man whose "affable nature" and whose learning admitted him both to aristocratic academies and to bourgeois clubs,[58] he turned to account all his knowledge and observation by writing plays of a new kind; in them he drew for plot material from the classic theater, from vernacular tales and—in this he was particularly original—from popular *contrasti*.[59] His enthusiastic publisher, Giovanni Greco, assures his "wise readers" with a little pardonable exaggeration, that the work of his author is "characterized by good morals and descriptions of virtue and vice, of truth and falsehood, marvellously observant of decorum . . . (containing) in them a great portion of moral philosophy, with such witty speeches that this alone, without the oddity of the different dialects, would suffice to delight and to instruct."[60]

Whatever efforts Beolco, like his friend Zan Polo, may have made to please his fellow-academicians,— and this preface shows he made some—his most genuine interest was undoubtedly in humbler life and in the representation of it to his audiences. His

[58] Preface to *Tutte le Opere di Messer Angelo Beoloho* (Vicenza, 1584). Cf. E. Lovarini, Gior. Stor., XXXIII, Supp. 2.

[59] *Contrasto* is a general term for dramatized debates, sometimes realistic, sometimes symbolic, similar to the Latin *Conflictus*, the medieval *Débat* or the primitive flyting. For old examples of *contrasti* cf. Carducci, *Cantilene e ballate* and Lumine, *Farse di carnevale*, etc., also Renier, *Appunti sul contrasto fra la madre e la figlia bramosa di marito*, Miscel. nuziale Rossi-Teiss.

[60] *Opere*, Lettera ai saggi lettori. Beolco himself probably would not have formulated his theory quite so exactly, as by the time this letter was written (1584) criticism had become much more precise than it was when Beolco wrote, sixty years earlier.

own part in his plays was that of a rustic fool—
whence his dialect nickname, Il Ruzzante, the rustic
speaker,—a kindly satirical portrait of the Bergamask peasant whose unmorality and stupidity, awkwardness and rough speech, he mimicked to perfection.[61] Not one of his plays is without a rustic
or a group of them; sometimes the setting is a
situation familiar to readers of French farces, in
which a thick-headed peasant husband is unmercifully baited by his lively wife and her lovers.
Again, as in *La Moschetta,* three or four country
folk work out in abusive flytings the author's answer
to a fashionable problem treated here and there in
the *Decameron,* as to the sinfulness of love between
godfather and godmother. Or as in the romantic
comedy, *La Rodiana,* played at Venice in 1549, the
low-class characters are introduced by way of
farcical relief to the monotonous propriety of the
principal lovers.[62] Through the conventionality of

[61] Ancona, *Origini,* II, 120, note 6, quotes a contemporary tribute
to Beolco's skill, dated Feb. 13, 1520, a description of a comedy
"a la vilanesca" done by a "certain Ruzante, a Paduan, who as a
peasant spoke most excellently." The rôle taken by Ruzzante himself varied from play to play, though it was given a kind of unity
by the name, dialect and peasant status of the character; he was
sometimes a lover, as in *La Fiorina,* sometimes a duped husband, as
in *La Moschetta,* sometimes a boasting soldier, as in *L'Anconitana.*

[62] This play is especially noteworthy for the number of dialects
used in it; one of the humbler personages speaks a Venetian patois;
another Bergamask; a third, an old man, swears immensely in still
a different lingo; a *negromante* uses something like Spanish mixed
with Latin and Italian, finally Corrado "Tedesco," talks in mimicry
of the German accent.

There has been a deal of discussion as to the authorship of this
play, which many critics ascribe to Calmo though it was first published
as Beolco's. Cf. Rossi, *Lettere,* etc., XXXVII f., and XLIV.

much of the characterization there penetrates a good deal of fresh observation and rather more sympathy than one finds in most sixteenth century representations of the despised third estate.

No matter how popular the material and how homely the art, such plays as these, written with quite elaborate artistic finish by a man of as much originality and as much interest in character as Beolco, offer very little resemblance to improvised intrigue farces which are almost entirely the extempore composition of several actors and actresses. It is probable that occasionally Ruzzante left some scene of clowning to the invention of the individual who took a comic part; indeed he is thought to have composed a dialog on rustic themes in which one of the stage directions reads, "Zilio the lover comes on singing and arguing with himself of the nature of love," a gap being left in the verses for this improvised soliloquy.[63] It is certain also that the liveliness of the comedies depended largely on the lazzi of the peasants, yet neither such jests nor the use of dialects were entirely peculiar to Beolco's work. Even granting in addition that some disguises were worn and that the stupid rustic was sufficiently stereotyped to be called a Mask, Ruzzante ought not to be regarded as the father of the commedia dell'arte.[64] One of its grandfathers, to keep

[63] Cf. Rossi, Lettere, etc, xxi–lii, note, and lxxix–lxxx.

[64] Sand, Masques et Bouffons, 35 f., following Riccoboni, Hist. du théâtre italien, 50 f., laid great stress on the relation of Beolco to the commedia dell'arte; he was imitated by Burckhardt, for criticism of whom cf. Bartoli, Scen. ined., cxxvii, note 3, and Flamini, Il Cinquecento, 304 f. Even so well-informed a student as Baschet says

to the trite figure, he might perhaps more justly be
named, for as a practical playwright and actor he
took, as I have said, the first step toward that fusion
of classic and popular themes and technic, of romantic story and satirical characterization which
provided later Italian actors with a common fund of
material for the plays peculiarly theirs. Yet no
scenario from his hand has been discovered and
there is no reason to think he wrote one; plot was
not his chief preoccupation and he was too much the
literary artist ever to have been content with out-
lining an intrigue for other and less skilful men to
fill in as the moment prompted.

This Venetian genius seems moreover never to
have organized or managed a troupe capable of expressing his ideas in words of their own. The
meager notices that remain to tell of his performances at princely festivals and before learned societies rather indicate that he relied for help on such
singers and entertainers as chanced in his way. In
1532 he had trouble in finding enough professional
actors to play a comedy before Ercole d'Este at
Ferrara.[65] Once however at a banquet in 1529, he is
mentioned with five other men and two women as
singing "most beautiful songs and madrigals" and
going around the table "chanting of rustic things
and in that (rustic) language most pleasingly, and
dressed in their new style."[66] Whether this were
an unusual occasion or whether he employed women

that Beolco "mis en vogue" the improvised plays, c. 1526-7; cf.
Les comédiens italiens, etc., 12-3.
[65] Rossi, Lettere, etc., xxx-xxxi.
[66] Ancona, Origini, II, 120, note 6.

regularly in his plays as well as for songs and
dances, is uncertain; probably he followed the custom of the dilettanti academicians, who distributed
heroines' rôles among their youngest men.[67] For
although the women among the mountebanks did not
hesitate to take speaking parts any more than to
walk the rope, dance, sing or play the lute, they
were too untrained to be given important places
in the academic productions, either Latin or Italian;
accordingly the noble youths themselves in their
quality of amateurs, at first played the comedies
written for them by Ariosto or Bibbiena or Grazzini,
and engaged professionals only for the clown's parts
and for the musical and spectacular interludes.[68]

Before 1550 there seem to have been few efforts
to bring together the professionals sporadically employed, in permanent troupes attached to specific

[67] As late as 1542 it is recorded that men took the women's parts
in an Italian play, the *Orbecche* of Giraldi Cintio; cf. Amicis, *La
commedia popolare latina*, 82.

Cecchini, *Breve discorso*, etc., says it is "scarcely fifty years since
women have appeared generally on the stage"; he speaks with the
authority of a long-lived actor who had traveled much and should
have known whereof he spoke. Riccoboni quotes him acquiescently
(*Hist. du théâtre italien*, 42) and indeed the statement has never been
seriously questioned so far as regular dramas are concerned; actresses
took part much earlier in courtly *intermedj* and in street farces, cf.
Ademollo, *Teatro di Roma*, xxii–iii.

[68] The prologs of Grazzini's comedies testify to this custom of
dilettante acting; cf. especially the prolog "alle donne" to *La
Gelosia* and the long prose prolog to *La Strega*, ed. of 1859, 10 and
171 respectively.

Cf. Ademollo, *Teatri di Roma*, 35 f., and *Una famiglia*, etc., x f.
Ancona, *Origini*, II, 137, note 2, describes a performance of the
Andria in 1539 in which a princess of the Este family took part; cf.
ib., 352, 494 and 551.

patrons. Even the theater-loving princes of Ferrara made no attempt to hold the actors they temporarily applauded; Ercole d'Este writes, February 5, 1496, to Francesco Gonzaga, Marquis of Mantua, that he regrets not being able to send him the comedy recently given at court; the rôles for each person, he adds, were written out separately and never put together, and as the actors had scattered the comedy was lost.[69] Such players as made a favorable impression at one palace were sure of engagement at another, but between these moments of glory and repletion the majority went back to the precarious hand-to-mouth existence of the unprotected stroller.

During the first half of the century however there must have been great progress made in the development of class-consciousness among the players, and consequently in their efforts to organize their troupes and to study their art. After 1550 public theaters began to be built and the best of the wandering bands to be formed into regular companies under the protection of noble patrons.[70] There were

[69] Letter quoted by Rasi, *Comici italiani*, II, 448; cf. ib., 703. The actors mentioned, all men, seem to have been professionals unattached to a patron.

Rossi, *Lettere*, etc., xxx f., discusses admirably the actor class in the Cinquecento.

[70] The dates for the foundation of theatres in the chief cities of Italy are thus given by Ademollo, *Una famiglia*, etc., introduction, and in *Teatri di Roma*.

Mantua, c. 1550.
Venice before 1565.
Siena, 1570.
Rome before 1575.
Florence, 1576.

usually some ten or twelve actors in one group, a
number that remained about the average for two
centuries; the Magnifico, the Gratiano, the Captain,
two pairs of lovers and from three to five clowns for
servants' parts or for inn-keepers, peasants and
magicians, were the essential characters, and they
were united in an organization more or less permanent according to their leader's strength and tact.[71]
This leader was licensed by some prince to choose
his companions and that difficult task accomplished,
was expected to recognize his first duty to his lord;[72]
at odd times he was allowed to play in public and
to reap the considerable rewards that came from
such representations.[73]

Milan before 1583.
There was a public theater in Naples before the end of the century,
cf. Croce, *Teatri di Napoli*, Chap. IV.
Ricci, *Teatri di Bologna*, Chap. I, thinks the Teatro della Sala in
Bologna was built in the first half of the sixteenth century. He
publishes in this book some interesting plans of early stages.

[71] Rossi, *Lettere*, etc., xxx f., says the earliest companies were not
formed before 1548. Ancona, *Origini*, II, 454, sets 1567 as the year
in which public performances were general.
There were ten persons in the Uniti in 1584. Tristano Martinelli
had in his "good and perfect company" (1621) ten or eleven persons
(Jarro, *L'Epistolario*, etc., 26–7). Riccoboni (*Hist. and Crit. Account
of the Theaters of Europe*, 68) says: "No Italian company ever contains more than eleven Actors and Actresses; of whom five, including
the Scaramouch, speak only the Bolognese, Venetian, Lombard and
Neapolitan dialects." Riccoboni's contemporary, the Italian actor,
A. Constantini, in his *Vie de Scaramouche*, 171, mentions as the
essential characters in an Italian troupe: "two lovers, three women,—
to wit, two for the serious parts, and one for the comic,—one Scaramouche, a Neapolitan; one Pantalone, a Venetian; one Doctor, a
Bolognese; one Mezzetin and one Arlequin, both Lombards." In
this company the Scaramouche would play the Captain.

[72] Jarro, *L'Epistolario*, etc., 22–7 and 36.
[73] Jarro, *op. cit.*, *passim*, especially 58.

Probably the atmosphere of freedom and the mixed company as well as the more certain pay, had something to do with making the actors feel most at home on a public stage. Coryat at least bears vivid witness to the simplicity and informality of one of the better Venetian theaters, describing it in detail: "I was at one of their Play-houses where I saw a Comedie acted. The house is very beggarly and base in comparison of our stately Play-houses in England; neyther can their Actors compare with vs for apparell, shewes and musicke. Here I obserued certaine things that I neuer saw before. For I saw women acte, a thing that I neuer saw before, though I haue heard that it hath beene sometimes vsed in London, and they performed it with as good a grace, action and gesture and whatsoeuer convenient for a Player, as euer I saw any masculine Actor. Also their noble and famous Cortezans came to this Comedy, but so disguised, that a man cannot perceiue them. For they wore double maskes vpon their faces, to the end they might not be seene: one reaching from the toppe of their forehead to their chinne and under their necke; another with twiskes of downy or wooly stuffe couering their noses. . . . They were so graced that they sate on high alone by themselues in the best roome of all the Play-house. If any man should be so resolute to unmaske one of them but in merriment onely to see their faces, it is said that were he neuer so noble or worthy a personage, he should be cut in pieces before he should come forth of the roome, especially if he were a stranger. I saw some men also in the Play-house, disguised in the same manner with double visards, those were said to be the fauorites of the same Cortezans: they sit not here in galleries as we doe in London. For there is but one or two little galleries in the house, wherein the Cortezans only sit. But all the men doe sit beneath in the yard or court, euery man vpon his seuerall stoole, for the which he payeth a gazet."[74]

It would be a little hard to realize to-day were not Elizabethan customs familiar to us, that in the public theaters the Italian players like the English were not free from obligation to their patrons. Numerous decrees and letters are extant telling of the favor or the tyranny from which supposedly protected companies rejoiced or suffered. In 1565 the governor of Milan, Don Gabriel della Cueva, prohibited all "Masters and players of comedies, herb-sellers, charlatans, buffoons, Zanni and mountebanks" "who are used to mount their platforms and to draw a crowd around them" to play on church feast days or in Lent or on stages near the church except after service, "on pain of whipping." The governor was a Spaniard and perhaps brought his country's manners with him, for the church and the state between them made an actor's life hardly worth living in Spain.[75] Yet Italian clerics were sometimes equally severe; the Gelosi had great difficulty in persuading Carlo Borromeo to allow them to play their "honest and pleasing comedies" in Milan, and were in fact only permitted to give those pieces that

[74] *Coryats Crudities*, II, 16–18.
[75] Rennert, *Spanish Stage*, 207 f.

had passed the censorship of "several learned and
pious theologians.'"[76] It would be interesting to
know which of the plays, all seemingly about on a
level so far as taste and morality go, this worthy
jury pronounced harmless to the public; probably
they only suppressed those containing a tinge of
heresy or blasphemy. Occasionally there are traces
of other limitations, such as that laid down by Sixtus
V in 1588, forbidding the Desiosi to employ women
in their comedies while in Rome and further requiring them to act by daylight.[77]

On the whole most Italian princes, secular or ecclesiastical, were less careful of the sacred interests of
morality than the few unfavorable decrees alluded
to would imply. Once the rage for theatricals was
started, the high and mighty fairly fought with each
other in the attempt to give beautiful and startling
spectacles and to procure the most accomplished
interpreters for their pieces. The Cardinal Orazio
Lancelloti, a creature of Paul V, had a little theater
of his own and a band of actresses,—some dressed as
men,—whom he trained and rehearsed himself.[78]
The Dukes of Mantua were among the first to establish their own companies and were such liberal and
obliging patrons that their favor was much sought.
In 1580 the then Duke of Mantua appointed Francesco Angeloni chief of the Mantuan "mercenary

[76] The whole of this interesting duel between the saintly archbishop and the most famous of the Italian companies has been ably
studied by Scherillo, La comm. dell'arte, Chap. VI, 139 f. Ancona
claims to have published the facts first, Origini, II, 183, note 2.

[77] Scherillo, op. cit., 138, and Ancona, op. cit., I, 416, note 5.

[78] In 1615 and after. Cf. Ademollo, Teatri di Roma, 5–6.

actors, charlatans and mountebanks" with permission to grant a written license to other players "to recite comedies or to sing in the street while selling chestnuts or other trifles.''[79] Again some years later the Duke's decree shows that the connection between the mountebanks and their more fortunate fellows was still close; Tristano Martinelli, the famous Arlecchino, is declared "superior to all mercenary players," to *Zaratani*, jugglers, . . . who put up their stages for selling oils, soaps, romances (*historie*) and the like articles: we make him superior to them all in this our State and also in the other of Monferrato, so that none of them, either alone or accompanied, may dare to recite farces or to sing on the platform . . . without a license from the said Martinelli in writing, nor to leave without license from the same, under pain of being stripped of all they have either in common or of their own, which shall be divided into three parts,''[80] one part for the treasury, one for the magistrate and the third, presumably, for Martinelli who was very avaricious. The decree goes on to state the toll that the monopolist was allowed to levy, and to say that Arlecchino was to supervise all festivals in order that neither scandals nor disorders should occur.

Such documents are interesting to us principally in their suggestions of the way that the popular elements in the strollers' performances were brought to

[79] Rasi, *Comici italiani*, I, 162, and Ancona, *Origini*, II, 474 and note 1.

[80] Jarro, *L'Epistolario*, etc., 11. Barbieri's *Supplica* furnishes valuable information on the relation of actors to patrons in the early Seicento.

the notice of educated audiences and learned dramatists. From about 1565 when an actor known as
Pantalone appears in a Roman lawsuit,[81] the Masks
begin to emerge from obscurity and to crowd into
the foreground of the only public attention that
counts historically, that of important personages
and letter-writers. Naturally it is in records of
carnival festivities when universal license was permitted and when the clowns were most in evidence,
that the most frequent mention is found of the Masks
and of the properties they require,—visards, beards
and the like.[82]   At the carnival of 1565 "ein Vene-
diger mit sein Knecht, Zane," entertained Ferdinand, Duke of Bavaria, in Verona so gaily that one
could "nit Peser noch wercklicher gedenkhen"; the
same letter describes a Prologus "dressed like a
Doctor, riding in on a donkey,"[83] probably a personage from a popular rustic comedy in which the quack
magician and the doctor were one and the same. In
1566 there is an allusion to the Spanish Captain of
comedy in a complaint of the Duke of Mantua's
secretary that "the Spaniard of the comedies" has
not come in time to act his part.[84] The same Mantuan archives note performances in 1567[85] by La
Flaminia (probably the "young Roman woman"
praised in an earlier document) and by the

[81] Rasi, *Comici italiani*, II, 231.

[82] Solerti, *Ferrara*, etc., exlix. The ducal accounts of Ferrara and
Mantua have been the most carefully searched for records of *comici;*
cf. Ancona, *Origini*, II, 510, note 1.

[83] Trautmann; *Italienische Schauspieler*, etc., 234.

[84] Ancona, *Origini*, II, 443, points out that the Spaniard must
have been a Mask, not a Spanish actor.

[85] Ancona, *Origini*, II, 447 f. and 445.

"Graziani," a company which took the name of its leader, a specialist in the Doctor's role.

That many of the plays given so successfully before these aristocratic audiences were *commedie dell'arte* is made fairly certain by the oldest surviving scenario (1568), a play so well developed in its main characteristics that it could not possibly have been unique. Moreover Henri III seems to have been entertained by two improvised plays of the Gelosi when he was at Venice in 1574; at least he peremptorily summoned the whole company to France two years later, begging especially that "the woman called Vittoria[86] and the Magnifique" should not fail to come,—an indication that the Masks stood out vividly in his memory.[87] There must still however have been a good many occasions when nothing so elaborate as a complete comedy was attempted and when the little interludes and debates from the mountebanks' portfolio were quite satisfactory. Pedrolino, himself the leader of a well-known company, did not disdain to amuse his patrons by some of these simpler tricks, as witnesses his practical joke at a banquet in the palace of Ferrara, 1580. He hid under the table unknown to anyone but the Duchess, and when Pantalone came to look for him, the clown stuck his head out of a large patty and informed the guests that he had been punished for his greediness, for that having gone into the kitchen

---

[86] Vittoria Piissimi, whom Garzoni calls a "bella maga d'amore," was one of the first actresses to attain recognition and to be largely rewarded; cf. Rasi, *Comici italiani*, II, under Piissimi, and for the Magnifico here mentioned, ib., II, 226–7.

[87] Baschet, *Comédiens italiens*, etc., 54 f.

6

"per gola" the cook had baked him into a pie; after this comic lament he disappeared under the crust and kept on talking from there.[88]

Another dialog between Pantalone and Zanni is described in a German account of a noble marriage in 1585;[89] one of the performers was represented "in the figure and dress of a Magnifico of the Venetian state, playing on a violin and singing . . . most ludicrously in the Italian tongue. . . . The other was in a very peasantlike costume, with wide long hose and a rare large hat which he knew how to turn and fold in all sorts of ways, and he spoke in Bergamask, and had a rake which he swung in a rustic manner, and moreover added every kind of amusing trick. . . . With their singing and springing they showed how much before all others their nation deserves the prize." A little song and dance like this is not formal enough to be classed with "professional" comedies, it rather belongs to the category of "things" half scornfully alluded to by Niccolò Rossi as "carried about by mercenary bands," unworthy of the name of art. In 1550 the actors who gave such shows were already dissociated from the charlatan's bench but they had further to learn concentration and to undergo a severe course of training in dramatic theory and practice before they could make their improvised plays famous over Europe.

[88] Solerti-Lanza, Gior. Stor., XVIII, 148 f.
For more details on Pedrolino cf. Rasi, Comici italiani, II, 241.
[89] Trautmann, Ital. Schauspieler, 226–7.

CHAPTER III.

If only the beggarly and base stages of public theaters had been open to professional actors the *commedia dell'arte* would never have advanced to the complicated form that we know; it would have remained unrecognized, merely the inartistic hodge-podge of clowning, old jokes and more or less hideous tricks that the mountebanks exhibited either on the street or at informal entertainments. But princely encouragement brought the quick-witted men and women among the strollers into contact with the interests of the intellectual world and forced them to modify their programs in accordance with academic theory. They learned that amateurs of the theater began to represent Latin comedies and then Italian plays modelled on them in the latter part of the fifteenth century; they were told of the discovery of twelve plays of Plautus in 1429[1] and of the publication of Aristotle's *Poetics* in 1498, two facts which gave an enormous impetus to critical theorizing and a great stimulus to dramatic activity. They were introduced into large halls set apart in palaces, and into private buildings erected specially for theatricals either by individuals or by academies, like the splendid Palladian structure, the Teatro Olimpico, described by Coryat in Vicenza;[2] perhaps

[1] Rossi, *Il Quattrocento*, 376.
[2] *Coryats Crudities*, II, 86. Cf. the recent account by Magrini of the *Teatro Olimpico*, especially p. ii f.

they were even allowed to take small parts in the classical dramas given here.

No doubt the actors soon came to realize that so noble a setting as that of the Olympian Theater was unsuited to anything except Greek or Senecan tragedies but in the smaller private halls they felt at liberty to give many performances of modern plays expressing the interests of their patrons.   These Italian comedies written by members of the academies were at first merely satirical "imitations of life" closely following Plautus and Terence; then came freer manipulations of romantic and sometimes of popular material with a central theme, it might be, dealing with Platonic love or working out a problem as to the relative values of duty, love, friendship and honor.[3] However large the canvas on which the action was painted there was always, in the sixteenth century at least, an attempt to observe proportion in plot development and to keep to the laws of unity as formulated by Aristotle's commentators and the laws of decorum as understood by Horace.[4]

[3] For the performances of classical and pseudo-classical plays at the ducal courts cf. Rossi, *Il Quattrocento*, 379 f.; Solerti, *Ferrara, etc.*, passim; Luzio-Renier, *Commedie classiche in Ferrara;* Rossi, *Commedie classiche in Gazzuolo.*

Ariosto's *Cassaria,* from the *Mostellaria* of Plautus, is now generally admitted to have been the first Italian comedy in the vernacular; it was written in 1488.   Bibbiena's *Calandra,* written about 1506–8 on the model of the *Menaechmi,* has often been called the first Italian comedy.   Both plays are classical in content as well as in form notwithstanding their Florentine color and their Italian names.

B. Accolti's *Verginia* on the other hand, played at an aristocratic wedding in Siena, 1494, is a romantic tragi-comedy from Boccaccio's story of Giletta of Narbonne, loosely constructed, and showing none of the Latin influence on technic.

[4] Cf. Spingarn, *Lit. Crit. in the Renaissance.* Minturno's *Arte poetica* is a mine of information on academic theory and practice.

It is not necessary to go into much detail in describing these written or "learned" plays; everyone who has read Gascoigne's *Supposes* or the *Comedy of Errors* or any of Chapman's comedies, knows the kind of plot and characterization that prevailed. Our concern here is with the literary influence such pieces exerted on Italian actors in the Cinquecento, and through them on their peculiar product, the "professional comedy." During the earlier half of the century as has been said, professionals were not often employed for the principal parts in academic productions; they gave their wit and grace mostly to the interludes. It was only the exceptionally gifted genius like Beolco or his Venetian follower Calmo,[5] who was clever enough to step to the front of the stage and take an important part in plays of his own writing. The majority were content to contribute to minor roles their quota of amusement, while absorbing what they could of academic ideas on the nature and presentation of regular plays. So by the time that organized companies began to be formed, about 1550–60, their managers were perfectly aware of what a noble audience looked for and criticized in a comedy, tragedy or pastoral, and were prepared to meet the demand by presenting literary drama in the approved manner. Perhaps it is worth while to quote in this connection part of a dialog on " scenic performances" composed under the influence of an academy between 1567 and 1590 by an actor-manager, Leone de Sommi,

[5] Calmo was as famous for his creation of old men as was Beolco for his peasants; cf. Rossi, *Lettere*, etc., introduction, passim.

a Mantuan Jew who was at the head of a company favored by the Duke.[6]

"In the first place," says Veridico, the spokesman of the author's opinions, "I should make every effort to procure a comedy that would satisfy me, with all the requirements that belong to such imaginative works (*tali poemi*), above all written in choice prose and not tiresome by reason of many soliloquies or long digressions or remarks not germane to the subject. . . . But I should also wish the comedy to be new if possible, or at least little known, avoiding as much as may be the printed ones however fine, because every new thing pleases; comedies that are known to the audience are usually little liked for many reasons, chiefly for this: the actor's great effort is to deceive and force the spectator into thinking the story presented is true, but if the hearer knows just what the actor is going to do and say, all will seem the veriest foolish lying. . . ."

As to division of parts in a play Veridico says: "After I had written out the several parts carefully and chosen the persons who seemed to me fittest . . . I would call them all together, and when I had distributed the parts as best suited, I would have them read the whole play, even to the boys that were in it—they would thus be taught the plot or at least as much of it as concerned them—impressing on their minds the kind of persons they had to represent; then I dismiss them, giving them time to learn

---

[6] The dialog is published by Rasi, *Comici italiani*, I, 107 f., from a MS. in the R. Bibl. of Parma. For De Sommi cf. Rasi, I, 106; Ancona, *Origini*, II, 403 f., and Neri, Gior. Stor., XI, 413, and Gior. Stor., LIV, 103 f.

their parts. . . . It is far more important to have
good actors than a good play, for truly I have often
seen a poor play well acted, succeed better than a
fine one badly played.   Therefore I choose . . .
those who can best imitate the different personages,
seeing to it that a lover is handsome, a soldier
muscular, a parasite fat, a servant agile, and so with
all. I also pay great attention to their voices for I
find it a precept of prime importance that . . . the
rôle of an old man should not be given to someone
with a childish voice, nor a woman's, especially a
young maiden's, to a gruff-voiced person.[7] If for
instance I wished to make a ghost speak in a tragedy
I would search out a voice naturally shrill, or at
least a trembling falsetto which would do for such
a part. As to faces I take less pains for there art
can supply nature, either by dyeing a beard or painting a scar, making a face pallid or yellow, or
healthier and ruddy, or whiter or browner, etc., as
may be necessary. But I never in any circumstances
use masks or false beards,[8] because they too much
impede utterance; if I were forced to give an old
man's part to a beardless actor, I would paint his
chin so that it looks shaved and add to the white wig
under his cap a few locks hanging over his cheeks
and forehead. . . ."

[7] This remark among others shows that De Sommi had in mind the
amateur performances of academicians rather than those of professionals.

[8] This is probably directed against the street actors whose use of
masks and other farcical disguises is often reproved by academic
writers, even by some of those of the actor profession; cf. Rossi,
Discorso sulla comedia, passim.

Veridico then discourses at some length and very sensibly on the manner of using the voice on the stage, making a great point of clear and intelligent enunciation. He next takes up a favorite critical problem—character decorum and the representation of typical persons: "It is not enough for the man who plays the miser's part to hold his hand constantly on his purse nor to look every minute to see if he has lost the key of his chest; he must also know how to represent the insanity that seizes him when he discovers that his son has robbed his hoard. If he plays the part of a servant he must know how in a moment of sudden joy to cut a quick and graceful antic, in a moment of grief to tear his handkerchief with his teeth; or in rage to pull out his hair, or with similar effective strokes to give life to the performance. If he plays a fool, beside answering off the point (which the poet will teach him by his words) he must be able to act the imbecile, catch flies, kill fleas and do the like foolish actions. If he plays the part of a serving-maid he must learn to shake his skirts coquettishly and if occasion demand it, to bite his finger for disdain,* and so on, things which the poet in his writing cannot fully indicate. . . ."

Massimiano, one of the interlocutors,—remembering the mountebanks, no doubt—remarks that he has seen some actors who at hearing a piece of bad news in a play turn as pale as if a misfortune had really happened to them, whereupon Veridico after quoting the *Ion* of "the divine Plato," goes on to

* Perhaps the thumb-biting among the servants in *Romeo and Juliet* is a relic of this stage tradition.

say that such talents cannot be taught but must come by nature, and praises some of his contemporaries for their rare gifts. "Among many accomplished persons who play perfectly in this age of ours . . . especially remarkable has always seemed to me the acting of a young Roman woman named Flaminia, who beside being adorned with many fair qualities, is adjudged so rare in this profession that I think the ancients never saw nor can there be seen among the moderns anything better than she on the stage, for one does not seem to see a concerted imitation of an action but something which really happens unexpectedly, so much she changes her gestures, voice and color according to the variety of incidents."

There follow some detailed instructions on posture and grace, summed up in the precept: "Always imitate and observe the characteristic nature of the person who is to be represented, fleeing above all things as one would misfortune, a certain pedantic manner of playing . . . like that of boys in school." In order further to emphasize the character of the persons in the piece dress is to be carefully considered: "I try to dress the actors as nobly as possible but with some difference between them . . . (above all things the action, time and place must be observed) . . . for sumptuous garments add much of dignity and charm to comedies and more to tragedies. Yet I would not dress a servant in velvet or in colored satin unless the habit of his master was so rich with embroidery and gold that a due measure was preserved between them." Meaner clothes are recommended for a miser or for a peasant, then after an allusion to the custom of the ancients in keeping to stereotyped costumes for old men, parasites, courtesans and others, Veridico speaks of the need for some variety: "Had I to dress three or four servants I should put one in white with a hat, another in red with a small cap on his head, another in livery of divers colors, another perhaps I might deck out with a velvet cap and a pair of netted sleeves. . . ."

Actors are bidden to disguise themselves thoroughly, so that the pleasure of the audience in the action may not be spoiled by the recognition of a familiar face, for that would break the illusion. Moreover "since every novelty is pleasing, it is a delightful sight to see on the stage foreign costumes, varying from our usage; hence it is that the most successful comedies are those costumed in the Greek fashion. For this reason more than any other I have arranged that the scene of the piece which, God willing, we shall present Tuesday, is laid in Constantinople, so that we can introduce for men as for women a style of dress unfamiliar to us here. . . . And if this succeeds well in comedy, as by experience we are sure that it will, all the more will it succeed in tragedy, in costuming which the greatest care must be taken, never dressing the actors in the modern manner but in the way that is shown in antique sculptures or pictures, with those mantles and that attire in which the persons of former centuries appear so charmingly. And because in the best spectacles one of the finest sights is a company

of armed men, I praise those who always bring into
the presence of Kings or Captains, some soldiers
or gladiators armed in the antique fashion. . . ."

"Of pastorals we will speak to-morrow . . . but
as to the dress of the shepherds . . . there should
be some variety among them, and their general style
as follows: cover their arms and legs with flesh-
colored cloth, or if the actor is young and handsome
it is not bad to have his arms and legs left bare,[10]
but never the feet, which should always be lightly
cased in sandals or socks; then there should be a
shirt of rough cloth or some material of a pleasant
color, sleeveless, and over this two skins (in the
manner Homer describes in the dress of the Trojan
shepherd), either of a leopard or of some other
pretty animal, one on the chest and one on the back,
bound together, with the feet of these beasts over
the shoulder and behind the back of the shepherd.
. . . Then let one have a small flask or a purse of
some fine wood at his girdle, others a scrip bound
on one shoulder. Let each have in his hand a club,
some stripped, some with leaves, and the more
extraordinary the more fitting they will be; their
hair, either their own or false, some curled, some
long and combed. . . . For the nymphs . . . women's tunics are needed, worked and varied, with
sleeves . . . girdles of silk and gold making folds to
please the eye . . . then some pretty colored silk
garment should be added from the belt down, girded

[10] These suggestions as to costume are undoubtedly the result of
much classical study, but there was on the stage of the *Sacre Rappresentazioni* a tradition in favor of a similar realism; cf. Ancona,
Origini, I, 446.

up to the ankles; the feet covered with a gilded buskin in the fashion of the ancients . . . the hair thick and blond, apparently natural, and some may wear their hair loose on their shoulders with a little garland on their heads, some may add a circlet of gold, others may knot it up with silken ribbons and cover it with a very thin veil falling over the shoulders. . . . These nymphs may have in their hands some a bow, with a quiver bound to their backs, others a single lance. . . . If the poet brings in a witch she ought to be appropriately dressed, or if a cowherd, let him wear rustic clothes that he may appear peasantlike. . . . And it adds much pleasure if the shepherd have with him at times one or more dogs, so also it would please me if the nymphs too had some, but gentler, with pretty collars and delicate little coats. . . ."

After having commented on all these weighty questions De Sommi returns to his rehearsal and says he always makes a point of calling over the list of names of the characters to see if they all understand what they have to do; then he draws up a list of the scenes in order, with the names of the persons in each, of the houses or streets from which they come out and at what place they must begin to speak. Such a paper, though Veridico does not say so, is practically the same thing as the scenario for an improvised play, perhaps slightly less full. But this admirer of the ancients and the aristocracy had no eye for anything so popular and irregular as an extempore farce; he shows his classic preferences by concluding his remarks with some directions on the prolog and interludes, always important parts of academic theatricals. He first commends the prolog in the manner of the ancients, when the poet himself or his representative came out in a toga and crowned with laurel, to speak with dignity and gravity: "Leaving aside for the moment those ingenious prologs into which the gods or other extraordinary personages are introduced. . . . I say that he who speaks in the poet's person should always direct his words to the spectators, contrary to the usage of the other actors, and should appear to them as their fellow citizen, giving them notice of what city the stage represents, of the kind of play and its name, asking for silence, and the like." As to interludes Veridico thinks that those of music are best for comedies, and that choruses only should mark off the acts in a tragedy; for pastoral poems something more elaborate is to be allowed.[11]

In his fourth dialog De Sommi talks of stage machinery and as in his remarks on costume, shows a taste for magnificence. Of pastorals he says: "The most of the plot and many kinds of plots, can be easily represented; in Bologna years ago I saw Amphion introduced in an *intermedio*, to the sound of whose music and singing the rocks piled themselves on each other until they made a wall for Thebes; in another an eagle appeared to carry off

[11] All the literary dramatists who had anything to say objected to the *intermedj*; Il Lasca bitterly complains in the preface to *La Strega* (1582) that "*intermedj* were invented to serve the comedy, now the comedy serves only as an excuse for the *intermedj*." Cf. with De Sommi, Ingegneri's *Discorso de la poesia rappresentativa* (1568), and also Macchiavelli's prolog to *La Clizia*.

Ganimede; then in the interval between the third and fourth acts Deucalion and Pyrrha came in, casting stones behind them, which stones rose up in the form of little naked children. And the fourth interlude was a giant who carried a very large ball, and having put it down on the stage he gave it several blows with his club and it opened and four Satyrs came out of it and danced a most charming moresca.''[12]

Obviously such splendid and costly spectacles were far beyond the resources of actors not in the employ of a prince or a wealthy academy. De Sommi himself was protected by Cesare Gonzaga, the founder of the Academy of the Invaghiti, a society for which the learned Jew managed dramatics in Mantua during several years.[13] These dialogs of his sound as though they had grown out of academic discussions of the nature of the drama, they certainly summarize the "correct" view of such matters. That theory should be so far developed to exact and dogmatic statement, marks the close of a long period of experimentation—nearly a century of familiarity on the part of educated people with classical canons and technic, and an even longer time spent on the elaboration of stage machinery.[14]

[12] Rasi, *Comici italiani*, I, 133.

[13] Ancona, *Origini*, II, 406-7.

[14] For the Italian stage and its gradual transformation cf. Flechsig, *Die Dekoration der modernen Bühne in Italien*. Descriptions of the *intermedj* abound in the literature and letters of the period and have been often reprinted; cf. Motta, Gior. Stor., VII, 386 f.; Arteaga, *Rivoluzioni del teatro musicale italiano*, III, 187 f.; Solerti, *Gl'albori del melodramma*, II, 17 f.; Mazzi, Nuova Ant., Ser. II, Vol. XXVIII, 577 f.; Saviotti, Gior. Stor., XLI, 42 f. Mazzi, *Congrega dei Rozzi*, I, 298 discusses *inframessi*, etc.

The professional actors, formerly so despised and so shut out from all real communion with their betters, had at last come to recognition; partly perhaps through the influence of Plato in that very *Ion* cited by Veridico, they were regarded, women as well as men, as in some subtle sense the instruments through which the divine fire manifested itself to humanity. Such at least is the sentiment that underlies many of the extravagantly complimentary poems addressed to players in the latter half of the Cinquecento.[15]

Platonic theories of inspiration, although their influence may have been really felt, must have contributed much less to the building up of the actor class than did its own advance in proficiency and culture. Very many players were taken into academies as regular members with the usual honorable ceremony of crowning with laurel, and such favored persons added their plays or poems or philosophic essays to the publications of these learned bodies.[16] In order to keep up their reputation and to deserve the name of scholars, the actors studied hard, learned Latin and Greek beside the dialects and modern languages needed in their plays, searched the classics for information on their art or for quotations to be used in their speeches, wrote songs

[15] Rasi's two volumes contain a wealth of material on this point as on many others; cf. especially the articles on the three Andreini, on Vittoria Piissimi, Maria Antonazzi, Vincenza Armani, P. M. Cecchini and his wife Orsola, Drusiano Martinelli and his wife Angelica.

[16] The most famous of the actor-academicians were Francesco Andreini (1548–1624), his wife Isabella (1562–1604), a member of the Pavian Intenti, and their son, Giovan-Battista, "academico Spensierato." There were many others; cf. Bruni, *Fatiche comiche* (1623), 9 f.

and sonnets and "conceits" to express their ideas
on the philosophy of love and on other intellectual
problems of the time, and not infrequently published
defenses of the theater based on their critical studies
and on their arguments in divinity and ethics.[17]
Antonio Molino, called Il Burchiella, the "Roscius of
his age," a friend of Andrea Calmo, was educated
"like any gentleman" as well as in the special arts
of song, dance, gymnastics and literary composition.[18] Isabella Andreini when she addressed one
of her patrons, that Duke of Mantua who had stood
sponsor to her child, was well enough seen in philosophy and the graces of compliment to begin her
letter thus:[19]

"Most Serene Lord: If in Ethiopia where there
are barbarous races, there are some peoples who
however barbarous yet adore two gods, the one immortal and the other mortal, the immortal as the
creator of the universe, the mortal as their bene-
factor, how much more here in beautiful Italy, garden of the world, where there is the light of faith
and the splendor of civilized customs, should be
adored the high and immortal God, supreme mover

[17] Solerti, *Albori*, etc., I, 16, calls the *comici* of this period "colti e
letterati," "critici delle questioni teatrali," etc. Bartoli, *Scen.
ined.*, cix f., gives a long list of the literary works of these men and
women.

Bonfigli in the introduction to his reprint of *Un Capitolo in morte
di Simone da Bologna* calls attention to the connection of the actors
with "penny literature" of all kinds, and points out that the mountebanks quite early in the Cinquecento began to write these little pamph-
lets. Cf. Perucci, *Arte Rappresentativa*, 195 f.

[18] Rossi, *Lettere*, etc., xxxi f. Cf. Rasi, *op. cit.*, I, 533.

[19] The letter is dated 14 Jan., 1587. Ancona, *Origini*, II, 490-1.

of the universe, and in the fair bosom of the most
noble city of Mantua Your Serene Highness as
mortal god, true giver of so many and notable
benefits.''

Since it might be a trifle wearisome to hear any
more proof of this kind of learning, let Vincenza
Armani stand as an example of all these accomplished beings; her funeral panegyrist, who to be
sure as her lamenting lover must be read with some
slight allowance, tells his hearers that the "divine
Signora Vincenza was born in the most famous city
of Venice," that "in cooking, in embroidery, nay in
painting with the needle, she outstripped the
Arachne of fable and Minerva herself, inventor of
these arts, . . . and before she finished the third
luster of her age she perfectly possessed the Latin
tongue, admirably explaining all its peculiarities,
and read and wrote so easily and correctly in Latin
and in her native idiom that the very discoverer of
orthography could not have done better.'' ''A
wonderful speaker, a sublime musician, herself a
composer of madrigals and of the music for them,
which she sang herself; an exquisite player on many
instruments, a sculptress in wax of the most skilful,
ready yet thoughtful in talk, and a very remarkable
actress. . . . She played in three different styles, in
comedy, tragedy and pastoral, observing the pro-
prieties of each so exactly that the Academy of the
Intronati in Siena which cherishes the cult of the
drama, often said this lady spoke better extempore
than the most finished writers after much thought.
. . . Everyone avoided arguing with her (in the

7

academic debates) for if at times she sustained the side of falsity she made it seem to those who heard her, the truth.'[20]   As might be expected her charms and her talent procured her many enemies and she died young, of poison.

The craze for culture was not the only result of learned influence on the actors. It was academic custom that started the practice, universal among professional troupes, of choosing a symbolic name and motto for their band,—the Gelosi, because "Virtù, Honor e Fama ne fèr gelosi," the Desiosi, the Fedeli; from imitation of a similar fad came also the habit of calling.individuals among them by their stage names,—Celia, Flaminia, Isabella,— sometimes with a punning significance; just as the academicians designated themselves by titles supposed, modestly, to express their leading traits,— the Stupid One or the Stutterer or the Idiot.[21]   The like small hobbies were only the outer sign of the deeper influence, that shift of point of view, that broadening of the intellectual horizon, which as I have said brought about such important modifications of the popular amusements.

The rough debates between Zanni and Pantalone or the Captain, or between the Doctor and the Signora of the mountebanks' stage were no sooner heard by learned ears than they became a subject

[20] *Oratione d'Adriano Valerini Veronese, in morte de la Divina Signora Vincenza Armani* . . . (Verona, 1570) cited Rasi, *Comici italiani*, I, 205.

[21] Everyone knows the absurdities to which this fashion led, how for instance, members of the academy of the *Umidi* took each the name of a fish, A.-F. Grazzini, the best known of them, calling himself Il Lasca, the Mullet. Cf. Mazzi, *Congrega*, etc., I, passim.

of discussion and criticism. They were so enjoy-
able that various excuses were found for them. Not
impossibly Aristotle's dictum as to the use of character names for the persons of comedy may somewhat have reconciled the theorists to the constant
reappearance of a certain limited number of farcical
Masks;[22] undoubtedly an early comparison of the
popular types to the figures in the Roman Atellanae
had a good deal to do with bringing them into a
more dignified position than they had ever held.
Moreover it is not difficult to see them as variations
from the characters of written plays. The boasting
bravo of the street platforms could very easily be
compared to the Latin Thraso or Pyrgopolinices;
were they not both arrant cowards, loud-mouthed in
their own praise but ready to start at a shadow on
the wall? The resemblance may be traced both
ways of course; if the literary figure influenced the
popular, it is quite as true that the captains in very
early written comedies such as Calmo's *Rabbioso* or
Dolce's *Capitano*, bear a strong resemblance, under
their predominantly Plautine color, to the vulgar
satiric conception of the bravo and the Spanish mercenary.[23] Again the charlatan Doctor of the *piazza*,

[22] *Poetics*, ed. Butcher, 4th ed., 35–7, section IX: "In comedy the
poet first constructs the plot on the lines of probability and then
inserts characteristic names,—unlike the lampooners who write about
particular individuals." Butcher (376–7) interprets the phrase to
mean that names in comedy should suggest certain traits, "humours"
or occupations.

[23] Cf. to Senigaglia's *Cap. Spavento*, Rasi, *Comici italiani*, I, 59 f.,
and Bartoli, *Scen. ined.*, clxix and liii f.; Scherillo, *Comm. dell'arte*,
chap. IV. Ancona, *Origini*, I, 590 f., studies the braggart in the

with his pretence of learning and skill and his extravagantly expressed belief in his pills and oils
could by a little analogy-forcing be confounded with
the "self-wise-seeming schoolmaster," the pedant
doctor, whom Sidney, true to the best critical ideas
of his time, mentions as one of the proper butts for
comedy.[24] This once seriously regarded medicine-
man of folk superstition when held up to the view of
politely cynical audiences lost all his prestige and
became merely one among several kinds of pedants,
unmercifully ridiculed for a show of wisdom they
have not, or for unbecoming seriousness over the
wisdom. they have.[25] Do not aristocratic dilettanti
always see a grimy Holofernes in a professional
scholar?

It is impossible to generalize too dogmatically
about any of these character types or to set off too
sharply the finished artistic version of any one of
them from its skeleton in a scenario. The Doctor in
an improvised play has usually quite as many traits
of the Latin *senex* as has Pantalone who regularly
filled the chief rôle of deceived father or husband;
both are equally remarkable for avarice, an amatori-

Sacre Rappresentasioni; Reinhardtstoettner, *Plautus*, etc., the literary type.

Rossi, *Lettere*, etc., lxxiv f., finds a closer relation between the
Capitano of Calmo's plays and that of the *commedia dell'arte* than
between the latter and the Capitano of any other written plays. The
same is true of Calmo's old men and Pantalone.

[24] *Defense of Poetry*, ed. Cook, 51.

[25] For the Doctor Mask cf. Rasi, *Comici italiani*, I, 406 f., and for
the principal actors of the part, Bartoli, *Scen. ined.*, clxv f. Dr.
Gratiano da Francolino is supposed to have made his first appearance
on the stage about 1560.

ous disposition and either gullibility or low cunning; both are altogether such unattractive persons that any sympathy for their invariable ill-fortune is absolutely impossible. Here academic theory bore out the popular judgment as to old men in love; they are among the proper subjects for comedy, says Minturno,[26] because they are always ludicrous, *A Cursing of old men in love,* written probably for insertion in a scenario by Isabella Andreini,[27] herself both an actress and a critic, expresses the usual view:

"Is it possible that you do not know that in this wrinkled forehead, these bristling brows, this colorless face, there is little, nay nothing, suited to a lover? . . . Ah, poor wretch! consider your folly, . . . love in an old man is nought but grief. . . . You ancients among many bad qualities have two that are intolerable, enviousness and evil-speaking, . . . so that no one escapes your slander. . . . As for your love letters they are audacities worthy silence if not laughter." The written plays almost always voiced a similarly unkind opinion and allowed little individuality to an ancient lover.

[26] *Arte poetica,* cited Spingarn, *Lit. Crit.,* etc., 2d ed., 61 f. For a study of the old man in comedy cf. Amicis, *L'imitazione latina,* etc., and Camerini, *Nuovi profili letterari,* II, 27 f. and 225 f.

Fresco, *Una tradizione novellistica nella commedia del secolo XVI,* (Camerino, 1903), studies the old man of Italian comedy as originating from two of Boccaccio's caricatures, Calandrino and Messer Simone, a view as one-sided as that which sees in the classic theater the only source of Renaissance drama. Boccaccio's influence was however tremendous. Cf. the befooled husband in Macchiavelli's *Mandragola* with *Decameron* V, 5 and 10.

[27] I. Andreini, Lettere, 21 f. This *Biasimo* might well have been used in Scala's thirteenth piece, *Il Dottor disperato,* Act II, where the direction in the scenario is "Oratio rebukes the Dr., an old man, for being in love."

In Calmo's comedies the peculiarities of the Venetian Magnificos and their Bergamask servants are
so constant that these personages may fairly be
called types, probably they may even have worn
some sort of conventional costume and mask; merely
the difference between premeditated and extempore
speech sets them off from Zanni and his masters.[28]
Indeed the hero's servant in most academic plays
is always the character who comes nearest to the
clown of street shows in his name, his dialect and
his lively manners. However consciously modeled
by his creator on the Latin *servus,* the lad must
naturally have taken the complexion of the strolling
merrymakers who from the first played the part in
otherwise amateur productions. As Zanni's traits
vary with his every interpreter he probably seemed
more amusing and individual than his stiffer counter-
part, forced as the latter was to keep to the lines
written for him by the poet; yet as Veridico had
advised the adept in fool's rôles to think up all
possible illustrative action for his lines, perhaps
there was really very little difference in the presentation of this character whether informal or
formal. Like Zanni the *servetta* owed little to
classical traditions; indeed even more than Zanni

* The relation of Calmo to the *commedia dell'arte* has given as
much trouble as that of Beolco; no scenario from Calmo's hand has
survived but Rossi thinks he may very likely have written up his plays
after a first extempore performance in which he tested their popularity. In the predominant interest in intrigue and in the kind of
persons in his plays as well as in the use of dialect and extravagant
concetti, his work is certainly nearer to the *commedia dell'arte* than
that of most of his contemporaries, naturally, as he was himself an
actor. Cf. Rossi, *Lettere,* etc., lxix f. and passim.

she is the shameless creature of the mountebanks' bench, who is brought into the play for the purpose of adding to the main intrigue a subordinate love plot, a parody on the principal interest.[29]

The lovers in the improvised plays on the other hand were taken bodily from the written comedies; young, inflammable, conscienceless they generally were, and, as Lamb says of the characters in our Restoration drama, not to be judged by the moral standards of every-day life. Their names were taken from life however, their faces were unmasked, their costumes those of ordinary well-to-do young people, their talk the Tuscan of the academies. Isabella Andreini, the most famous of *prime donne*, not only gave her name to her rôle in Scala's plays and in many later ones but wrote volumes of speeches appropriate to the part in their expression of love as the Petrarchists and Platonizers conceived it. Like the conceits for the Doctor and the Captain and the extravagances of the heroes and heroines in written plays, these "tirades" are full of mythology, classical quotations and allusions and far-fetched figures.[30]

---

[29] The critical tradition of there having been but four Masks, two of them belonging to the old men and two to distinct kinds of Zanni,— the knave, Brighella or Pulcinella, and the fool, Arlecchino,—seems to go back to Barbieri's *Supplica*, in which the actor-author says "The first servant . . . provokes laughter . . . by most subtle tricks and ready replies; the second by foolishness." Goldoni probably did not know Barbieri but he expresses the same opinion, *Memorie*, II, 185 f.; L. Moland, Sand and Symonds all adopt this statement as the basis of their exposition of the *commedia dell'arte*.

[30] P. M. Cecchini in his *Frutti delle moderne commedie* says, "They who play the difficult parts of lovers enrich their minds with a pretty lot of noble discourses suitable to the variety of matter which the

Where the scenario notes, "Isabella despairs as a despised lover," or "Isabella raves against Love and Fortune," she might say:[31] "If I did not complain of Love I must have been born mute. So great are my misfortunes that not only must I complain of him but must lament that I have not all the tongues, all the languages of the world, that I might better sorrow over his injustice; he rewards my pain with grief, wills that I feed on wormwood and hemlock, wills that I suffer patiently . . . wills that I dissimulate my woe and cruelly commands me to show a smiling face, rejoicing while my miserable heart in its bitter pain bitterly bewails its sorrow. . . . I renew the torture of Tantalus and long for the food and drink of love which are not given me." Or "My days fleet on with the months and the seasons. The sun changes the trees, alternating with his sister in giving light, my sorrow alone remains the same.[32] That changes neither its character nor its place nor gives way to any pleasure. Yet what do I say? My

stage should treat . . . (by) a frequent reading of elegant books so that there remains in the reader's memory an impression of most heightened style, which when their speeches are heard produce the effect of springing from native genius."

[31] I. Andreini, *Lettere*, 9 f.

[32] It is hardly necessary to note the commonness of this Petrarchan conceit. The most familiar Elizabethan statement of it is in the Earl of Surrey's sonnet, "Wherein each thing renews save only the lover." The antithesis appears often in Isabella's *Lettere* and is the theme of a song in her pastoral *Mirtilla*, Act I, scene 2, of which one quatrain is:

> E quanto il ciel di più bel fior dipinge,
> E più le cose allegre
> Tanto al mio tristo core
> La fiera doglia accresce.

grief changes only too much; from ill it goes to worse, from cruel and bitter to unspeakable and unbearable . . . so that now my harsh laments weary town and village, mountain and valley, rivers, seas, meadows, woods and even tireless Echo herself.''[88]

Debates on the nature of love were also suited to the lover's rôle, therefore Isabella, a philosopher and academician as well as a poet, wrote, doubtless as she spoke on the stage, ''You say that love is a mode of behavior of the soul, that the soul is eternal and that therefore love will be eternal. I admit that the soul is immortal, but love is only one of its attributes (*cade in lei per accidente*), . . . since it is not credible that an attribute of the soul is, like it, eternal, why do you wish me to believe this? Love in others, moreover, is fed on hope and happiness, yet you say he is fed in your breast by despair and pain. . . . Everyone follows, you add, his own good, and you alone your own enemy, desire your harm and seek it.''[84] So for many pages the fine-spun sentimentalities of the sonneteers are restated in more or less inflated and pedantic language, not at all different from the style of lovers in the most affectedly Italianate Elizabethan plays.

Sometimes elaborate and vicious punning gave a kind of symbolic force to a lover's argument,—again a manner imitated by the Elizabethans. In one of the conceits in dialog form written by Domenico Bruni, a youth argues with his former sweetheart, whom in her page's dress he does not recognize, that

[*] I. Andreini, *Lettere*, 143.
[**] *Ibid.*, 143.

his present love is fairer and worthier than his first. She defends herself ingeniously by pointing out that his first love's name was Celia, and that in offending her he has offended Heaven (il Cielo), "and whoever offends Heaven is damned to Hell. . . . I have heard (she goes on) that names indicate in themselves fortunate or unhappy destinies; therefore this name of Lavinia (his present mistress) does not please me; for Lavinia was that most unfortunate creature sung by Virgil who started the war in Latium, caused the death of Turnus and the sorrow of Aeneas; moreover if you take the second syllable of this name, which is *Vi,* and place it first, you compose a name which is *Vilania,* or villany. Now Villanies dishonor men, whence you may conclude that the possessing this lady will only dishonor you." Fulvio, the victim of this lecture, cannot avoid retorting, "How well up in worldly wisdom you are, my Lucio!"[35]

Thus the lovers in the best *commedie dell'arte* of the Cinquecento exhibited their refinement, their learning and their powers of expression, nor did they forget to inveigh at proper intervals against Cupid and Fortune, the bugbears responsible for all the ills they suffer. In similar manner Doctor Gratiano and the Captain and even poor old Pantalone made the most of their academic accomplishments in the speeches they wrote for their parts. The Doctor was especially given to the insertion of Latin, usually of the maccaronic variety, and to the

[35] Bruni, *Dialoghi scenici,* a MS. of the Seicento, published in part by Basi, *Comici italiani,* I, 521 f.

elaboration of platitudes and the laboring of etymologies in a way that makes us suspect him of laughing in his sleeve at the diversions of the learned societies before which he played. Soldano Aniello, one of the earliest specialists in the Bolognese rôle, wrote a whole book of *Fantastic and Ridiculous Etymologies,* sometimes little plays to be used as prologs, sometimes mere conceits for the Doctor to insert in the comedy at the right moment.[36] A late *Tirade for a Gratiano* gives the etymology for *soldato* in a monolog which begins:

"This word divides into three syllables, *sol, da, to.* *Sol* means that the soldier must be like the sun, (*sole*) in giving light to the whole world of soldierdom; alone, (*sol*) in touching mud without being defiled, water without wetting himself, fire with being burned," etc.[37]

A different kind of speech for the pedant's part is the *Persuasion to Study;* an example quoted by Perucci fairly reeks of the library: "The man in this world who is without wisdom is *sicut asinus sine capistro,* because lacking the bridle that leads him along the road to virtue, he goes headlong to the precipice. He is just *sicut porcus in luto;* he who does not fatten himself on the drink of knowledge will remain ever dry and thin as a starling,

[36] An early instance of this fascinating pursuit of the derivations of words is noted by Monnier, *Le Quattrocento,* 142, in a description of how Marsigli's free school debated in 1389 the origin of the word *prato.* The academies kept up the exercise constantly.

For Aniello cf. Rasi, *Comici italiani,* I, 164 f. He flourished c. 1590.

[37] Quoted by Bartoli, *Scen. ined.,* lxxxvi, note 3, from an unpublished MS.

and cannot thicken the soup of conversation. . . . You will be the ass, but bridled by my discipline, (i. e. after studying with Gratiano) the pig, but fattened by my learning," etc.[38] Whatever the Doctor said, whether studied or extempore, was apparently marked by irrelevance and lack of sequence in its propositions, for Captain Spavento, in one of his dialogs with Trappola says, "Apropos of Bacchus, I remember a dispute I once had with Death," and the Zanni takes him up with, "This remark of yours sounds to me like a speech of Gratiano,—your saying 'Apropos of Bacchus I remember Death!' Master, beware! pay attention to what you speak, how you speak and where you speak, else those who don't respect you as I do, may cast 'fool' in your teeth."[39]

The old men's plague and the lovers' enemy, the Captain, had many famous interpreters, and none better than Francesco Andreini, the redoubtable Captain Spavento of Hell-Valley, some of whose words have just been quoted. This gentleman, for gentleman he was, knew intimately the soldiers of written plays, had often acted their overbearing demeanor toward servants and women and had learned their speeches, loaded with ancient mythological ornament and absurd exaggerations. He was familiar with their tales of "shattered legs, crushed arms, rolling heads, cries of terror from one party, threatening roars from the other, and

---

[38] Perucci, *Arte Rapp.*, 279 f., says the actor of the Dottore must study Fidenzio "to learn his phrases" and must "strengthen himself" in the style of Merlino Coccai and Stoppino.

[39] Andreini, *Bravure*, I, Rag. 17.

blood, always blood."[40]   He knew how among other exploits, Martebellonio, son to Mars and Bellona, killed Death, or Mona Viva—Lady Life—as she was called before this hero took her throat between two fingers and "strangled her like a quail."[41] Therefore when he came to write set "tirades" for his part in the improvised plays he imitated the tales of these braggarts and shook the stage by stories of his battles with giants, gods and Death herself.

"Know," he says to Trappola, his Zanni, "that one day Death and Cupid got drunk and went to sleep in the temple of Bacchus—Lyaeus, Bassareus, Father Liber, which you please—and when they woke each took the bow and dart of the other; so they went about their business."

Trappola, "A nice sight! Cupid and Death drunk and tramping through the country like a couple of Germans!"

Captain, "I happened to be passing, full of pride and glory, across the ridge of the Caucusus . . . as I walked Death (whom I despised) shot a mortal bolt to take away my life; instead it made me fall in love with the Queen of the Amazons, who stood delighting me in the window of her palace. I felt myself wounded and wrenching the arrow from my breast, I threw myself against Death, who was at once caught in the snare of love for me, and said, 'Captain Spavento, my soul, I am yours!' . . . But I so burned with contempt instead of love that I

[40] Senigaglia, *Cap. Spavento*, 93.
[41] G. B. della Porta, *I due fratelli rivali*, I, sc. 4.

seized her by one foot and slung her at the head of Heresy."[42]

Elsewhere the warrior tells of so wearying Death by the number of his victims that she begged him to assume her office for a month.[43] At still another time he took Death, Love and the Devil prisoners,[44] and finally, like Theseus and Pirithous, he went to Hell to steal Proserpina.[45] No wonder that he describes himself as "King of the Proud, Emperor of the Ambitious, Monarch of the Wrathful, . . . who with my head threat the East, with my foot press down the West, with my left hand bind the south wind and with my right tame the cold, icy north,"[46] "the brave, the unconquered, unconquerable, invincible, a lightning flash, an eagle, a scourge in war."[47] He admits that he arms himself fantastically and oddly with Mt. Taurus on his head as a helmet, the labyrinth of Crete as a cuirass and the pyramids of Egypt as bolts.[48] What a pity that we are haunted by memories of the way, in the scenarios, this same tremendous talker flees from a ghost or a boy!

He is as proud of his learning as of his valor and to prove his accomplishments quotes from the classics and from Petrarch, Tasso, Marini, Ariosto, even a line from Dante, though ascribing this last

[42] *Bravure*, Part I, Rag. 17.
[43] *Ibid.*, I, Rag. 22.
[44] *Ib.*, I, 13.
[45] *Ib.*, I, 39.
[46] *Ib.*, I, 6.
[47] *Ib.*, I, 23.
[48] *Ib.*, I, 2.

to Petrarch.[49] He also takes part in a famous academic quarrel and in two discourses defends Tasso[50] as "he who in the Tuscan tongue and the heroic style conquers every other poet . . . who is considered worthy to fill the second seat on Parnassus, by the side of the most famous Petrarch." Trappola's comment is, "This is a right honorable end to the scholastic battle, to recognize as poet such a man, the honor of our age and of all poets, whose honor was yet questioned by some envious of his glory, who have tried though vainly to obscure it with slander. . . . It is enough now to say *Tasso,* and everyone knows we mean *poet.*"

The Captain's love affairs as told by himself are quite as astounding and much more unquotable than his warlike deeds or the proofs of his learning. Goddesses are rivals for his favor,[51] the Moon forgets Endymion for him,[52] and innumerable mortals break their hearts for his inconstancy. In a scenario of later date than Andreini's dialogs the Captain opens the play by telling Coviello that he has conquered Cupid in battle and has forced the god to name the most beautiful lady in the world; she is Isabella, daughter to Dr. Gratiano, and the

[49] Bartoli, *Scen. ined.,* xxv, note 4, remarks on this and cites still other poets mentioned by Andreini.

[50] *Bravure,* I, 45. Cf. I, 40, the *Defense of Tasso in the Inferno.*
Probably the position of the Gelosi, Andreini's company, as protégés of the ducal houses of Ferrara and Mantua gave the impulse for this defense. The question is interesting as showing that the professional plays, like some of our vaudeville, made a kind of journalistic appeal to their patrons.

[51] *Bravure,* I, 26.

[52] *Ib.,* I, 51.

soldier is here to seek her, sure of success. Unfortunately his talk in this case as always is based on vain imaginations and after some ridiculous Tweedledee-Tweedledum mock-fights with Gratiano, the hero is obliged to retire discomfitted, leaving the damsel to her young lover.[53]

Although as I have said Zanni has more traits of the mountebank's clown than the other persons in the improvised plays, even he does not entirely escape the prevailing infection of pedantic talk. The set speeches for his part are not so numerous as those for the Captain, the Doctor, Pantalone and the lovers, yet he does have his soliloquies—for use either as prologs or epilogs or in the body of the comedy—his laments and love rhapsodies parodying his master's, his prescriptions parodying Gratiano's, more rarely his bombastic ravings meant to be taken seriously but ludicrously out of keeping with his character. Of these last one must suffice; it is supposed to be spoken by the much-traveled Zanni, Ganassa, who addresses a lament to his master:

"Alas, dear master, let me weep, me who have a real cause to be the most unhappy and unlucky man alive to-day, because the dearest friend and companion I had is dead! Why have I not the eloquence of Demosthenes, of Cicero and of Quintillian, that I might describe the worth of his merits and the passion of my soul! He was joined to me by the closest ties of friendship that have existed since the days of Theseus and Pirithous, Titus and Gisippus, Pylades and Orestes. . . ."

[53] *Flaminio disperato*, Nuova Antologia, Ser. II, Vol. LI, 223 f.

Pedrolino, in Scala's *Faithful Pilgrim Lover* (Gior. XIV) proves his education to have been as liberal as Ganassa's, for in one scene he "lists the famous men at-arms who have loved and been the servants of love" and meditates the proportionate values of a soldier's and a scholar's career,—an ancient problem debated time and again by the academies and found in not a few medieval *contrasti*.[54] Sometimes Zanni invented genealogies, boastful tales, lawyer's quibbles and the like which savored more of the study than of the charlatan's bench,[55] yet on the whole his singing and tumbling and jesting were more usual and certainly seem far more congenial to him than the arduous searching of the classics necessary for his literary efforts.

If there were space to quote soliloquies either mournful or gay from written comedies it would be apparent how closely modeled on them was much of the high-sounding talk in the improvised pieces. Love, honor, fortune, examples illustrative from Ovid and Virgil, sentiment and philosophy from the Italian poets, all these elements were seething in the proficient actor's memory as he had learned their expression in literary dramas. Nothing could be more natural than that he should draw on this store of polite knowledge and adorn his farces with em-

[54] Stoppato, *Comm. pop.*, 90, mentions two famous medieval debates on this theme. The same subject recurs constantly in the *Decameron* and is a chief interest in one of the farces of the Rozzi, cf. Mazzi, *Congrega*, etc., I, 325.

[55] Cf. Bonfigli, introduction to *Capitolo in morte di Simone da Bologna*. Simone had played the Zanni's part under the name of Zan Panza di Pegora and in this poem is learnedly mourned by two other Zanni, his comrades.

broideries in which both material and pattern were cut from something of solider and richer design. Supplemented by his private studies, the literary plays in his repertory also taught him a more important thing than the use of ornament, they taught him how to construct a plot, how to make a central love interest the framework for dialog between the clowns of his troupe, and how to enliven it all by the *lazzi* his experience had forced him to invent. He discovered that the Signora of his company in her masculine attire, was more interesting if she put on doublet and hose for a purpose,—say to allow her escape from an over-strict father or her following an inconstant lover, than if she wore them always and as a matter of course.[56] He found it possible to use the familiar fools, the Magnifico and Dr. Gratiano, in the rôles of the old men of the play, thus making their vices and their foolishness tell in the development of an intrigue. Finally he made the most of the gymnasts and lithe Zanni in his band by casting them for servants' parts where they could turn all their gifts to advantage and bring in their tricks and their music with least outrage to the fable.

It was through changes and innovations such as these that the Gelosi toward the end of the sixteenth century, made good their boast of having raised the standard of professional entertainments;[57] one of

[56] Cecchi's *I Rivali* and *Gl'ingannati* (by a member of the Intronati of Siena) are two of the best known of innumerable written plays in which the heorine resorts to masculine disguise.

[57] F. Bartoli, *Notisie istorische*, etc., says Scala was "the first who to the professional comedy gave fitting order, with all the proper dramatic rules." Vol. II, under *Scala*.

Francesco Andreini's prefaces says that "this marvellous company in which each actor was superlatively excellent" had showed the public and all
future players "the true method of composing and
presenting comedies, tragicomedies, tragedies, pastorals, spectacular pieces, interludes and other scenic
devices." The same comedian in his prefatory
letter to Scala's collection of scenarios praises his
author thus: "Signor Flavio (Scala's stage name)
could have written out his works in full . . . but because to-day there are so many printed comedies
that . . . are very offensive to dramatic rules, he
wished with this his new invention to put forth only
the outlines, leaving to excellent wits . . . the sup-
plying the words,—if they do not disdain his labors,
composed to no other end than to delight." It is
true that Scala's plots do not offend against the
rules; they are carefully planned to observe the time
and place as well as the unity of action. Even his
extravaganzas are regularly laid out after academic
patterns, following in general style the gorgeous
theatrical mongrels which critics allowed to be appropriate to princely feasts.

No little effort and study and a considerable length
of time must have been given to perfecting of pieces
so complex as those in the repertory of the Gelosi.
In just what order, if in any one order, the various
ideas going into the formative process occurred to
the managers of this company and of others like it,
just what was the exact method by which their people
acquired the habit of improvising dialog on an outlined plot, is not known and probably never will be.

For my part I think Veridico's account of the way he rehearsed his troupe offers a valuable suggestion on the latter point; De Sommi could hardly have been the only director who made analytic abstracts of the plays in his repertory, noting places, actors on the stage, entrances, exits and a hint of the action. Very likely he and his kind started the custom which Perucci describes a century later, of hanging the outline of the comedy in a prominent place behind the scenes where every member of the caste could refer to it constantly.[58] It is well-known that Italian actors were particularly apt in improvising dialog—they had had enough practice on the charlatan's bench—and in changing their program according to their audience. When they were performing as they often did, for weeks together at some aristocratic house where the one cry was for variety, they would naturally be unable to learn by heart the great number of plays demanded, and would be forced to help out their memories by their wits. If they followed De Sommi's advice to present only little known pieces and preferably those not yet printed, their patrons could not have the text under their eyes to refer to in case some remark on the boards sounded too free or not quite in the poet's style; so no one could be blamed if on the basis of the trainer's outline, some of the players should rave and joke extempore.

Impromptu speakers could not of course go far wrong when, like the best of the professionals, they were thoroughly in touch with the intellectual inter-

[58] Perucci, *Dell'arte rappresentativa*, Parte XIV, p. 364.

ests of the day, the kind of plot and technic considered correct, the types of character appropriate to
comedy, tragedy and pastoral, the proper stage-
setting required for each and the proportion in
which realistic satire should be combined with
romance. The professional actors had moreover the
readiness that came from acquaintance with the
world; they knew city squares and country commons
in their own land and many others, for they were
always on the road from place to place; they knew at
first hand, because to a large extent many of them
were, charlatans of the *piazza* and their Zanni; they
knew the village priest, the rustic magician, the
peasant of the country and his buxom wife and her
lovers. They were also, as we have seen, trained
from childhood, women as well as men, to please all
kinds of spectators and in the most various manner;
they had on their tongues' end language for every
situation, from Petrarchan sublimities for the joys
and despairs of lovers to the vilest Billingsgate for
comic quarrels. In the improvised plays they managed to produce from all these experiences and ac-
quirements they delighted everyone save an occasional over-squeamish moralist; the academic purists
found their own creations reflected with a difference,
—and a difference making for gaiety,—and soon
justified the "professional comedies" by resorting
to their usual excuse, a classical comparison; fashionable Platonizers found their favorite themes
woven into the more serious scenes, sometimes even
developed with eloquence as by the Andreini; aris-
tocrats and parvenus greedy of splendor were re-

galed with spectacle, ballets and rich costumes; last and perhaps most important, the universal liking for the lively jest that stirs heartiest, most unthinking laughter, would here be fed to the full,—for who could censure *lazzi* of the broadest in amusements confessedly so farcical and free?

It is always just as impossible to pick out a certain year and say "here began" . . . whatever literary form it may be that is under discussion, as it is to define a genre so exactly that all or even the majority of its exemplars are brought under its wing. The rise of the *commedia dell'arte,* which I have sketched in broadest outline, is so intimately bound up with the history of the actors, and of the literary and popular drama of the sixteenth century that the threads are particularly hard to disentangle, whereas the difficulty in dating the process comes from our ignorance of how many old scenarios may be lost and of what proportion of rustic farces were improvised,—written scenes naturally alone survive. Yet perhaps a more important thing than the drawing of such hard and fast divisions, is just to recognize the general relation of the improvised plays to the actors and the century that produced them, persons and an age of which they have left pictures like distorted grimaces half-seen in a darkening mirror.

CHAPTER IV.

Never was the irony of definition-making better illustrated than by the fact that the oldest scenario of the "professional" Italian comedy records a play given by amateurs. As early as 1568, it appears, the actors' peculiar resources, their Masks and *lazzi* and extempore repartee, were well enough known to be imitated by noble dilettanti with the aid of only two professional musicians. The comedy is still further peculiar in that it had no women in it and that it never became part of the repertory of a troupe. Yet notwithstanding these variations from normality the little farce is so characteristic and so full of reminiscences of the mountebank's bench as to be worth quoting in full.

Massimo Trojano, the court choir-master, who invented the "delightsome plot," reports the play at first-hand in a conversation with a friend, a dialog which is one of several describing the entertainments at the Duke of Bavaria's wedding in Munich.[1] After explaining that the "improvised comedy" was thought out in a day, the principal speaker in the dialog says: "At first there was a peasant 'alla

[1] Book II, Dialog II, p. 183 f., of *Discorsi delli trionfi, Giostre, Apparati,* etc., *di Massimo Trojano di Napoli. . . . In Monaco. . . .* MDLXVIII. The scenario is quoted in full by Stoppato, *Comm. popolare in Italia,* 131 f. It is in three acts, like most scenarios and is distinctly a court spectacle like the piece published by Toldo, Gior. Stor., XLVI, 128 f. I translate literally, keeping the confused tenses, etc.

cavajola'² so ridiculously dressed as to seem the very
ambassador of laughter.'' He then goes on to tell
his hearer that there were ten persons in the play
and that the parts were so divided as to give him,
Massimo, three, namely, the prolog, Polidoro (the
young lover), and the Spanish "disperato." The
other parts were taken as follows: a Magnifico,
Messer Pantalone di Bisognosi (played by Orlando
di Lasso, another professional musician); the Zanni
(Giovan-Battista Scolari, of Trent); the servant of
the young hero (Don Carlo Livizzano); the Spaniard's lacquey (Giorgio Dori of Trent); the courtesan beloved by Polidoro (the Marquis of Malespina);
her servant (Ercole Terzo); and a French servant.

"To return to our comedy (continues the narra-
tor). When the prolog had been spoken, Messer
Orlando (Pantalone) had a sweet madrigal sung
while Massimo who had played the peasant, took
off his rustic garments and all in crimson velvet
with broad cuffs trimmed top and bottom with gold,
and with a black velvet cap lined with the finest
sables, came out with his servant, praising Fortune
and boasting that he lived happy and content in the
kingdom of love; when behold, the Frenchman, servant of Fabritio, his brother, came from the country
to summon him with a letter full of the worst news,
the which Polidoro read aloud; with a great sigh,

---

² The *farse cavaiole* were so-called because they represented doings
of the peasants of Cava, a south Italian town. Cf. Croce, *Teatri di
Napoli*, Archivio per le provincie napol., XIV, 583 f., and Ancona,
in Arch. per lo studio delle tradizioni popolari, II, 239. Torraca,
Teatro italiano, etc., prints an example of these realistic little farces,
431.

having finished the letter, he had Camilla called, and after having told her the necessity of his going away, kissing her, he took leave and departed. From the other side of the stage entered Messer Orlando, dressed as a Magnifico, with a doublet of crimson satin and Venetian hose of scarlet, and a black mantle long enough to touch the ground, and a mask which just to see made everyone laugh, and with a lute in his hand, playing and singing:[3]

> Who passes through this street
> And does not sigh, fortunate he!

After repeating this twice, he stopped playing and began to complain of Love and say: 'O poor Pantalone, who cannot pass through this street without sending sighs through the air and tears to the pavement of earth! . . .' and everyone began to laugh as much as possible so that as long as Pantalone was on the stage nothing was heard but laughter, all the more that after Pantalone had made a long discourse with himself and his Camilla, Zanne appeared, who had not seen his Pantalone for years and, not recognizing him as he walked distraught, gave him a great shove and after quarreling, they at last knew each other; then for joy Zanne took his master on his shoulders and they turned like a windmill . . . and then Pantalone did the same to Zanne; at last both fell to the ground; then they rose and talked a

[3] In the dialog, p. 146, the second speaker remarks upon Orlando's versatility in being able to play the Venetian when he was himself a Fleming; Zanne's speech was equally remarkable, however, for it is described as Bergamask "so good that it seemed he must have practiced it fifty years."

little, Zanne asked his master how his old mistress was, Pantalone's wife, and hears she is dead, and then Pantalone begins to howl like wolves and Zanne to shed tears, thinking on the maccaroni and mince-meat[4] which she used to give him to eat; then leaving off their tears, they returned to cheerfulness and the master bade Zanne carry some pullets to his beloved Camilla; Zanne promised to speak for him but did the contrary. Exit Pantalone, and Zanne went to the house of Camilla, all trembling; Camilla fell in love with Zanne (and this is not astonishing, for women often leave the better to turn to the worse) and made him enter her house. And here there was music by five *viole da gamba* and as many voices. You can imagine whether or not this act was amusing; I swear by heaven that at all the comedies I have seen I have never heard so much hearty laughter. . . .

"In the second act Pantalone appeared wondering that Zanne was so slow in bringing an answer. Then Zanne came out with a letter from Camilla saying that if he desired her love he must disguise himself in a way that Zanne would explain to him orally; at this joyful news Pantalone and Zanne went to exchange clothes, and the Spaniard entered, 'with his heart drowned in the sea called jealousy' and told his servant of his great and valorous deeds and of the many souls, hundreds and hundreds, he had sent to Charon's boat; and that now a wretched woman had taken his mighty heart away. Com-

[4] In the second edition (Venice, 1568) Zanne regrets his mistress's "maccaroni e raffioli," in the first is preserved the dialect form he probably used, "maccarù e sbruffedei."

pelled by love he goes to salute his Camilla, and begs her to let him enter her house; Camilla with flattering words accepts a necklace from his hand and promises him fair for that evening; he goes away content. Then Pantalone and Zanne came in dressed in each other's clothes, and after they had entertained awhile by teaching how to act the Magnifico, they entered Camilla's house. Here there was music by four voices, two lutes and other instruments.

"In the third and last act Polidoro (who kept Camilla) returns from the country, goes into the house and finds Pantalone in poor clothes; asking who he is and being answered 'a porter' and that Monna Camilla wished him to carry a box to Sister Doralice at San Cataldo, Polidoro believes this and says he'd better take the box soon; Pantalone on account of his age is not able to lift it, and after a little talk, says he is a gentleman; Polidoro disgusted at this, took a stick and belabored him so hard (to the sound of loud laughter of the spectators) that he would remember the blows a long time. Poor Pantalone ran out and Polidoro entered the house, very angry at Camilla. Zanne, who had heard the noise of blows, found a sack and got into it; Camilla's maid drove him out on the stage, tied up in the sack. The Spaniard, furious at not having received the promised summons, is about to leave, and raising his eyes to heaven, is beginning to say, 'Alas,' with sighs, when he stumbles on the sack containing the miserable Zanne and both he and his servant fell full length; rising in great wrath he untied the sack, shook out the Zanni and with a stick dusted his bones

very thoroughly[5] and the Zanni fleeing and the
Spaniard and his servant after him, they left the
stage. Polidoro with his servant, and Camilla with
her maid then entered, Polidoro saying to Camilla
that she ought to marry, because he for an excellent
reason did not wish to support her any longer; she
after saying 'No' many times, finally resolves to do
as Polidoro commands her and so agrees to take
Zanne for her lawful husband. During this discourse Pantalone came in armed with firearms, and
Zanne with two arquebuses on his shoulder, eight
daggers in his belt, a buckler and sword in his hand
and a rusty helmet on his head; both are seeking
those who beat them; after making several thrusts
which seem to show that thus they will slay their
enemies, Camilla bids Polidoro speak to Pantalone.
He points out Zanne to the old man and Zanne,
frightened, motions his master to begin the fight,
Pantalone does the same to Zanne; Polidoro, understanding the cause they both have, calls by name
'O signor Pantalone!' and puts his hand to his
sword; Zanne does not know which of his weapons
to take first and so there is a ridiculous hurly-burly.
This lasted awhile till finally Camilla held Pantalone and her maid the Zanni and peace was made
and Camilla was given to Zanne as his wife. In
honor of the wedding they danced an Italian dance

[5] The sack *lasso* seems to have a perennial charm for all audiences
who like farce or uproarious amusement. There is an example of it in
one of the mythical tales in the *Mabinogion* (*Pwyll, Prince of Dyved*)
and it occurs again and again on the stage; cf. the two *Farces
tabariniques* in Fournier's *Théâtre français au XVIe et XVIIe siècles*,
I, 502 f.

and Massimo for Messer Orlando begged pardon if the comedy fell short of the merit of their Most Serene Highnesses. . . ." So with a conventional apologetic and complimentary epilog the simple little farce ends.

In such a play as this there is evidently not the least philosophical intention, not the slightest idea of mingling with its "delightfulness" that ethical teaching which theorists of the academies insisted was the function of comedy; the whole thing is merely to amuse. There is no strain on the attention of the audience, no plot complications such as in many plays of the period gave rise to long debates on the relative values of love and honor; all the merit of the spectacle consists in its liveliness and in the skill with which all kinds of ancient laughter-moving devices are used. At the very first there is the appearance of the well-known figure of the rustic, so often satirized in farces and May-plays and popular tales, tricked out in his usual rags and talking nonsense, no doubt in dialect. The same kind of comic appeal is repeated in Pantalone's entrance in the second scene, again a satiric portrait more or less familiar to the spectators from the Magnifico's performances in carnival processions and from his similarity to the old man of literary comedies; it is worth remarking perhaps, that here he is perfectly detached, that is, he is not, as so often in written plays and in later *commedie dell'arte,* the father of either hero or heroine, he makes therefore not the slightest sympathetic impression, only the ridiculous one of an old man, love-mad. His antics, including song and lute-playing, are all highly burlesque without a thread of real character to bind them together; there seems to be no reason, for instance, why a person so energetic as to go through the gymnastics with Zanni should have been unable to lift a box, but such small inconsistencies never troubled the actors of improvised farces. The windmill business just alluded to, the affray between Polidoro and Pantalone, the entanglement of Zanni in the sack with the resulting complications, and the absurd mock battle at the end, are all the simplest and oldest ways to rouse immediate, unthoughtful laughter. More subtle are the suggested parodies on the academic follies of the time,—Polidoro's first speech in praise of Love and Fortune, Pantalone's serenade and grandiloquent meditation thereon, the Spaniard's still more inflated *bravure*. Academic and literary also is the influence that formed what there is of plot, the slender intrigue in which the chief persons are as it were the shadows of Latin comic characters.[6] The courtly demands for splendor of costume, for music whenever possible and for a dance at the close of the play, were as carefully regarded by Massimo Trojano as by his followers in the creation of scenarios; such adornments must really have been needed by an aristocratic audience as relaxation and variety in the continual horse-play of these farces.

The modern editor of this comedy considers it so complete as to indicate that the high-water mark of

[6] This comedy is unlike most of the improvised plays in the fact of the heroine's position; she is generally a girl of good family who loves only the youth she means to marry,—not, as here, a courtesan.

the *commedia dell'arte* must be placed in the middle of the Cinquecento,[7]—rather a rash conclusion in view of the fact that it is the only surviving scenario of the period and that it is so much simpler than most of those of later date.[8] Scala's collection may and doubtless does contain several plots as old as the one just described, but since the collector did not edit each of his pieces with modern scholarly accuracy, speculation on the subject is unsafe.[9] Two of his numbers may be at least conjecturally dated before 1578 and about 1589 respectively, though such proof as there is may seem rather shadowy. In the *Portrait*[10] the assumption as to date hangs by the slender thread of a name and one hypothesis dependent thereon; the principal heroine,—not as in most of Scala's pieces a respectable girl of the bourgeoisie but an actress of very free life called Vittoria,—must, I think, have been played by Vittoria Piissimi, whose character was of just the kind suggested here. Now La Vittoria was with the Gelosi only a few years and left them finally to establish a company of her own in 1578. Granted, and the supposition is at least probable considering the Italian practice, that she created the chief rôle in

[7] Stoppato, *Comm. pop.*, 139 f.

[8] Solerti, *Ferrara*, etc., cc–cci, mentions an improvised play given in 1577 by noble persons, so the Munich performance was not unique.

[9] Re, Gior. Stor., LV, 329, thinks that Scala's plays must have been mostly composed late in the Cinquecento.

[10] *Il Ritratto*, Giornata XXXVIII of Scala's book, has been fully reported, translated into French by Moland, *Molière et la com. italienne*, 81 f.

For the discussion on *La Pazzia* cf. Solerti, *Gl'albori del melodrama*, I, 42, and Solerti-Lanza, Gior. Stor., XVIII, 184–5.

the *Portrait*, giving it her own name, this scenario
must have been written before 1578 or the play would
not be found in the repertory of the company to
which until that year she belonged.

La Pazzia, played at Florence in 1589, has not
been identified with absolute certainty.[11] It may
have been a pastoral or it may have been the improvised comedy I am about to describe; a contemporary account calls it merely a "comedy by Isabella
Andreini of the company of the Gelosi, attended by
the Grand Duke . . . with the same interludes that
served for *La Zingara* by Vittoria," and says
further it was played superlatively well, especially
"with genius and eloquence by Isabella."[12] The
occasion was the wedding of Ferdinand I de'Medici
to Christina of Loraine, May 13, and the comedy, if
it were really the one of the same title preserved by
Scala, was much more elaborate than that given at
the Bavarian fête. As there seems to me a fair
chance of Scala's piece being this royal entertainment and so of its dating next in age to the *Portrait*,
I give a brief synopsis of it here.

The argument tells a romantic story. Oratio, on
his way to marry Flaminia, is captured by Turks
and taken as a slave to Algiers, leaving his mistress
to retire to the cloister. In Algiers the tale of
Joseph in Potiphar's house is repeated and continued,—the wife of Oratio's master falls in love
with the young captive and agrees to turn Christian
if he will flee with her and marry her. She arranges

[11] Solerti, *Gl'albori*, etc., II, 18.
[12] Ancona, *Origini*, II, 495 f., recounts the rivalry of the two companies and especially of the *prime donne*.

the escape, taking her small son with her. After various adventures during which the lady's husband and son are killed, Oratio conducts her to Genoa where she is baptized under the name of Isabella and where the play opens before the couple have been married. In the first act we hear from Flavio that Flaminia has left the convent, that he loves her but she is cold to him. Pedrolino tells the facts about Isabella and Oratio which the argument had previously summed up, adding his opinion that the two "are living in sin." The next scene is a passionate conversation between Isabella and Oratio, she accusing him of unfaithfulness in not marrying her as he had vowed, he promising to fulfil his oath very soon. Isabella withdraws, making an opportunity for an exchange of the noblest sentiments by Flaminia and Oratio, confession of mutual love and mutual encouragement to prefer honor to love. After their tearful parting, the Captain enters with Arlecchino, looking for a "Christianized Turkish woman"; the pair go to the Inn where the Captain makes love to the innkeeper's sweetheart, Ricciolina, fights with one of her admirers and is deluged with water thrown from a window by a servant,— true *commedia dell'arte* fun. The act closes by the revelation of Pantalone's determination that his son Oratio shall no longer live in sin but shall marry Isabella at once, a resolution imparted to the youth with the effect of throwing him into a violent rage and causing him to quarrel with Flavio, Flaminia's other lover; Isabella looks on and weeps the while.

The heroine as the second act opens tells Flaminia

9

she will rather die than force Oratio to marry her; the two ladies then vow friendship and "compliment" each other, until Pedrolino interrupts them with an account of the duel between Oratio and Flavio. This recital finished, the Captain enters, recognizes Isabella as the woman he seeks and tells Flaminia her story; as he is going on to make love to Flaminia, Oratio arrives and finds a second quarrel on his hands. Quiet on the stage is restored after much noisy confusion, and Flavio has a chance to urge Pantalone against postponing Oratio's marriage any longer. Isabella listens until she seems to go mad and assaults Flavio with a knife; he falls hurt and bleeding, she tells Oratio that she has revenged his wrong, but in fact leaves Flavio to make capital of his wound in pressing his claims on Flaminia. Very soon Oratio leads Isabella out again, caressing her and assuring her that he does not care for Flaminia, and sending her in finally "quite consoled"; he has himself of course to remain to inform the audience in a soliloquy that he is true to Flaminia in his heart but that honor is master of his acts. Flaminia interrupts these fine words by asking sarcastically when he means to marry his "amazon"; he is furious, so is Isabella at the window; honor takes wing very quickly as Oratio declares he will only marry Isabella to get rid of her and to fulfil his vow, and that then he will remove her by trickery or poison. Isabella really goes mad this time, "raves against love and fortune," tears her clothes and throws them about and at last rushes off in despair.

Oratio and Flaminia are overcome by remorse at the wrong done their victim—the third act shows— and they join with Pantalone in begging Dr. Gratiano to try to cure her; the mad woman is brought in, bound and "doing her insane tricks," Pantalone accuses Oratio of having caused this by his love of Flaminia, the young man "despairs." The Captain is greeted by Isabella as one of the constellations, and is then violently beaten by her. Gratiano next enters with hellebore, to cure Isabella "instantly," she frightens him by suddenly appearing and bidding him be quiet while Jove sneezes. To Oratio's greeting, "You are here, my soul," she learnedly replies: "Soul according to Aristotle is spirit" and goes on with divers other absurdities of a semi-academic nature, until she is seized and bound and made to drink Gratiano's dose of hellebore. She soon comes to herself, receives Oratio's penitent apologies and agrees to marry him at once. Flavio is immediately betrothed to Flaminia, Burattino to Ricciolina and Pedrolino to Franceschina so that the play may end properly.

Most of Scala's pieces are, like this one, intrigue comedies on a considerably more developed scale than that evolved in a day by Trojano. The relations between the persons are carefully thought out, or rather they are adaptations of those in the motherless households of written drama;[18] again as

---

[18] The absence of a respectable matron from the scene is by no means so invariable in the written as in the improvised plays; cf. Cecchi, *Gl'incantesimi* (Venetia, 1550); Cenci, *Gl'errori;* Gonzaga, *Gl'inganni* (Venetia, 1592), all romantic intrigue comedies containing numerous farcical scenes like Scala's scenarios, which emphasize the

in the written plays there is a large romantic element in most of the plots and a good deal of talk about love and fortune in the dialog; the settings for the first forty numbers—the comedies—shows still another literary influence, a Roman tradition, for they all represent street scenes calling for the same simple stage arrangements. When the plays were given in private before wealthy patrons these settings, canvases painted in perspective, would often be done by the best artists,—Raphael did not disdain to design the scenery for a comedy given before Leo X,[14] and there are records of other illustrious representations of realistic and beautiful backgrounds for academic plays. There were almost always, whoever the designer of the scene, three main houses shown, one at each side and one at the back, leaving two streets as well as the house doors

humanly pathetic interest of the plot largely by bringing into it an unhappy mother. Of course the *commedia dell'arte* had nothing to do with pathos and therefore left the mother out of account and made the father so vicious or foolish that he could not be pitied.

[14] A performance of Ariosto's *Suppositi* in the Castel Sant'Angelo, March 8, 1519. Cf. Graf, *Attraverso il Cinquecento*, 369.

Grazzini in the prolog to *La Strega* played before a Florentine academy, says: "La scena si conosce benissimo esser Firenze; non vede tu la cupola?" Evidently this was as realistic a representation as that of Cecchi's *Incantesimi* in the prolog to which the author says. "Voi conoscete che questo proscenio è in Firenze, che'l Cardo e la Cupola e la piazza che è qui, ve la figurano assai chiara." So also an Italian artist painted the scenes in *La Calandra* to represent Florence when that comedy was given at Lyons in 1548 before Henri II and Catherine de'Medici (Baschet, *Comédiens italiens*, etc., 9).

As early as 1518 Bibbiena had a comedy given in Rome for which the scenery was painted to represent a characteristic bit of Mantua. The description is found in a contemporary letter cited by Flechsig, *Dekoration der mod. Bühne*, etc., 64.

for entrance and exists.[15] The middle house certainly and the two others probably, had balconies from which Isabella and Flaminia could exchange insults with each other or compliments and vows with their lovers, and over the balustrade of which Arlecchino could leap and Oratio could climb.

Properties for these comedies were often as simple as this setting, the only absolute requirements were "clubs for beating," formidable weapons for keeping the Zanni and the Captain in order and for helping the lovers execute their vengeance on the old men. Scala here and there lists various other "necessary things"; according to the play may be required an Inn-sign;[16] a long bench for the charlatan, with a handsome trunk, a lute, charlatan's wares, two bottles of wine;[17] a pair of shoes, a sharp knife, a chest of food, a roasting spit;[18] many lanterns and night-shirts, a woman's dress for Arlecchino;[19] a garden at one side of the stage, a small table with two seats, confections, arms;[20] a large felt hat, a bundle of faggots for Pantalone, two loaves of bread, a cheese, a bottle, a plate with seven fritters;[21] a tall mirror standing on feet, two

[15] Bapst, *Essai sur l'histoire du théâtre*, 167, and Rennert, *Spanish Stage*, 96, call attention to the need for regarding chronology in any study of stage arrangements. The Italian street scene seems to have been a norm for improvised comedies from the latter part of the sixteenth to at least the middle of the seventeenth century.

[16] Giornata I.
[17] Gior. II.
[18] Gior. IV.
[19] Gior. IX.
[20] Gior. XI.
[21] Gior. XV.

similar rings;[22] a chest with many letters in it;[23] two Alexandrian carpets, a suit for a Turkish merchant, slave's habit for Pantalone;[24] slaves' suits and iron chains, eight barrels of water, a palace with throne and columns.[25] All these articles, except the palace and its columns, were perfectly ordinary everyday supplies, easy for the poorest company to produce. Not so the gold and silver vessels, the rich robes, the carved furniture, the jewels and flowers, to say nothing of the painted scenes pastoral or marine, required for the mythological and heroic part of the repertory. For those the Gelosi had to draw on the treasury of the dukes of Mantua or the kings of France before whom they played.

Not until the seventeenth century had multiplied and cheapened stage devices and had brought the professional actor some independence of his private patrons could Scala's last nine pieces have been given in public. One of these, a tragedy called the *Mad Princess,* must have required at least one painted cloth representing the seashore, and calls for, among the properties: "one very beautiful ship, two skiffs, one pavilion, four elegant trunks, four lighted torches, four silver basins, one water-ewer, divers lances, a head resembling the Prince of Morocco, one moon which shall seem to set, a throne for the king of Fez." The *opere miste* that follow the tragedy make still larger demands for machinery

[22] Gior. XVI.
[23] Gior. XXIII.
[24] Gior. XXVI.
[25] Gior. XXXVI.

and properties. There are transformation scenes that needed skilful manipulation and rapid changes of tableau in which the usual stage direction is, "the middle scene (*prospettiva di mezzo*) falls, showing" —whatever the climax demanded, temple of Pan or palace of a king.[26] In *L'Alvida*, a "royal work" (Gior. XLII), are listed "a wood, a fine grotto, a large tree to place in the center" and among the dramatis personae, "a lion, a bear and an ass."[27] In *The Enchanted Tree*, a pastoral (Gior. XLIX), greater demands are made: "a painted tree for the transformation (of a nymph into a tree), a tree with apples attached which shall rise, a grotto for the witch, a cape in the sea which shall suddenly appear, two fires with perfumes, two rays which shall flash

[26] The battlements, trees, etc., needed for these plays were probably canvas structures like those mentioned as required by the Italian players at Windsor in 1573; cf. below, Chap. V, and Feuillerat, *Documents concerning the Revels*, etc., for numerous entries in the Revels Accounts of payments made on "one Citty & one battlement of canvas," etc.

[27] Ancona, *Origini*, I, 318 and 511 f., describes some of the remarkable machinery used in the *Sacre Rappresentazioni* at a quite early date,—devices for representing sea-fights, making a temple fall in ruins, etc.

Animals on the stage both in the Mysteries and in *intermedj* were perfectly familiar to Italian audiences. Cf. Ancona, *Origini*, I, 513, and Flechsig, *Dekoration*, etc., 12.

In the dramatic diversions at the court of Mantua during the carnival of 1591 elaborate settings were used; there was one painted cloth with "a noble palace painted in chiaroscuro," another with trees and a third of a city with battlements and with transparent paper in the windows, also a mountain for the temple "adorned with flowers and ivy-leaves." The Gelosi were quite accustomed to acting in entertainments as gorgeous as this; cf. the account of the spectacles at the wedding of Ferdinand I de'Medici, 1589, Solerti, *Albori del melodramma*, II, 19 f.

(presumably to imitate lightning), and an earth-
quake.'' Gold and silver utensils, handsome furniture, a chariot drawn by four spirits, shepherd's
attire, princely robes with crowns and scepters, new-
born babes, battlemented cities and a forest in
Persia—such were a few of the articles that gave
magnificence to this curious group of plays.

The first of these extravaganzas is an example of
the compound plays so popular at the time, consist-
ing of three or more separate little pieces sometimes
on the same theme, sometimes as in this case connected very loosely by a thread of plot.[28]   The scene
is conveniently laid in the Peloponesus so that the
conventional ideas of Sparta and of Arcadia may be
utilized, but the classicism of the three parts is of
the most diluted academic character.   The comedy
is pure farce; an old Spartan father, called Pantalone of course, ignoring his daughter's love for
young Oratio, son to Dr. Gratiano, promises her
hand to one of Orestes' Captains; the soldier is
however soon summoned to the wars and when he
returns he finds that Pantalone has been prevailed
upon to betroth the girl to Oratio.   Scenes of jealousy and misunderstanding follow but are cleared
up so that a triple wedding closes the act.   Then
comes a pastoral interlude built on a much tangled
love plot, with the scene laid in ''Spartan Arcadia'';

---

[28] In England the best-known work of the kind is Beaumont and
Fletcher's *Four Plays in One*, but there were many others which have
perished; cf. Feuillerat, John Lyly, 341, note 3, and *Henslowe's Diary*
for 1592 and 1597. One of the outline plots of the period surviving
in England is of the second part of such a play, Tarlton's *Seven
Deadly Sins*, for which cf. below, Chap. V.

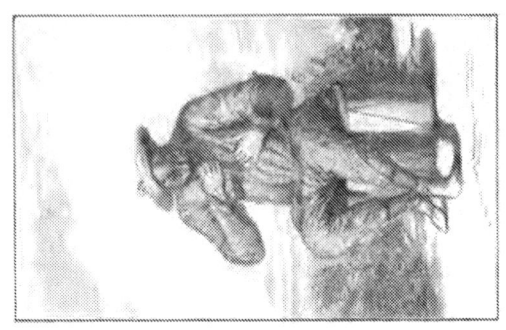

Fillide, daughter to Pedrolino (factotum at Pantalone's villa), pretends death to follow her lover, Sireno, and after she has been put into the vault flees in the disguise of a shepherd. Before she finds him the faithless swain sees and loves Amarillide, who is pining for Tirsi, who in turn loves Fillide and mourns her as dead. Fillide after many tearful recriminiations and after wounding Sireno with an arrow when she finds him with Amarillide, is at last converted to care for Tirsi by her rival's decision to marry Sireno. Ridiculous scenes between peasants relieve the lachrymose dolefulness of this act. The most fully described *lazzo* is a trick of Lisetta, a shepherdess, to calm two fighting cowherds; she promises them a plate of food if they will allow her to tie them back to back; she then sets the dish on the ground, urging them to eat and laughing at their struggles to reach the maccaroni. Finally one succeeds in bending over far enough and goes out eating and carrying his hungry fellow on his back. The pastoral ends conventionally with music and a marriage procession to the temple.[29]

The tragic third of this "three-plays-in-one" deals with Spartan royalty, with the love of King Orestes for Altea, daughter of his guest Bramante, king of

[29] Cf. De Sommi for the probable costuming of these pastorals, above, Chap. III.

Solerti, *Albori*, etc., gives descriptions of other musical and mythological *commedie dell'arte*. He calls Orazio Vecchi's *L'Amfiparnaso* (1597) "a real true *commedia dell'arte* to which has been applied madrigalesque music." (I, 17.)

Ancona, *Origini*, II, 451, describes a comedy played as early as 1567 in which Cupid frees Chloris, a nymph who had been turned into a tree; but this was not an improvised play so far as is known.

Mycenae, with his murder of this guest and further with the revenge taken for the deed by Oronte, king of Athens. A slight connection of the three parts is made in the last by the appearance of Pantalone and Gratiano as ambassadors to the Athenian monarch, who present him from their master with a silver basin containing Bramante's head. Altea does not long survive her father, for she chooses in the manner of her kind death rather than dishonorable love; we see her, decapitated, borne across the stage on a "car of justice" while Pantalone and Gratiano, like a Greek chorus, "discourse on the swift turns of Fortune." The play ends with a messenger's account of the death of Orestes in battle and the people's joyful proclamation of the "ancient liberty" of Sparta, henceforth a republic.

Contrasted with this tripartite drama is the long drawn out epical trilogy, *L'Orseida*, interesting especially on account of the folk and fairy elements in its first part. The Elizabethans would have found no difficulty in compressing into one piece the varied events of so romantic a history, but to the Italians under the critical eyes of their academic theorists the preservation of the time unity was an ever-present anxiety; consequently they often strained probability to the breaking-point in order to bring about their climax within "one revolution of the sun." Scala, if he were the author of the *Orseida*, frankly begged the question by presenting in three separate tragicomedies the three important moments of his action. In the first, a half-serious, half-farcical parody on the Beauty-and-the-Beast theme, Dorinda, daughter of Pan's chief priest, is carried off by a ferocious bear against whom all Arcadia has for years been in arms. Her father's despair is mitigated by a vision of the god and a prophecy that Dorinda will be happy in the devoted love of a divine husband and that she will be the mother of heroes. In the second part, supposed to take place some time later, the bear is killed by Trineo, a prince searching in Arcadia for his friend and his love; the main point of the action is however so obscured by Trineo's other adventures, by the comic legerdemain of the servants and by spectacular changes of scene, that it is a surprise to find the third part motived by the monster's death. This concluding portion begins in the manner of the usual revenge tragedy by the hero, Ulfone, vowing vengeance on Trineo for having murdered his father, "although a bear." Many are the complications in the way of fulfilling this simple resolution, but justice is at last done and Ulfone receives a bride and a triple kingdom at the hands of the priest of Pan.

After all this confusion comes, in Scala's book, a milder piece, a pastoral, *The Enchanted Tree.* The argument states that Fillide, daughter of the old shepherd Ergasto, loves the young Arcadian Sireno, an exile from his country; the uncle of this youth, a "magician enchanter," disapproves his love for Fillide and therefore makes him insane and by that means forgetful of the nymph. She disguised as Lisio, a shepherd, flees from her father's home in pursuit of her lover but "by chance" she also goes mad and is even, through the machinations of a rival, believed to be dead. At last by the art of the Mage all are "contented." This is largely a musical play, there being frequent directions to Corinto (one of the shepherds) to enter "playing his pipe" and to the nymph Clori to sing. For the rest the play is made up of *commedia dell'arte* jests, partly absurdities of the two insane characters, partly tricks of the magician. Among the latter are fireworks which issue from the cell of the wise man whenever anyone tries to go in, an instantaneous change of scene in which the back curtain falls to show a "maritime cape" and an enchanted tree with spirits and demons dancing about it; the tranformation of a nymph into another tree and later her restoration; the bewitching of Arlecchino into the form of a wild crane who makes much mirth by stretching his neck in reply to questions. The final spectacle must have been a triumph of stage machinery for in it the blood of Timbri, who had stabbed herself for love of Selvaggio, restores to human form the maiden of the tree amidst a shooting of flames "all over the stage," flames so potent in their magic that they bring back to life Timbri herself and change Arlecchino from a bird to a man. Three marriages close the action and the Mage, as in *L'Orseida,* resolves to become a benevolent being.

If I have dwelt on these extravaganzas a little it is because they combine in a peculiarly intimate way, popular and literary elements. For example such ancient folk motifs as disguise, transformation, death-and-resurrection, the use of blood as a means of restoration to life, the humanization of animals for dramatic purposes, are quite recognizable even though so overlaid by convention that it is perhaps a trifle absurd to try to disentangle them. On the other hand the academic commonplaces which Scala as a practical, successful manager and a supporter of the best theatrical usage of his day felt bound to maintain—the idealistic conception of love and honor, the pastoral and heroic machinery, the classic legacy of myth and theory—are just as evident as the popular material.[30] During the seventeenth century plays like these hybrids became increasingly numerous, growing more and more spectacular until their place was taken by the *melodramma* and the comic opera.

Notwithstanding the importance of the "mixed works" it is hardly fair to leave Scala's book without a glance at one more of the comedies that make up its chief bulk. This time instead of summarizing another romantic intrigue like *La Pazzia*, I will give one of Scala's reworkings of a classic theme, the *Menaechmi* situation, because this serves better than some others to show how the freedom given by a merely outlined action favored farcical treatment of plot material. The heroine Isabella is the wife of Captain Spavento who has been away for six years in search of his lost brother, a Captain also. The play opens on the day of Spavento's return from

---

[30] There were written plays also of the same mixed character called sometimes "regiacomica," sometimes "tragicomica." Spanish influence on these heroic extravaganzas was strong; cf. Bartoli, *Scen. inediti*, lvii f.; Croce, *Teatri di Napoli*, 139, and Maddalena in *Wiener Sitzungsberichte*, CXLIII, part 16.

his unsuccessful quest, and at once portrays the state of affairs at his home. The first scene shows that an explanatory prolog was not necessary, for here Isabella tells her sad story to her maid Franceschina and her neighbor Flaminia, and confesses that during her husband's absence she has fallen in love with Oratio. This gentleman is the lover favored by Flaminia and accordingly Isabella's admission is followed by a lively and abusive dialog between the ladies and that in turn by a bout at fisticuffs. Oratio enters in time to save Isabella from Flaminia's fury, only to be rewarded by accusations of infidelity from his mistress. More blows are exchanged with so much noise that Pantalone and Gratiano, fathers of the girls, rush to the rescue; Isabella runs into the house gesticulating like a lunatic and Flaminia pretends to be bewitched; the two old men follow to see if they can do anything. Spavento then enters to the Inn (which is the third house on the stage), disguised in order to find out quietly what his wife has been doing in his absence; Pedrolino, the inn-keeper, promises to care for the stranger and his servant Arlecchino. When the boards are clear again Oratio explains in a soliloquy his adoration of Flaminia and his fear that she has fallen into a causeless jealousy of Isabella; his fear is not much relieved by information from Franceschina that her mistress (Isabella) has gone mad with love of him. However, as she begs him to visit the lady disguised as a doctor, he compassionately agrees, puts on a long gown and a false beard and is about to enter Gratiano's house when Flaminia, who has been listening from the opposite window, runs out, throws herself on Oratio, pulls off his beard and robe, beats him and in her jealous rage puts everyone to flight.

The second act begins by Spavento's telling his friend Flavio some of his adventures and asking for news of Isabella; the Captain gets no satisfaction from Flavio but overhears Oratio and Pedrolino talking of Isabella and her unfortunate love. The men go off, making way for an explanation between Flaminia and her father Pantalone, followed by Franceschina's additions to Flaminia's confession. Arlecchino hears the maid say that her mistress loves Oratio and not the Captain, and with true Zanni officiousness goes to tell his master of his discovery. Then, with the entrance of the other Captain, begins the tale of mistakes and blunders that has always been the chief attraction of this type of play. Flavio takes this Captain for Spavento, his friend, and both speak at cross purposes. After they go out a comic scene between the maid and Spavento shows that Franceschina in revenge for a beating is capable of slandering her mistress very freely; Arlecchino confirms the girl's story by what he has just overheard and is rewarded by the flogging that closes the act.

The plot begins to clear up with the reconciliation of Oratio and Flaminia after an angry conference spied upon by Pantalone. The old man is seen by the lovers as soon as they make up their quarrel and is begged to consent to their marriage. No sooner is he persuaded than the two Captains enter, the brother first and for a moment only, Spavento

immediately after; Arlecchino informs the latter
that Pedrolino will turn them both out of their
lodging unless they pay him at once, whereupon
Spavento angrily beats his servant off the stage.
The other Captain appears again and in answer to
Pedrolino's furious reproaches gives him money.
Next Gratiano draws near and begs the Captain to
go to his wife at once; the soldier denies having a
wife and calls the Doctor ugly names, giving him the
lie in his throat as well. As soon as he goes off
Spavento greets Gratiano and tries vainly to ap-
pease him. Exeunt severally and enter Isabella and
Franceschina debating whether or not the master of
the house will be glad to see them; on the appearance of the stranger Captain they both fall at his
feet with prayers for forgiveness—a tableau seen by
Spavento as he comes from the wings. The husband watches till the Captain raises the lady and
then rushes forward sword in hand to avenge his
honor; instantly however he recognizes his brother,
embraces him and Isabella,—and the play ends
merrily.[31]

A glance at the titles in any list of scenarios will
show how largely all through its existence the commedia dell'arte made capital of such farcical im-
broglios as those just related, that is to say, of com-

* For other abstracts of Scala's plays cf. a paper in Mod. Philology, April, 1911, in which I have summarized two more of his
comedies and his one tragedy; Moland, Molière et la comédie italienne,
81 f.; Scherillo, in La vita ital. nel seicento, 311 f., and Klein,
Geschichte des ital. Dramas, I, 913 f., give still other examples. Klein
gives a full account of Scala's Gior. XXX, drawing from it some
rather unwarrantable conclusions as to its connections with Shakes-
spere's Twelfth Night.

plications resulting from the disguise of one person like another or the resemblance of one person to another. In the seventeenth and eighteenth centuries these motifs became more and more extravagant, there being sometimes two or more couples of twins on the stage, sometimes three or even four "similar" Arlecchini or Pulcinelli. The improvised plays did not always however intend to be pure farce or even mainly farce. Such a tragedy as *The Queen of England*,[32] is for the most part taken from some serious treatment of the death of the Earl of Essex in the reign of Elizabeth, probably from a written tragedy, possibly from a distorted memory of the actual facts. Some of the properties needed for the piece indicate its tragic nature: "One paper head which looks like the Earl; mask and mantle for the Queen; pistol; ribbon;

[32] Bartoli, *Scen. inediti*, 54 f. Cf. another scenario on the same theme, Brouwer, Rendiconto, etc., 345. It is impossible to date this scenario exactly though it seems to belong to the end of the seventeenth century. As to its literary affiliations there is an equal amount of doubt; the Abbé Boyer wrote a French tragedy on Essex's death, *Le conte d'Essex*, acted 1678. P. Corneille's tragedy of the same title was published in the same year and contains an allusion in the preface to M. de la Calprenède's successful treatment of the same subject "thirty or forty years ago," a play I have not been able to see. N. Biancolelli's *La regina statista d'Inghilterra e il Conte d'Essex*, etc. (Bologna, c. 1664), I have also failed to find. This may be the source of the scenario though the latter has also been traced in part to a Spanish heroic play, *Dar la vida per la sua dama*.

With the English revenge tragedy by J. Banks, *The Unhappy Favorite or the Earl of Essex* . . . (1685) the *commedia dell'arte* has, I am quite sure, nothing to do. There may of course, as Professor Thorndike suggests to me, have been some common source for all these versions of a well known story, or they may have been composed separately on a historical basis.

10

bunch of keys; basin; throne of state; gold chain for
the servant; ridiculous costume for the same; letters
and petitions; inkstand; small table and bell; two
silver candlesticks with large candles." After this
list the play opens with the return of the "Conte di
Sex" to the English court after a victorious campaign
in France; he is discovered at night facing the
garden-gate of the Princess Lucinda, explaining to
his servant Cola that he must see his love before he
greets the Queen; he is condescending enough to add
that he loves Lucinda only as second choice, because
the Queen has recompensed his long devotion by
cold neglect. After he has entered the garden Cola
sleeps on the ground and talks comically in his
dreams until wakened by a shot and by the flight of
three masked villains from the garden; the Count
and Queen follow, the Count wounded in the arm, the
Queen trying vainly to discover his identity and reward him. Though he refuses his name he allows
her to bind up his arm with a ribbon and so they
part. The next scenes are partly comic and have
to do with the courting of Lucinda by the Prencipe
del Delfino (the Dauphin?), with her repulse of him
and with Cola's satire on the situation. Lucinda
next greets the Count and confides to him her plot
to kill the Queen and seize a crown which was by
right her father's. (If there is a reminiscence of
Mary Stuart here it is not clear, though it does suggest itself.) The Count pretends to be willing to
help in the plan but secretly thanks heaven for the
chance to prove his loyalty to his sovereign.

The court then assembles and after the aged

councillors, Ubaldo and Pandolfo, the Pantalone
and Gratiano of the play, have advised the Queen in
various burlesque ways Cola announces his master's
return from France. His reward is a fine gold
chain and rich costume, for which he attempts to
thank the Queen by a kiss. When the Count enters
he receives as the meed of his victories the appoint-
ment of Governor-General. The Queen asks the
hour of his return and noticing his confusion tasks
him with a secret love affair. Essex denies her
charge and is just about to lay bare Lucinda's
treason when the Princess herself enters followed
by one of the councillors; the old man takes the
Queen out but not before she has seen and recognized her ribbon on Essex's arm. Lucinda's jealousy of her royal mistress and her vows of revenge
are both so violently expressed as to drive her lover
from her, leaving the lady to give Cola an important
letter for her brothers. In a final burlesque scene
Cola is robbed of his new finery by the two other
Zanni, Trappola and Bagnolino.

The second act opens quite simply where the first
left off, with a continuation of the servants' fight;
Cola after driving away the others by pointing a
pistol at them, attempts to excuse himself to the
Count for neglect of his master's affairs. The Earl
pardons him and bids him lock up the Queen's
ribbon carefully—vain counsel to a Zanni, for no
sooner is Cola preparing to obey than Lucinda con-
fronts him and forces him to give her the treasure.
There follows a romantic talk between Essex and the
Queen in which she tries to make him understand

j

"in ambiguous words" her love for him, chiefly by means of a page's ditty, "the lover revealing his love." But the noble refuses to take the meaning to himself, still worse, he maddens the lady by telling her that the great have no right to indulge personal feelings; she replies by the commonly accepted statement that love equalizes all estates,—"Not monarchs and their subjects," says her loyal servant. Lucinda at this points interrupts the conference, appearing with the ribbon on her arm. Fatal token! The Queen recognizes it, angrily sends her off and turns a much-changed face to the Count, bidding him fly the kingdom within three days or forfeit his life; yet a moment later, seeing his confusion and grief, she repents, reverses her doom and confesses her love for him—a scene surely calling for the histrionic powers of a Bernhardt! The Earl retires rather overwhelmed with so much passion, and Delfino comes to tell the Queen that Lucinda wishes to marry Essex; she again flies into a jealous rage, summons Lucinda, has a violent altercation with her and concludes with a vow of vengeance on her lover.

Next come two typical *commedia dell'arte* scenes, the first between the Count and Cola, abuse on the one side, excuse on the other; the second, Bagnolino's *lazzi* as he prepares throne and table for the Queen. The court meets, the Queen takes her place and as she looks over various papers tears up the Count's petition to serve her as Captain of her Guard. The effort to control herself evidently exhausts her, for when the Council is dismissed she falls asleep in her chair. This gives the Earl a

chance to enter quietly and to expatiate on her
beauty and his long-established love for her; she
also is enabled to reveal still more plainly her adoration of her subject by talking in her sleep. Just as
the Count stoops to kiss her Lucinda rushes toward
the throne with pistol pointed; as she fires Essex
strikes up the weapon, the traitress runs away, the
Queen wakes, the Count is suspected, arrested,
carried off to prison, all in a moment. Cola is next
seized and searched and Lucinda's unsigned letter
taken from him. A silly *lazzo* relieves the end of
the strenuous act; as the three servants quarrel over
Cola's wardrobe Cola pretends to tie his shoe and
as he stoops down, catches Bagnolino and Trappola
each by one foot, overturns them both and flees.

To the Earl in prison lamenting the disillusion-
ments of a life at court comes a masked lady (the
Queen), with offers of aid; in his gloom he declines
help and only sighs out his love and devotion to his
sovereign. She is touched to the point of giving
him a key and bidding him escape, something he so
little desires that he ungratefully flings the key into
a well, protesting his innocence the while. Cola,
disguised, now visits the cell for the purpose of
begging to be remembered in his master's will; the
Count at once draws up the instrument, bequeathing
land and money to his servant, then gives Cola a
letter for Lucinda, a warning that Essex will not
always be at hand to save her. The catastrophe,
absurdly enough motived, follows close upon. The
Queen sends Ubaldo to the prison but bids him not
execute justice unless she twice calls out his name.

She then takes the judgment of the court on the situation and finds it to be unanimous: "traitors should be punished." There is a moment of suspense, for as Cola passes just then and with his usual complaisance surrenders the letter for Lucinda, the Queen finds in the Earl's words proof of his innocence. Overjoyed, she cries out loudly to Ubaldo, who thinking he hears the signal, executes his prisoner and appears shortly with Essex's head in a basin. The Queen can only lament over it in despair till unable longer to endure the thought of her injustice, she kills herself.

The Queen of England is a little unusual among scenarios in giving for all its absurdities and its farce and its impossible characters, an indefinable sense of reality.. It is not often that an improvised play rouses even the tritest reflections on life, yet here in the very unreasonableness of the story and the illogicality of its climax there seems to be a recognizable representation of the actual tragedy of Essex; as in the historic situation inconsistencies of passionate natures and small accidents and misunderstandings bring about a melancholy end where a happy one might seem just as possible. There must I think have been some definite literary source for the scenario to which should be attributed such little power as it may have. The tone of the written plays differed from the improvised chiefly by a consistent maintenance of just such seriousness as haunts us fitfully here; of course the professional actors' main care was only to amuse uproariously, not as with the regular dramatists, to bring some definite idea to finished expression. This diversity of aim accounts for such formal differences as the shortening of the five acts in written prose and verse to the regulation three in improvised prose;[88] the substitution of the Masks for the more highly differentiated persons of literary drama, and the multiplication of *lazzi* in the professional plays.

Yet the plot fabric of both forms was at bottom the same and so were many of the ornaments with which professional actors tried to grace their freer plays. Scala, we learn from various contemporary references, used gorgeous mythological prologs and interludes when he performed for private audiences and even when he was giving his more economical public representations he may very likely have followed academic fashion in putting the substance of his argument into an introductory speech, perhaps at times into a brief dialog. Whether a prolog were appropriate or not seems to have mattered little,—actors and poets composed sheaves of them for miscellaneous recital—and Scala quite probably varied his salutations according to his audiences.[34] The written plays were almost always prefaced by one or more introductory addresses,[35] invariably semi-

[88] Only one five-act scenario has been found among the five hundred and seventy-nine in existence, all the rest have three acts; cf. Brouwer, *Ancora una raccolta di scenari*, 395, note 4.

[34] Domenico Bruni, a member of the troupe of the Confidenti, published two volumes of prologs and miscellaneous speeches mostly in verse: *Prologhi* (Bologna, 1623) and *Fatiche comiche* (Bologna, 1623).

[35] Grazzini's *La Gelosia* (1551) has a prolog addressed to men and another to women; the play was written for academic performance by amateurs and is particularly literary in tone.

boastful, semi-apologetic, occasionally stating the subject of the comedy, more often taken up with a discussion of some critical problem,[36] not infrequently setting forth in allegorical manner either the leading theme of the piece or a delicate compliment to audience or patron;[37] or again they are in Jonson's style, entirely independent, and consist of a lively monolog or dialog in which one or more lads make the spectators laugh at their stupidity or their wit.[38]

Many of these amusing trifles would have done quite as well, and probably were actually annexed for service in improvised plays, as in the academic productions they adorn in print; they belong to the class of unattached prologs already referred to, those written originally no doubt for some special

[36] Grazzini's *La Strega* is prefixed by a prose debate on the nature and function of comedy, as Cecchi's *La Romanesca* by a poetic definition of the *farsa*. Similar philosophic efforts are to be found here and there in Lombardo's *Nuovo Prato di Prologhi* (Venetia, 1628). Lombardo probably played with the Uniti c. 1584; cf. Rasi, *comici italiani* II, 45.

[37] Of these an elaborate specimen that may have been used for *commedie dell'arte* was written by Soldano Aniello, for himself as Dr. Spacco Strummolo to speak in praise of the city of Bologna, presumably at performances there; it is a debate between various Olympians on the origin of the name of that city. Cf. Rasi, *Comici ital.*, I, 165 f. Cf. also Martucci in Nuova Antologia, 15 maggio, 1885, 222.

[38] One of Bruni's prologs is called "for a boy," and begins: "Most noble lords: Plato in his *Banquet*—it wasn't Plato—ah! I remember. Aristotle in his *Politics;* it wasn't Aristotle either—plague take these great fantastic authors, they've in a way turned my head, so I can't recall the prolog nor anything else." (*Fatiche comiche*, 6 f.)

performance but afterwards incorporated into a collection of miscellaneous poems. Bruni wrote several prologs to be spoken by Pantalone, one of them in Venetian dialect begins by discussing a fashionable problem thus:

If honor be the reward of virtue, why may not a man who lives virtuously even though his wife is little less than a harlot, be regarded with honor? And if honor be the garment of the soul of him who does well, how can the acts of another make him despised? And if all the virtuous actions of a woman cannot make honorable an infamous man, why should the infamy of a woman dishonor a worthy man?

This is one of Bruni's not uncommon labor-saving devices; he often wrote speeches which like this one would do equally well for prologs to a number of different comedies or for insertion in the main body by the play at a crisis in the old man's ill fortunes.[39] The honor theme in Pantalone's mouth reminds us once more how close were the relations between the professional and literary theaters of Italy. The fact of this cousinship can hardly be too much stressed or accounted for too carefully. Beyond the causes for it already suggested—the intimacy of actors with their patrons and the liberal attitude of

[39] A later volume, Bocchini's *Corona macheronica* (Bologna, 1663), contains a number of speeches for the "Zagno," the *servetta*, etc. Cf. p. 13, *Prologo per un Zagno in Bologna*, beginning:

> "No ve ste più à stupir,
> Brigade, se qua suso
> Me vedè comparir
> Con maschera al muso
> In scena cantando. . . ."

learned playwrights toward their interpreters—lies another reason, habitual flexibility in the method of rendering a given plot. During all the history of the *commedia dell'arte* written plays were reduced to scenarios for freer treatment and scenarios were expanded into full prose or verse dramas, the changes being made sometimes by the authors themselves, sometimes by hack-writers or actors, and often in such a manner that it is impossible to tell which is the earlier version. So far as is known Fabritio de' Fornaris, a far-traveled member of the Confidenti, set the fashion in 1585 by writing up and printing in Paris his comedy of *L'Angelica*, which during some years previously had been played from a scenario by his own company. Giovan-Battista della Porta, author of many literary comedies, left two versions of one of them, a scenario and a fully written piece, *La Trapolaria*.⁴⁰ Niccolò Barbieri in the dedication to his *Inavvertito* (1630), says he publishes the comedy because the plot has become so popular that every actor possesses a different form of it. A letter of 1632 survives in which a poet is asked to expand into "playable verses" the enclosed "plot of a comedy to be given at the next carnival."⁴¹ Such are a few examples of the interchange of form which serves to explain similarities between literary and professional plays. In some cases, naturally, the written dramas do not correspond closely to the scenarios bearing the same name; again a title was

---

⁴⁰ Scherillo, *Comm. dell'arte*, Chap. VI, 117 f. Cf. F. Bartoli, *Notizie istoriche*, I, 230 f.

⁴¹ A. Bartoli, *Scen. inediti*, lix, note 4.

sometimes altered for an improvised piece though the latter was in plot exactly identical with a written source.[42] In short so many kinds of relationships existed between the two methods of dramatic art that there is no excuse for wonder at their obvious correspondences.

After the middle of the seventeenth century when the popularity of the *commedia dell'arte* was declining, the tradition derived from the practice of its actors contributed several elements to the favorite amusements of the time, the *melodramma* and the opera bouffe. Certain parts of these "mixed pieces" were regarded as beneath the dignity of being set to music or put into verse, and so were left to the extempore invention of the actors who took the masked parts. This combination of prose fooling with musical numbers on a thin plot basis survives in the modern extravaganzas of our own comic stage, yet it is only in such old-fashioned operas as the *Mariage de Figaro* that there is still traceable anything resembling a direct influence of the *commedia dell'arte*. During the eighteenth century, as will shortly appear, the Masks ceased to be prominent in the better theaters and dropping out of fashion were relegated to the places from which they sprang, the humble amusement halls of the common people and the booths of country fairs. So humiliating a

[a] Groto's *Emilia*, for instance, was played with improvised dialog as *Le furberie di Scappino;* cf. Bartoli, *Scen. inediti,* lix.

Bartoli gives a long list of titles of scenarios (ib., xxix f.) with, in the notes, corresponding titles of written plays. Cf. Brouwer, *Ancora una raccolta di scenari,* 395 f.

downward progress however did not begin till all Europe had become familiar with Pantalone and Gratiano and their families, and until mimics of their grotesque selves grimaced on every important foreign stage. It is with this intermediate moment of success and glory that we must deal before pointing to the disappearing Masks in their hungry, out-at-elbows, poverty-stricken old age.

CHAPTER V.

Among the many causes for the Italianate character of the Renaissance in western Europe not the
least is to be sought in the performances of Italian
actors in the sixteenth century. These troupes were
great travelers, even more given to jaunting about
than were their English rivals, and naturally they
introduced to the courts of Paris, Madrid, Vienna,
Munich and London, their own rich and varied culture, chiefly in the early years of the century the
music of their country, later, when they had become
better organized, the improvised pieces which were
their peculiar professional glory, and the "learned"
plays of many of their academic friends. Whatever the proportion of tragedies to comedies and of
written to extempore plays in their repertory, there
is no doubt that farcical *commedie dell'arte* were
everywhere the main favorites and that they became
famous far and wide; the *lazzi* of Arlecchino, merry
and easily understood as they were, pleased not only
the foreign rabble but princes and their courts no
less, just as they had done at home in Italy. In
1560, to instance a typical expression of aristocratic
approval, Catherine de'Medici in unmistakable
terms announced that she wanted no more tragedies
played by the Italian company, but, Brantôme adds,
"she gladly heard their comedies and tragicomedies, even those of Zanni and Pantalone, taking

great pleasure in them and laughing her fill at them like everyone else, for she always enjoyed a laugh.'"[1] Her amusement was by no means singular; she is but one among many powerful patrons who applauded the Italians in foreign lands, and who contributed to the vogue and success of the Masks among strangers.

With the oldest records of traveling Italians we have little to do for they do not concern the *commedia dell'arte*. That Henry VIII had several Italians among his minstrels, that "Maistre André Italien" was commissioned in 1530 by the governor of Paris to "make and compose the most exquisite farces for a royal entry,'[2] and similar facts, are interesting proofs of the cosmopolitanism of the Italian strollers but they are otherwise insignificant for us. The *commedia dell'arte* could not begin its triumphant progress abroad, of course, until it had taken shape at home, that is, until its creator-actors had become firmly enough established and permanently

---

[1] Cited by Scherillo, *La vita italiana*, 317.

[2] The musician Masacone at the English court in 1517 has been traced to Italy by Professor Cunliffe; cf. Pub. of Mod. Lang. Assoc., XXII, 147–8. Collier, *Hist. Eng. Dram. Poetry* (1831), I, 83, quotes from a document which he says is of Henry VIII's reign, a list of eighteen of the "King's minstrels," among whom are Nicholas Andria and Antony Maria; as the document is undated there is no way of telling whether these men can be identified respectively with the Maistre André who was in France in 1530 and the Antonio Maria who according to the Royal Accounts of France was paid for entertaining the court of Charles IX in 1572; both identifications could hardly be true if the list is *bona fide* and of Henry VIII's reign; yet in view of the long professional careers of some of the Italian actors, there is a possibility of either. Cf. Baschet, *op. cit.*, 36–7, for the record of "Anthoine Marie" in France, where he was at the head of a company in 1572. Cf. Rasi, I, 185.

enough banded together to work out in groups this
cooperative product,—a result not achieved until
nearly the middle of the century. It is therefore
after about 1550 that Italian names in foreign
records begin to have a meaning for us, and it is
from that time on that we must search for traces of
the *commedia dell'arte* in other countries.

Not till 1548 when Bibbiena's *Calandra* was given
magnificently by an Italian troupe in Lyons,[3] does
there appear a sign of any but single and scattered
musicians and jugglers in any foreign court. At
nearly the same time however other little companies
seem to have crossed the Alps to seek their fortunes
in different directions; at least there is in 1549 a
note of one small band, five Venetians, who were
paid one florin by the "Rechner" of Nördlingen, for
some kind of a dramatic performance.[4] Their leader
is unidentified; he could hardly have been the famous
Giovanni Tabarin of Venice, afterwards so familiar
to Teutonic audiences, him whose company was recorded at Linz in 1568–9 and at Vienna often between
1568–74.[5] Although in the course of these twenty

[3] A full description of this splendid occasion is given from the
original documents by Baschet, *Les comédiens italiens*, 6 f.

[4] Trautmann, *Ital. Schauspieler*, 225–6.

The group who played in Nördlingen in 1549 was probably organized for real dramatic performances and with some degree of perma-
nence, since a little later they were paid by "four florins and good
words" after representing "an old Roman history of Hercules."

Vettori, *Viaggio in Allemagna* (Paris, 1837), says, p. 173, that
Italian comedies were known in Germany in 1507 but the statement
is on the face of it improbable, and the author is notoriously un-
reliable.

[5] Tabarin was under the direct protection of the Emperor with the

years a few meager notices testify to the presence of strolling bands in foreign palaces, they unfortunately throw little light on the repertory presented, and are therefore no more worth citing here than the records of the musicians just alluded to.

When however a little later some plainer hint evokes more vividly the ghost of a bygone spectacle, it must not escape us. Such is the note describing the performance by a Florentine, Antonio Soldino, and his troupe, of a tragedy before "the Roman Imperial Majesty" in 1570,[6] and that other record of the generous reward paid the same man by Charles IX in Paris, 1572, for the representation in the royal palace of "comedies and pleasing diversions," or as is elsewhere stated, "comédies et saults."[7] Soldino's men were evidently able to give "regular" pieces—witness their tragedy before the Emperor—and probably among their lighter "diversions" included a few *commedie dell'arte*. Again in March, 1571, the special ambassador from Elizabeth to Charles IX, Lord Buckhurst, gives us a glimpse of an Italian play in a letter to the Queen:[8]

title "player to his Imperial Roman Majesty." Trautmann, *op cit.*, 228 f.

Ancona, *Origini*, II, 458–68, brings together some facts about Tabarin who, he says, was the first to take troupes to foreign countries; if this were so we should probably have to suppose him to have played at Lyons in 1548 as well as in Germany in 1549. Cf. Rasi, II, 555 f.

Ancona states (*op. cit.*, II, 405–6) that about 1567 Italian *comici* began to travel; the German records cited above would change the date to about 1548.

[6] Schlager, in Wiener. Sitzungesberichte, phil.-hist. Klasse, VI, 167.
[7] Baschet, *Comédiens italiens*, 34 f.
[8] *Calendar of State Papers, Foreign Series of the Reign of Elisabeth*, 1569–71, 413.

"The 4 of this month the King procures the duke of Nevers to invite me to diner where we found a sumptuous feste and of gret honour adorned with musick of a most excellent and straunge conserte, and with a Comedie of Italians that for the good mirth and handling therof deserved singular comendacion."

M. de Nevers was Lodovico Gonzaga, younger brother to the Duke of Mantua, by all his training and traditions a patron of the theater; but what this company was by which he entertained his guest or what kind of play was given, the Englishman does not detail..

The Earl of Lincoln in a letter dated June 18, 1572, is a trifle more explicit: "At after dynar Monsieur and his brother brought us to a Chamber wheare there vearie many sortes of exelent musicke; and after that he had us to another large Chamber wheare there was an Italian playe and divers vantars (vaulters?) and leapers of dyvars sortes vearie exelent; and thus that daie was spent.'"

From this time on the records are full of quite definite allusions to Italian actors, especially in France, where between 1599 and 1624 at least eight companies performed. Ganassa whose first appearance is in a comedy at Mantua, 1568,[10] was one of the most restless of them all; after playing at Lucrezia

Baschet, *Comédiens italiens*, 14 f., assumes the play to have been a *commedia dell'arte*; the original statement is however too vague to be interpreted dogmatically. The company may possibly have been Soldino's.

[9] Nichols, *Progresses, etc. of Queen Elizabeth*, I, 304.

[10] Ancona, *Origini*, II, 455.

11

d'Este's wedding in Ferrara, January, 1570,[11] he went to serve Phillip II, playing in Madrid, as Father Ottonelli says, "in our manner," teaching the Spaniards "modest and not obscene comedies.'"[12] On August 18, 1572, he and six companions acted at the marriage of Henri de Navarre and Marguerite de Valois in Paris, and as good Catholics undoubtedly witnessed and approved the St. Bartholomew six days later.[13] So far as is known Ganassa was the first to introduce the Bergamask Zanni to Parisians, playing either in *contrasti* or in *commedie dell'arte* with Pantalone, as the Sieur de la Fresnaye Vauquelin notes:

> . . . le bon Pantalon, ou Zany dont Ganasse
> Nous a representé la façon et la grâce.[14]

The same pair of comic figures was especially successful in Germany and Vienna, if we can venture such a deduction from the facts that they are the most often described and are the most prominent in the frescoes at Schloss Trausnitz where they are portrayed with the Doctor, the Captain, the lovers and the *servetta* grouped about them.[15]

---

[11] Solerti, *Ferrara*, etc., xcii.

[12] Cf. Ottonelli, *Della christiana moderatione*, etc., II, 37. Barbieri's statement in *La Supplica*, 105, is the source of later accounts of Ganassa in Spain. Cf. F. Bartoli, *Notizie istoriche*, I, 248–9.

Ganassa was not the first Italian actor in Spain; for others cf. Rennert, *Spanish Stage*, 22 and 29, note 1.

[13] Baschet, *Comédiens italiens*, 42 f.

[14] In the second book of his *Art poétique*, a poem begun in 1574; cited by Baschet, *op. cit.*, 45.

[15] Trautmann, *Ital. Schauspieler*, 193 f. The sixteenth century frescoes at Trausnitz may commemorate the performance of Trojano's play at Munich, 1568, but more probably they are generalized representations, having nothing to do with a particular comedy. Rasi, *Comici italiani*, II, 1024, reproduces a small portion of the frieze.

Pater.

MARCHE COMIQUE.

Voyez-vous ce docteur sur sa digne monture,
Qu'accompagne Pierrot suivi d'autres bouffons,
Et qui pour annoncer sa grotesque figure,
Remplit l'air de ses mauvais sons?

It is perfectly to be expected that the improvised plays with their bizarre Masks and their *lazzi* would have been more appreciated in foreign halls than the sometimes tedious regular dramas, yet there is not the slightest reason to think that the actors confined themselves to farces or that they did not play abroad the varied repertory they gave their home audiences. They spoke Italian to be sure, but that language was as well understood then by educated people as is French to-day, so that at least before the courts the strangers could act their literary pieces.[16] As Sorel describes the Italians and their "naive and ridiculous antics" he admits "an extraordinary charm" in their plays, even though they are unable to abstain from mingling buffoonery with their more serious efforts, for such fooling "is too natural to them to be omitted"—they are, he adds apologetically, so instinctively expressive.[17] Popular in the extreme there is no doubt they were with whomever saw them,—the frequency of their visits to Paris alone proves that; just how general and insistent was the demand for their services will perhaps be clearest if the history of the most famous of the companies is briefly outlined.

The Gelosi are first heard of in Milan, where they acted in 1569 with "that sweet siren" Vittoria

[16] Trautmann, *Ital. Schauspieler*, 235, proves that the Italians used their own language at the imperial court of Vienna and in Germany; in Madrid the same was true (cf. Rennert, *Spanish Stage*, 260) and in England there is record of at least one play translated into Italian for performance, probably by an Italian company. (Fleay, *Chronicle History*, etc., I, 26.)

[17] Rigal, *Théâtre français avant la période classique*, 48.

Piissimi as their bright particular star. In May, 1571, they furnished a dramatic entertainment for a royal baptism in France, at Nogent-le-Roy, whence they went to Paris, only to regret their distance from their protector the king; Parlement insulted them by prohibiting from acting in public all "players of farces and such like common amusements" who were not properly authorized. The Italians in vain produced their permits from the king in which they were called "Comédiens du Roi," —Parlement referred to them indeed a little more politely as "actors of tragedies and comedies" but reiterated in November the interdict. The company under its chief, Alberto Ganassa, seems to have gone home again directly, for in the spring of the following year they played at Milan.[18] The autumn found them at Genoa, the next summer at Ferrara; here upon an island in the Po where the Estensi had a splendid villa, they gave the *Aminta* of Tasso before Alfonso II and his train, unfortunately only to be rewarded by "little gain and many insults"[19] though a contemporary says they were at this time "most ready in the imitation of every kind of person and all human actions, especially those that are apt to move laughter."

In the winter of the same year they were in Venice,

[18] The outline of the movements of the Gelosi I have taken from what seem to me the most careful studies of the subject, Solerti-Lanza, in Gior. Stor., XVIII, 159 f., Ancona, *Varietà*, II, 283 f., and Ademollo, *Una famiglia*, etc., xxxiv f. Baschet, *Comédiens italiens*, 16 f., gives a detailed account of the trouble with Parlement, citing the documents.

[19] Solerti, *Ferrara*, etc., xciv.

whither they returned in 1574 after a brief trip to Milan, to play before Henri III of France in a tragedy by Frangipani and two improvised comedies, the latter elaborately staged and "adorned with interludes." I have already referred to the impression made on Henri by this company, especially by Vittoria and the Magnifico, Giulio Pasquati; to this ineffaceable memory was due the summoning of the Gelosi to Paris in 1576 after two years of successful performances in Milan, Florence, Ferrara, perhaps even in Vienna, where Pasquati had gone in 1576.[20]

The second journey to France was not without adventure for the whole company was taken prisoner by the Hugenots near La-Charité-sur-Loire and had to be ransomed by the king before they could appear in January at Blois; the same evening they arrived they showed their gratitude by giving one of their comedies in the great Salle des Etats, to the huge diversion of Henri and his court.[21] In May they established themselves again in Paris, where they played to large crowds and at some profit as they were allowed to charge four sous entrance fee.[22] But as in 1571 Parlement—no doubt at the instigation of the Confrérie de la Passion, the dramatic monopoly

[20] Trautmann, *Ital. Schauspieler,* 229; cf. Rasi, *Comici italiani,* II, 226.

[21] Baschet, *Comédiens italiens,* 61 f. They were allowed to collect a demi-teston (fifteen sous) apiece from the audience, an unusually large sum.

[22] In 1541 two sous had been the price fixed by Parlement for a place at a public performance; from 1609-20, five sous was the price in the pit and ten in the gallery and boxes, a sum increased in 1634 to nine or ten sous for the pit and nineteen to twenty for boxes. Cf. Rigal, *Théâtre fran. avant la période classique,* 156-7.

in Paris—put an end to their performances, this time with a definite accusation to the effect that plays like theirs only served to teach "paillardises et adultères" and "were a school of debauchery to the youth of both sexes." As before the Gelosi presented the king's letters, yet now with better results than formerly, for after a short time they began to play again "at the Hostel de Bourbon . . . by the express permission and order of the king." "I desire that it be done so and that there be no mistake," says Henri's note of command to the city authorities, "for I have pleasure in hearing them and have never heard more perfect."[23]

The atmosphere may have cooled in France notwithstanding the favor of the court, or that favor may itself have turned to some newer object, for the Gelosi were back in Italy in 1578, when at Florence they lost La Vittoria and made some other changes in the company. The next year they had more trouble. A decree of the Duke of Mantua is extant, dated May 5, 1579, exiling "from the City and State of Mantua the comedians called the Gelosi who lodge at the sign of the *Bissone*, and also Signor Simone, who plays the part of the Bergamask, and Signor Orazio and Signor Adriano, who play the parts *amantiorum*, and Gabriele called delle Haste, their friend."[24] There is no record of their offense; whether their plays were too free either in morals or in political or personal satire, or whether like Pedrolino's company in 1576, they were forbidden

[23] Baschet, *Comédiens italiens*, 76.
[24] Ancona, *Origini*, II, 464 f.

to act because of the scandalous lives of some of their number, nothing remains to tell.[25] Perhaps the machinations of Vittoria, who was by this time the star of the Duke's most favored company, the Confidenti, were to blame for the exile of her former confederates.

It seems almost necessary to suppose some plot or inimical influence working against the Gelosi, for they were quite certainly not inefficient. That same summer they played before Prince Ferdinand of Bavaria and were by him pronounced "die best Gesellschaft so in gantz Italia von Comedianten."[26] Moreover in 1580 they conquered the reluctant good will of Carlo Borromeo, Archbishop of Milan, and caused him to modify his prohibition of their plays so that they were allowed to perform in such pieces as were approved by an episcopal commission,—a triumph to which perhaps is due their reinstatement at Mantua in 1582. Fortunately the Gelosi were not under the exclusive patronage of the Gonzaghe at this period, for in 1583 Francesco Andreini declined the Duke's offer of a position in his new company with the excuse that he is engaged to the "most famous S. Alvise Michiele, manager of the hall at Venice," probably the director of a public theater. For some years the Andreini and their friends seem to have been rather more bound to the noble family of Este than to any other, for they played at Ferrara quite regularly at carnival time. Between 1580 and 1599 they traveled from city to city in northern

[25] Rasi, *Comici italiani*, I, 242.
[26] Trautmann, *Ital. Schauspieler*, 235.

Italy, making a name for themselves chiefly through the beauty and genius of their leading lady, Isabella Andreini, and the successes of her husband in the Captain's rôle.

In 1599 the Gelosi apparently went for the third time to France; they performed at court without molestation but of course as soon as they tried to take money for public plays at the Hôtel de Bour-gogne, the Confrérie de la Passion again had them restrained. Eight days after they had received the writ from Châtelet, however, a permit was granted them, probably as a result of their having paid a large sum for the privilege.[27] By 1600 all trace of them in Paris has disappeared and the court is ap-plauding a new and equally excellent troupe called the Accesi, protêgés of the Duke of Mantua. But one more bow the Gelosi certainly made to French royalty, in 1603–4, just before the death of Isabella Andreini and the consequent retirement of her hus-band from the stage threw their fellows into such despair that they disbanded temporarily, to reor-ganize later under a different name.[28]

Though the Gelosi deserve all credit as pioneers they were by no means the only actors who familiar-ized French audiences of the sixteenth century with the plays of their country, plays so much more lively

[27] Rigal, *Théâtre français*, etc., 48–9, and Baschet, *Comédiens ital.*, 103 f. The Italians were used to similar monopolies at home, cf. Jarro, *L'epistolario*, etc., *passim*, for details on the monopoly granted T. Martinelli by the Duke of Mantua.

[28] For biographical details on this interesting couple, who added the example of the most scrupulous regularity of life to their professional triumphs, cf. Rasi, *Comici italiani*, I, under Andreini, and Bevilacqua, Gior. Stor., XXII, 109 f.

and dramatically effective than the pieces in the repertory of the Confrérie de la Passion. The Accesi, whose Arlecchino set the fashion for a long line of imitators,[29] the Confidenti in 1584 and after, and especially the Fedeli, who under the leadership of Giovan-Battista Andreini preserved the scenarios and carried on the traditions of the Gelosi,[30]—all these did their part toward making the French stage ready for Molière. They were all exceedingly well-known and are often alluded to in the writings of the time. French poets rimed "histories" on the misadventures of "Pantalon Bisognoza,"[31] or wrote sonnets to Isabelle, "one of the gods disguised as a mortal," and to "admirable Arlequin, whose very posture is expressive."[32] The Sieur de Rosni used the familiar Masks as illustrations in his pungent satire of courtly vices,[33] and the Cardinal de Retz in his *Memoirs* constantly pillories his enemies under the stage names of the Italians,—Mazarin for one as a "vulgar Pantaloon" or as "Trivelino Prince."[34] Malherbe censures Arlecchino's production of *I dui*

[29] For the Accesi and Confidenti cf. Ancona, *Origini*, II, App. II. For the Martinelli, *ibid.*, Ancona, *Lettere di comici italiani*, and Jarro, *L'epistolario*, etc., *passim*.

Bruni, a member of the Confidenti, writes of them in his *Prologhi* and his *Fatiche comiche*.

[30] G. B. Andreini made astonishing advances in staging; he was particularly fond of presenting mythological-allegorical spectacles such as his own *Centaura*, three plays in one, in which all the characters of the first part are centaurs.

[31] Loret in 1654; cf. Moland, *Molière*, etc., 185–7.

[32] Isaac de Byer in 1600 and 1603; cf. Baschet, *Comédiens italiens*, 134, 119.

[33] In 1603. Cf. Baschet, *Comédiens ital.*, 136–7.

[34] In 1652 and after. Cf. Moland, *Molière*, etc., 187 f.

simili, "which is the *Menaechmi* of Plautus," uncertain whether "the sauces were bad or my taste corrupted," but sure that he came away "with no contentment except from the honor the Queen did me by her invitation."[35] Whether corrupted or not his taste must have been singular for Martinelli, the Arlecchino of the occasion, some ten days later writes to a Mantuan friend, "The comedy was most successful, contrary to all expectation; but they are wild about comedies here so everything seems good."[36]

Before going on to follow the fortunes of other traveling companies in other countries it may be well to pause awhile and ask just how much influence these strangers and especially their peculiar plays can be proved to have had on a foreign art greater than their own. Here again as in the case of the Roman Mime there is danger of taking one set of facts out of their connection and of seeing them so isolated as more analogous to another set of facts than in their proper setting they really are. It will not do to stress too much an influence that was only one small element in the stream of Renaissance life. The *commedia dell'arte* was not responsible for the mixture of classical and romantic material in Hardy's plays and in the English and Spanish drama,—a mixture quite as characteristic of the written as of the improvised Italian comedies, and very general in the theater of the period—nor was it responsible for the theory of love that underlay

[35] Baschet, *op cit.,* 242–4. This was in 1613 on Martinelli's second visit to Paris.

[36] Jarro, *L'epistolario,* etc., 57–8.

the conceits of its young heroes and heroines—
these were ideas adopted by the actors in deference
to academic taste, as we have seen. Nor is the habit
of improvisation, of which a good deal has been made
in studies of the Spanish *gracioso* and the Elizabethan fool, to be traced exclusively to imitation of
the Zanni; improvisation, especially of sharp
repartee, topical allusion and comic *lazzi*, is a universal characteristic of any really popular stage,[37]
and if Shakespeare's or Lope de Vega's fools filled
out their meager lines by quips of their own, they did
it just as circus clowns or minstrels do it to-day,
because they are moved to free expression by the
nature of the entertainment they offer, not because
they ape clever improvisatori, Italian or other.

Neither can the many *lazzi* of the *commedia
dell'arte* be made a fair test of their influence;
farcical tricks, disguises, mock-fights and the rest
are, like improvisation, very general appeals to
groundlings and are found in medieval French and
English plays long before there was any possibility
of interaction with Italy. Moreover masks, inherited
from the medieval theater, were sometimes worn on
the stage as late as Shakespeare's or even Molière's
day; Quince, you remember, silences Flute's
scruples as to acting Thisbe when he has "a beard
coming" by assuring him he may wear a mask,[38]
and Corneille remarks on the effectiveness of substituting an actress with uncovered face for a masked

[37] Cf. Hunter, *Popular Romances*, etc., 390, for a St. George play
in which the prose parts are improvised.
[38] *Midsummer Night's Dream.*, I, 2.

man, in female rôles.[39]   For character types the
same warning holds good; resemblances are not to be
too jubilantly noted between Pantalone, for instance,
and the old fathers of French, English, Spanish
plays of this period, for the Magnifico was probably
not responsible for what may be due to a direct imitation of a common source,—some Latin or Latinate
Italian model—or to a similar expression of conventional ideas as to the universal unlovely traits proper
to all old men.

In looking for signs of the *commedia dell'arte* in
other countries therefore, I have left aside as irrelevant much that might perhaps be construed into evidence and have regarded as conclusive only the
plainest references to peculiarities undoubtedly
belonging to the extempore plays.   The most satisfactory of these are naturally direct allusions either
to the Italian practice of improvising on a scenario,
or to some of the Masks, or—of more uncertain
value—to a typical *commedia dell'arte* motif, if there
may be said to be such, a mountebank's performance, for example.   Interesting but not so germane
to the matter are resemblances of plot and character,—due quite as probably, I repeat, to a common
source as to imitation.   Finally there are likenesses

---

*Corneille, Examen of *La galérie du palais*. "Le personage de
nourrice qui est de la vieille comédie et que le manque d' actrices sur
nos théâtres y avait conservé jusqu'alors, afin qu'un homme le put
représenter sous le masque, se trouve ici metamorphosé en celui de
suivante, qu'une femme représente sur son visage."

Women on the French stage were known as early as 1545 but were
not generally countenanced until nearly a century later. Cf. Bapst,
Essai sur l'hist. du théâtre, 177–8, and Rigal, *Théâtre français*, 181.

in comic *lazzi*, the most shaky of all evidence on which to found a theory of interaction.

France felt the Italian actors' influence somewhat more definitely than other countries, as one might expect from the frequency of the visits of the foreign troupes to Paris and the intimacy of their association with their French competitors. In the earlier half of the sixteenth century a number of the most popular Italian academic plays had been turned into French by Parisian dramatists; the nine free versions published by Larivey must have given in themselves alone a powerful impetus to imitation.[40] When it is remembered that such pieces as these, performed by French professionals or amateurs,

[40] This is not the place to go into the question of the relation of Italian written plays to the French seventeenth century theater, yet the influence was so important that it ought at least to be noted in passing. As early as 1543 Charles Estienne translated *Gl'ingannati*. P. de Larivey, himself of Italian extraction, followed Estienne's example by issuing in 1579 his first six *Comédies facétieuses*:

Les esprits, from Lorenzino de' Medici's *L'aridosio*. (1521.)
Le morfondu, from A. F. Grazzini's *La gelosia*. (1551.)
Les jaloux, from V. Gabbiani's *I gelosi*. (1545.)
Les escoliers, from G. Razzi's *La cieca*. (1563.)
La veuve, from N. Bonneparte's *La vedova*. (1568.)
Le laquais, from L. Dolce's *Il ragazzo*. (1539.)

In 1611 three more translations from the Italian were issued by Larivey.

La Constance, from Razzi's *Costanza*.
Le fidèle, from Pasqualigo's *Il fedele*.
Les tromperies, from N. Secchi's *Gl'inganni*. (1562.)

Cyrano de Bergerac's *Le pedant joué* is an adaptation of Bruno's *Candelaio*, and so many other plays of the end of the sixteenth century and the beginning of the seventeenth are to be traced to Italian originals. Cf. *Ancien théâtre français* in the Bibl. elzévirienne for all of Larivey's comedies edited by Viollet-le-Duc. E. Fournier, *Théâtre français au XVIe et XVIIe siècles*, I, 139 f., reprints *Les esprits*, with an introductory note.

were supplemented by the Italian actors' presentation of still others of their written plays and of *commedie dell'arte*, it is no wonder that the work of the greatest French comedian is full of trans-Alpine reminiscences.

Molière in his youth must certainly have seen many Italian plays both in these translations and in the original, the latter sometimes improvised, sometimes fully written, and he as certainly learned from them, even if he was not, as tradition says, partly trained by the famous Scaramouche.[41]   On his return from the provinces in 1659 he found Scaramouche and his company established since 1653 in the Salle du Petit Bourbon, and for a few months the two troupes shared the hall, playing on alternate days; a similar arrangement was made at the Palais-Royal in 1662 and lasted till Molière's death, the actors continuing on good terms, occasionally rivals but often associated together in entertainments before the court.[42]

So intimate a connection between Molière and his foreign co-workers no doubt gave rise to the story of

[41] Moland, *Molière et la comédie italienne*, 177, quotes a description of a probably imaginary lesson given Molière by Tiberio Fiorillo, "le grand Scaramouche"; the legend of such a relation between the two actors was well-known in the seventeenth century and the Italian's picture was often published with the verses,

> Il fut le maître de Molière
> Et la nature fut le sien.

For Scaramouche cf. Rasi, *Comici italiani*, I, and Croce, *Teatri di Napoli*, 582 f.   The apochryphal *Vie de Scaramouche* by his associate, Angelo Constantini has been proved a tissue of falsehoods.

[42] Moland, *op. cit.*, 7 f., 178 and 252.   This book, though superseded in some points by later investigations, remains the basis for all study of this particular connection.

his having stolen his plots from the widow of an Italian actor who had preserved her husband's scenarios.[43] The legend is still further colored by numerous likenesses of dramatic method and in his earlier work, of theme and characterization, between the plays of the great French comedian and the Italians. The two little farces, his first essays in play-writing, *La jalousie du barbouillé* and *Le médecin volant*, are both quite frankly imitative, apparently of scenarios.[44] The groundwork of both the pieces he brought back with him on his return to Paris were taken from Italian plays, *Le dépit amoureux* from *L'interesse* of Niccolo Secchi,[45] and *L'étourdi* from Niccolo Barbieri's *L'inavvertito*, the latter a comedy written up from a scenario and given in Paris as early as 1627.[46] The extraordinary mixture of satire, wild burlesque and tragedy in *Le festin de pierre* is the result of the poet's having

---

[43] Toldo, *Molière en Italie*, Jour. Comp. Lit., I, No. I.

[44] Neri, Gior. Stor., I, 75 f., publishes *Il medico volante*, a "commedia dell'arte distesa," i. e., an originally improvised play, written out fully after performance. Toldo, *Alouni scenari*, etc., 462, summarizes the discussion of the relation of Molière's play to Italian versions; there remains some doubt as to whether the French or the Italian form were the original.

[45] First edition, Venice, 1581. Riccoboni, *Hist. du théâtre italien*, 141, called attention to this source of *Le dépit amoureux* long before any one else noted it. Moland prints *L'interesse* in his edition of Molière, *Oeuvres*, III, 53 f. Rigal, *Molière*, I, 97, points out some other connections between Molière's comedy and Barbieri's *Inavvertito* and still other Italian plays.

Cf. on this subject Despois, *Théâtre français*, etc., 59-60, for an argument on the question of Molière's indebtedness to the Italians.

[46] Moland prints *L'inavvertito* in Molière, *Oeuvres*, II, 159 f.

L'étourdi also contains borrowings from Groto's *Emilia* and Fornaris' *Angelica;* cf. Rigal, *Molière*, I, 56 f.

borrowed his material not directly from the ultimate
Spanish source but from a reworking of the story
in a scenario, *Il convitato di pietra*, played in Paris,
1657; Mozart's *Don Giovanni* reproduces the spirit
of the scenario more nearly than Molière's play,
which is always just on the edge of escaping from
burlesque and never quite succeeds in doing it.[47]

Tartuffe, one of the greatest and most original
dramatic creations of the world, does not perhaps
owe his existence to the Italian theater, for had
Aretino's Hypocrite and Scala's Pedant never trod
the boards, Molière would probably have unmasked
hypocrisy in the form of his famous Jesuit.   Yet as
he had before him two convenient plots each effective ·
ly showing up an unctuous *faux dévot*, he took from
them both and especially from the scenario, hints
and more than hints for his own drama.[48]   Aretino's
Hypocrite may have been drawn on the model of a
pedant whom he knew in real life and whom he described as "the most oily, the most disgraceful, the

[47] Moland, *Molière et la comédie italienne*, 191 f., reproduces this
scenario, one of the gayest and most extravagently farcical ever
plotted. Cf. Despois-Mesnard, Molière, *Oeuvres*, V, 13 f.

For a scenario probably influencing Molière's *Monsieur de Pourceaugnac*, cf. Toldo, Gior. Stor., XLVI, 128, and *Alcuni scenari*, etc.,
474 f. Scenarios of apparent date c. 1660 contain the same plot and
similar *lazzi*.

[48] Neither Moland nor Despois-Mesnard say anything about Scala's
scenario but Moland in *Molière et la comédie ital.*, 209 f. analyzes
Lo ipocrito. After I had noted the resemblances between *Tartuffe*
and *Il pedante*, I found the same connection mentioned in Vollhardt,
Archiv für das studium der neueren Sprachen, etc., XCI, No. I, and
in Toldo, *Figaro*, etc. Toldo, *Alcuni scenari*, 481, discusses the old
scenario of *Basilisco di Barnagasso*, which tradition says influenced
Tartuffe.

most villainous you ever saw", a man who became
the master of a large house through his hold on its
mistress, and who lorded it over everyone including
the lady's husband.[49] The comedy so mordantly
satirizing this person or another like him, undoubtedly contributed much to Scala's scenario,[50] one of
the most effective of his plots.

In the first act of *Il pedante* Cataldo, the pedant,
appears as a mediator between Oratio and his
father Pantalone, and is so plausible that the youth
feels obliged to enlighten the audience in an aside
on "the miserable nature of the pedant." In the
second act—Cataldo drops out of sight in the *lazzi*
and love-making scenes of most of the first—the
hypocrite tells Pantalone that he will help him keep
order in his house and prevent Isabella, the old
man's young wife, from disgracing her husband. A
little later there is a comic scene between the pedagog and his pupil Fabio, "pedantic rimes made by
Fidentio, master of all pedants", and then a soliloquy in which Cataldo muses on his skill in cover-
ing "under the mantle of dissimulation and moral
pretensions" all his rascality. The speech pre-
ludes a conversation between him and Isabella; he
accuses her of flirting with the Captain, she weeps,
acknowledging her fault, and Cataldo with great
dexterity insinuates she would do better to bestow
her love on someone nearer home, namely, himself;

[49] Cited by Graf, Nuova Antologia, Ser. III, Vol. V, 412, from
Aretino, *Ragionamenti*, Part I, Gior. II.

[50] Scala, *Teatro*, etc., Gior. XXXI.

For the influence of others of Scala's scenarios in France cf. Toldo,
Études sur le théâtre de Regnard, Revue d'hist. lit. de la France, X, I.

she consents on condition that he pacify her angry husband.

After more love scenes between the children of Pantalone and Gratiano, Cataldo tells his patron that Isabella is "the most honest woman in the world", calls her out and insists on peace and an exchange of kisses. In the third act Isabella informs her husband of Cataldo's treason just at the moment when Pantalone is congratulating himself on having such a faithful friend. The old man will hardly believe her, repeating that he is sure the pedant is a "tremendously good man", but he at last consents to the plan his wife outlines, in order to discover the truth. He accordingly begs Cataldo to take charge of his house for a few days during his absence, an invitation immediately accepted with "many fine little words of praise for everyone." No sooner has Pantalone turned his back than Cataldo tells Isabella he dies for love of her, and she "to catch him with fair promises" bids him go to her room and wait for her. She then tells the two Zanni of her victim's helplessness in the house and they go in to execute a barbarous punishment. After yells from within, the unfortunate is brought out in his shirt, "bound with good cord"; he kneels to confess his scoundrelism and to beg for mercy, and the Captain recommends that he be let off with a sound beating and exile from the city. He is therefore flogged "very well" with three large clubs and driven off as "an infamous man and most hurtful, an example to all other pedants." Molière adopts this "moral" conclusion rather than the more cynical one of Aretino, in which the hypocrite goes entirely unpunished.

Molière never quite emancipated himself from the prevailing Italianate fashions, although only in one other play did he take an Italian plot entire and adapt it to French taste in his own manner. *Don Garcie de Navarre* follows quite closely the outline of Cicognini's *Gelosie fortunate del prencipe Roderigo,* itself probably from a Spanish source.[51] The intrigues of *L'école des femmes* and *L'avare* are indeed of the Italian classical type but are so freshened and changed by the powerful characterization of the principal figures that they deserve to be called original in every respect.[52] On the other hand *Les fourberies de Scapin,* with its plot influenced by a scenario based on Groto's *Emilia,* shows that as late as 1671 Molière found it easy to slip back into the imitative habits of his youth.[53]

Moreover all the comedies in which Sganarelle takes a leading part, either as servant or rustic, husband, father or tutor, contain decided reminiscences of the Italian style. The intrigue of *Le cocu imaginaire,*[54] the absurd *lazzi* in *L'école des maris,*

[51] Moland, edition of Molière, *Oeuvres,* II, and Rigal, *Molière,* I, 127. Cf. Toldo, *Alcuni scenari,* 481.

The French "opera eroica" reminds one now and again of the last nine extravaganzas in Scala's book, except that it is in far better form than they and more homogeneous in tone.

[52] The plot of *L'école des femmes* is found in a Neapolitan scenario, *L'astute semplicità di Angiola,* cf. Toldo, *Alcuni scenari,* etc., 469. It is uncertain whether the scenario is prior to the play or is based on it.

[53] Bartoli, *Scenari ined.,* lix f. There is a chance that here too the Italian scenario is from Molière's play.

[54] Moland, *Molière et la comédie ital.,* 255, cites the scenario *Il*

the choruses in *L'amour médecin* and the doctor's
lingo in *Le médecin malgré lui*—to mention but a
few of many Italianate motifs—prove how power-
fully in small details Molière was influenced by the
dramatic tastes of his popular neighbors. But there
is no need to point out many analogies of this kind,
and certainly none to say anything about the indebtedness of ballets like that in *Le bourgeois gentil·
homme* or *Le malade imaginaire* to Italian example,
—the *commedia dell'arte* has little part in this relation. Neither is it necessary to examine in further
detail Molière's burlesque doctors, his old men, his
comic servants or his lovers, who owe much to the
Masks but who are yet so individual. Anyone familiar with Scala's and Bartoli's scenarios will note
here and there as he reads *Le malade imaginaire* or
another comedy, an old Italian joke skilfully re-
furbished, a hackneyed situation vivified, or will
catch a likeness to Gratiano or Pantalone or Arlecchino as Argan or Monsieur Jourdain or Sganarelle
gesticulates or turns a grinning face to the audience.
Such occasional suggestions of tricks and comic
peculiarities of character, probably semi-consciously
noted and later used to good purpose, seem to sum
up Molière's indebtedness to the *commedia dell'
arte,* aside from the plots he drew from scenarios.

Looking back into the seventeenth century it is
apparent that in no other country of Europe did
the Italians find so apt and illustrious a disciple

ritratto ovvero Arlecchino cornuto per opinione as a doubtful source
of *Le cocu imaginaire;* the scenario as we have it seems of later date
than the play. Cf. Toldo, *Alcuni scenari,* 481, for another scenario
of a similar character.

as Molière. Their adventures in Germany and Austria after 1560 seem to have left little trace except in their patrons' expense accounts and occasional letters. The musicians who got up the improvised play for the wedding of the County Palatine in 1568 had no company with them and do not seem to have stirred any German dramatist to imitation.[55] The small troupe led by Jacopo of Venice which gave *La Calandra* at Munich in 1569, perhaps the first organized company in Germany,[56] pointed the way to many followers,[57] yet as has been said, beyond their pictures on the walls of Schloss Trausnitz, they left no permanent memorial behind. Giovanni Tabarin, Antonio Soldino and others whom we meet often in France, were in Vienna in 1568 and after—some of them got as far as Dresden in 1600[58]—but there was no Teutonic genius to take lessons from them and evolve masterpieces out of their skeleton plots. They doubtless helped to spread Italian culture,[59] theatrical devices and customs, though even in this their example worked more slowly here than elsewhere; for instance it is not until 1654[60] that we hear of a performance on a German stage, at Basle, by a "well-practiced com-

[55] Orlando di Lasso did however leave some marks on German music; cf. Bohn, *Orlandus di Lassus als Komponist weltlicher deutscher Lieder*, Jahrbuch f. Mün. Geschichte, I, 184 f.

[56] Trautmann, *Ital. Schauspieler*, 223–4.

[57] Cf. the records listed in Trautmann, *op. cit., passim*, and in Meissner, *Die engl. Komödianten*, etc., 190–1, and elsewhere.

[58] Schlager, Wiener Sitzungsber., VI, 147 f., and Trautmann, *op. cit.*, 292 f.

[59] Reinhardtstoettner, Jahrbuch f. Mün. Geschichte, I, 93 f.

[60] Cohn, *Shakespeare in Germany*, cii–ciii and note I.

pany" who boasted "repeated changes of expensive costumes, a theater decorated in the Italian manner" and "skilful women" in the cast.

Spain received the Italians more sympathetically, probably because dramatic conditions and the status of actors in the two countries were very similar. Cervantes' description of the strollers of his own time and nation is equally true of Italian players in the Cinquecento: "In the sweat of their brows they gain their bread by insupportable toil, learning constantly by heart, leading a gypsy life from place to place and from inn to tavern, staying awake to please others. . . . With their calling they deceive nobody, for continually they bring out their wares on the public square, submitting them to the judgment and inspection of everyone."[61]   There was the same difference between well-paid private and uncertain public performances, the same alternation between prosperity and misery, for these playthings of a fickle world; the same difficulties with the authorities,—questions about the morality of comedies, doubts as to the advisability of letting women take part in a public representation, condemnation of dances and farces, limitation of the hours and days of performance, regulation of the prices to be charged.[62]   Yet in spite of all opposition, probably all the more sturdily because of it, the Spanish drama grew and throve, and welcomed the visiting

[61] Written c. 1565. Cited Rennert, *Spanish Stage*, 160. Of course conditions all over Europe were much alike at this time (cf. Rigal, *Théâtre français*, etc., *passim*) but Italy and Spain offer particularly close resemblances.

[62] Rennert, *Spanish Stage, passim.*

actors who gave so much to it and in turn learned much from it.[63]

Ganassa's repertory in Madrid, 1574,[64] was, according to a contemporary, "comedias mimicas . . . y bufonescas," "trivial and popular," containing "the persons of Arlecchino, Pantalone, the Doctor," improvised pieces undoubtedly.[65] The next year Ganassa lent money toward building a public theater in Seville where he engaged to give sixty performances; whether because he was involved in this financial venture or because he found Spain a lucrative field for his efforts, he returned several times with his company and seems always to have found a ready welcome. Others of his countrymen followed him to Madrid,—an Italian acrobat with his tumblers in 1582, "the new Italians" later in the same year,[66] and in 1587–8 the brothers, Tristano and Drusiano Martinelli, with Madonna Angelica, wife of the latter.[67] Martinelli's company was quite

[63] Spanish and Italian actors played side by side in other countries as well as in Spain, cf. Trautmann, *op. cit.*, 250 and 305. Such contacts help to explain the influence of the romantic Spanish drama on the *commedia dell'arte*, shown in Scala's extravaganzas.

[64] Ganassa is the first Italian actor-manager in Spain of whom much is known; that he was not the first there, is shown by the record of a troupe which gave a comedy by Ariosto at Valladolid in 1548. Cf. Creizenach, *Gesch. des neueren Dramas*, III, 167.

[65] Baschet, *Comédiens italiens*, 49, note 1, and 50. Cf. Rennert, *Spanish Stage*, 28 f.

[66] Rennert, *Spanish Stage*, 44, noting this company conjectures they were I Cortesi; I should be inclined to identify them with I Comici Nuovi, formed at Mantua early in 1580 with Drusiano and Angelica at their head. (Solerti, *Ferrara*, etc., xcix f.) There is little proof for either identification.

[67] Ancona, *Origini*, II, 478 f., gives many letters from and about the Martinelli; cf. Rasi, I, under Martinelli and Jarro, *L'epistolario*, etc.

certainly the Confidenti, then favorites of the Duke
of Mantua, a prince whom with his son Angelica
numbered among her lovers.[68]   This lady humorously
enough was licensed to play in Spain not on account
of her beauty and talent, but because she was a
married woman and in the protection of her husband.   The authorities seem to have blinked the fact
that it was never to Drusiano his wife looked for
protection.[69]

All these companies pretty certainly played
written as well as improvised comedies, yet since
they spoke Italian they probably in Spain as elsewhere reserved their liveliest pieces, where gesture
largely supplied speech, for the public theaters; the
uncultured rabble could enjoy *lazzi,* songs and
dances and catch the easy drift of a simple plot
without knowing the language. "Learned" plays,
pastorals and interludes were more appropriate for
the court and for noblemen's halls.   In 1556 Lope de
Rueda translated one of the best known academic
comedies of the Cinquecento, *Gl'ingannati*—which
Estienne had put into French as early as 1543—and

Solerti, *Ferrara,* etc., xcix, note 4, quotes a letter of 1582 describing
how much in love with Angelica the Duke of Mantua was at that time.

[*] Rennert, *op. cit.,* 45–6. Cf. Ancona, *Origini,* II, 523, a letter of
1598, from a certain captain who complains to the Duke of Mantua
that he has supported Angelica and their son for years with the
connivance of Drusiano, and that the husband now claims the child as
his own, and abuses his wife, forcing her to go about begging "over
di aprir bottega publica."

[*] The Confidenti had petitioned to be allowed to act with the women
in their band—there were three—because they were "helpless" without them, and it was in answer to this request that the authorities
modified their prohibition of women's acting, in favor of married
women.

throughout his life he seems to have been influenced by both Italian theory and practice.[70] Lope de Vega, from his youth a frequenter of Italian plays, began his artistic career by the imitation of an Italian pastoral, *Jacinta;* his comedies show that he had taken lessons in the same school as Lope de Rueda, for like the *commedia dell'arte* they have three acts—though unlike them they are written and in verse—his lovers are often called Fulvio, Valerio, Ottavio, Isabella, Lucinda, and his clown has traits of the Zanni we know. With Calderon the influence worked the other way; Biancolelli took his scenario of *L'impegno del caso* from Calderon, a plot that was in turn borrowed by Thomas Corneille for his *Engagements du hazard.*[71] Such are a few examples of an interrelationship that awaits further investigation in the future.

[70] V. de Amicis, *L'imitazione latina*, etc., 5–6.
[71] Moland, *Molière et la comédie italienne*, 369.
Cf. also Brouwer, *Ancora una raccolta*, etc., 395, note 1, for another scenario from Calderon.

CHAPTER VI.

If owing to lack of published records traces of the *commedia dell'arte* in Spain are hard to find, the difficulty in England is rather that there is there too great wealth of accessible material and consequently a danger of seeing too many connections. Yet if we resolve to confine our notes on this small part of the Italian stream to unmistakable evidences of the Masks and other peculiarities of the improvised plays, there will be no excuse for straying too far along seductive by-paths of analogy; nor on the other hand will such a limitation prevent recognition of the undoubtedly close connection between Italian and Elizabethan drama.

The relation that existed between the stages of the two countries is, as in France, here explicable mainly, I think, through direct contact between actors rather than through printed texts.[1] Not only were Italian actors often in England, playing both at court and in the city, but they acted almost side by side with English companies on the continent, in Vienna frequently and in Paris and Spain at times.

[1] The only studies I know of the *commedia dell'arte* in England seem to me to have erred from taking the problem too broadly. Scherillo (*La vita italiana*, 338 f.) suggests Italian parallels for some of Shakespeare's characters and high-flown *concetti* which are probably due to a general Renaissance fashion, far wider than the *commedia dell'arte*. Schücking (*Stoff. Beziehungen*, etc.) is ready to see *commedia dell'arte* influence frequently when there is nothing to justify him.

On September 18, 1604, an English troupe gave a tragedy before the Dauphin—the Gelosi and the Fedeli were then in Paris also[2]—and according to Thomas Heywood such royal favor to British players was not uncommon. "The French king (he says) allows certain companies in Paris and Orleans, besides other cities; so doth the king of Spain in Civill, Madrill, and other provinces."[3] Nash, who was perhaps a member of one of these favored bands, tells of a meeting he had with a well-known Italian Zanni while he was on his travels: "Coming from Venice the last summer, and taking Bergamo in my ways homeward to England, it was my happe, sojourning there four or fiue days, to light in felowship with that famous Francatrip' Harlicken, who perceiuing me to be an Englishman by my habit and speech asked me many particulars of the order and manner of our playes which he termed by the name of representations: amongst other talke he inquired of me if I knew any such Parabolano here as Signor Ciarlatano Kempio. Very well (quoth I). . . . He hearing me say so, began to embrace me anew, and offered me all the courtesie he colde for his sake, saying that altho' he knew him not, yet for the report he had heard of his plesance, he colde not but bee in love with his perfections being absent."[4]

[2] Rigal, *Théâtre français avant la période classique*, 50, note.

[3] *Apology for Actors* (Shakespeare Soc., 1841), 58. Cf. Cohn, *Shakespeare in Germany*, cxxxiv f.; Meissner, *Die engl. Komödianten*, etc., *passim*; Baschet, *Comédiens italiens*, 100 f.; Mezières, *Prédecesseurs de Shakespeare*, 35; Collier's edition of *Memoir of A. Munday* (Shak. Soc., 1851), xxxv.

[4] *An Almond for a Parrat* (1590), ed. McKerrow, Nash's *Works*, III, 342. Rasi notes no real Francatrippa; the Zanni mask was often called by that name however.

As we know in general the repertories and the
habits of the Italians who rubbed elbows with Englishmen in all these foreign towns, as we recall how
lively and amusing or how beautiful and impressive
their plays could be and as, further, we take into account the then universal custom of pirating plays
from hearing them instead of copying them from
printed versions, nothing seems simpler than that
the English actors should learn directly from their
rivals.   But before dogmatizing on this point it may
be well to deduce in more detail the reasons for such
an hypothesis.

Italian musicians have already been mentioned as
visiting England in the first half of the sixteenth
century; in the latter half there is much clearer
evidence of regular companies of actors at court,
though unfortunately as in other countries the
records here are unsatisfactorily incomplete, the
foreigners being alluded to only by their first names
or even more vaguely, and very little information
being vouchsafed as to what they played.   In 1550
the Privy Council ordered one hundred pounds to be
paid to "Alberto, Franciso, Ambrosio, Vincentio
and Marck Antonio, the Kinges Majesties violen
players, by way of his Hignes reward," for how long
a term of service or for what kind of performances
we are not told.[5]

⁵ *Acts of the Privy Council*, II, 88. The man last named may quite
possibly be the same "Marcantonio, veneto," who with a neapolitan
and a bolognese companion recited comedies with "music, singing
and dancing" at Mantua, 1567; cf. Ancona, *Origini*, II, 477. For
the others I have found no probable identification unless Franciso
may be the same who in 1569 played at the imperial court; cf.

Other payments are made to other Italians by the
Privy Council from this time on, and the Revels Accounts also refer occasionally to the representations
by "the Italian players." Between February and
November, 1573,[6] "Ffor the Progresse to Reading
and Lykewise ffor the Ayringes, Repayryngs, Trans-
latinges, preparing, ffytting, ffurnishing, Garnish-
ing, Attending, and setting foorth, of sundry kyndes
of apparell propertyes, and ffurnyture for the
Italyan players that ffollowed the progresse and
made pastyme fyrst at Wynsor and afterwardes at
Reading," various payments are made; a list of
"Implementes and Expences" for these same actors
includes "a plank of ffyrr and other pieces of sawen
wood. Golde lether for cronetes. Thred and
sheperdes hookes. Lamskynnes for Shepperds.
Horstayles for the wilde mannes garment. Arrowes
for Nymphes. Lightes and Shepperdes staves.
Hoopes for Garlandes. Baye Leaves and flowers.
: : . The hyer of a Syth for saturne." Another
entry about the same occasion under the caption,
"hyer of Apparell," is: "iij devells cotes and heades
and one olde mannes fries cote for the Italian
prayers (sic) at Wynsor." Leone de Sommi could
not but have approved the elaborateness of a piece
in which nymphs, shepherds, wild man and Saturn
were so appropriately equipped! Probably so much

Meissner, *Engl. Komödianten*, etc., 190. Meissner mistakenly identi-
fies "Francesco Ysabell" of the Viennese record with the Andreini
(who were not acting as early as 1560) and their company with the
Gelosi.

[6] Feuillerat, *Documents relating to the Office of the Revels*, etc.,
225 f.

preparation was for a written pastoral, not merely for an improvised play.[7]

Other companies followed close upon. "Alfonso Ferrabolle and the rest of the Italian players" were rewarded on February 27, 1576,[8] for some kind of an exhibition at court, and Laneham in his lively style has given us an idea of what such a performance may in part have been.[9] He says at the Kenilworth festivities in 1576:

"Noow within allso . . . *waz thear showed before her Highness by an Italian, such feats of agilitie, in goinges, turninges, tumblinges, castinges, hops, jumps, leaps, skips, springs, gambauds, soomersaults, caprettiez and flights; forward, backward, sydewize, a downward, upward, and with sundry windings, gyrings and circumflexions; allso lightly and with such easiness, as by me in feaw words it is not expressible by pen or speech. . . . I bleast me by my faith to behold him, and began to doout whither a waz a man or a spirite. . . . Az for thiz fellow I cannot tell what to make of him, save that I may gesse his back be metalld like a lamprey, that haz no bones but a line like a lute-string."

On January 13, 1577, the Privy Council directed

[7] Wild men were favorite characters in the allegorical *mascherate* and *intermedj* of Italy; in a typical Florentine entertainment of 1543 they are made to sing a song as they conduct Reason to the city. Cf. *Tutti i trionfi*, I, 533. There was also a tradition in England in favor of wild men and their appearance in court masques; cf. Chambers, *Med. Stage*, I, 185, note 2, also A. H. Thorndike, Mod. Lang. Notes, XIV, No. 4.

[8] E. K. Chambers, Mod. Lang. Review, II, 5.

[9] *Laneham's Letter*, in Nichols, *Progresses*, etc., *of Q. Elizabeth*, I, 440-1.

"the Lord Mayor of London to geve order that one Dronsiano, an Italian, a commediante and his companye, may playe within the Cittie and the liberties of the same betweene this and the firste weeke of Lent."[10]   Although the name is spelt with an *n* instead of a *u* in the first syllable there is no doubt that the manager referred to is Drusiano Martinelli, who was in Spain with his wife and brother in 1587–8 and perhaps in 1582.   It was in 1577–8 that the Gelosi were in Paris—they were in Blois in January, it will be remembered—and there seems no improbability in Drusiano's having come from Italy with this company to which his brother later belonged, and in his having taken some of the players across the Channel; there was however another company in Lyons in November, 1576, and it may be that this was Drusiano's band.[11]

Whoever they were these people with Martinelli must certainly have presented *commedie dell'arte;* not only was their leader, like his brother, a well-known Arlecchino, but they played in the city of London, and as has been suggested, the public performances of the Italians were more likely to be the readily-understood improvised pieces than the written ones comprehensible to a courtly audience.[12] They may very possibly have performed at court

[10] *Acts*, etc., X, 144. The identification of Dronsiano with Drusiano, first made by Collier (*Hist. of Eng. Dram. Poetry*, 1826, III, 398, note), has been accepted by all Italian authorities without attempt to prove it from unpublished documents.

[11] Baschet, *Comédiens italiens*, 71 f.

[12] For Drusiano as head of the Duke of Mantua's men (1595), cf. Ancona, *Origini*, II, 518 f.

too, perhaps in pastorals and interludes, like the
troupe for whom the speeches in a *Masque of Amazons and Knights* were translated into Italian in
1579.[13] They may also have occasionally given in
the city a written academic comedy like the *Inganni*
compared by Manningham to *Twelfth Night*.[14]

By all their repertory the foreigners probably
scandalized the staid part of their London audiences,
and that in more ways than one. Performances by
women on the stage, a custom which Coryat had
heard "hath been sometimes used in London," were
unknown to the native British theater and even had
the women acted only in the most moral tragedies,
they would have met with little favor.[15] Since their
repertory consisted of "rather jigs than plays"
with no emphasis on "teaching" and a great deal
on "delightfulness" it is small wonder that the cock-
neys took in reference to such antics a tone of repro-
bation or contempt. Hear Nash for one speak of
the "players beyond the sea" as "a sort of squirting
baudie comedians that have whores to play womens'
parts and forbeare no immodest speech or unchast
action that may procure laughter," and, proudly,
"but our Sceane is more stately furnisht than euer

[13] Fleay, *Chronicle History*, etc., I, 26. In view of all these Italian
performances it is not strange that as M. Feuillerat says, "entre 1578–
85 on a l'impression d'assister, probablement sous l'influence de
l'Italie, à un brusque épanouissement du genre" (i. e., the pastoral).
[14] *Manningham's Diary*, Feb. 2, 1601/2.
The play has been identified with *Gl'ingannati*, by a member of
the Intronati.
[15] Women did not appear on the English stage regularly till after the
Restoration. Cf. Toldo, in *Rev. d'hist. lit. de la France*, April, 1896,
260 f.

it was in the Time of Roscius, our representations
honorable and full of gallant resolution, not consist-
ing like theirs, of a Pantaloun, a Whore, and a Zanie,
but of Emperours, Kings and Princes."[17] The un-
flattering judgment is echoed by Whetstone in the
dedication to *Promos and Cassandra:* "At this daye
the Italian is so lascivious in his comedies that
honest hearers are greeved at his actions," and
Gosson blames foreign example for the taint in
English plays, "Baudie comedies in Latin, French,
Italian and Spanish have been thoroughly ransact
to furnish the playhouses of London."[18] Indeed it
is. only an occasional aristocratic academician like
Gascoigne or Sidney who can be found to admit that
"Italian toyes are full of pleasant sporte"[19] and
that the abuse of the unities, so common in English
drama, is something which "at this day the ordinary players in Italy will not err in."[20] Thomas
Heywood in similar strain speaks of "all the doctors, zawnyes, pantaloons, harlakenes, in which the
French, but especially the Italians have been excellent" and considers, like the Italian critical theo-

---

[17] Nash, *Pierce Penilesse* (1592), ed. Grosart, 92. Nash knew more
than a little of Italian written plays, especially of Aretino's. Cf.
Summer's Last Will and Testament, ed. Grosart, 146, ll. 1520–1;
Strange News, 182, and *Lenten Stuffe*, 234, the last an allusion to
Aretino's *Puttana Errante.*

[18] Gosson, *Plays confuted in five actions* (1582).

[19] Prolog to the *Glasse of Government.* Cf. *Stele Glas,*

These interludes, these newe Italian sportes
And every gawde that glads the mind of man.

Marlowe also alludes to Italianate courtly *intermedj, Edward II,* I, 1.
[20] Sidney, *Defense,* 48. "Ordinary players" as contrasted with
dilettanti academicians, of course.

13

rists, that comedy should have in derision "foolish innamorates" and "Pantaloons that have unthrifty sons."[21]

Other specific allusions to the Masks are numerous enough. Shakespeare more than once uses "the old Pantaloon," the "lean and slippered Pantaloon," "the old Magnifico,"[22] as terms of contempt for some exemplar of old age's folly. Harvey in one of his letters refers to "a sorry Magnifico,"[23] and Middleton's Doctor in the *Changeling* (I, 2) hopes to improve the state of his idiot patient though hardly to stretch him up "to the wit of a Magnifico"—surely no great advance beyond imbecility! Later dramatists seem to have been just as severe toward "under-hearted, dull-blooded Pantaloon,"[24] who is portrayed as Pantaloni at his ugliest and silliest in Brome's *Novella*.

The Zany, as the Elizabethans agreed to call the Italian servant-clown, frequently served to point a comparison in an English comedy. Biron speaks of

> Some carry-tale, some pleaseman, some slight zany,
> Some mumble-news, some trencher-knight, some Dick
> That smiles his cheek in years and knows the trick
> To make my lady laugh when she's disposed.[25]

Malvolio mentions the "fool's zanies" in the sense of foolish servants to the fool,[26] while Jonson more

[21] *Apology for Actors*, 43 and 54.
[22] *Taming of the Shrew*, III, 1, line 37. *As You Like It*, II, 7, 158. *Othello*, I, 2, 12.
[23] *Foure Letters*, ed. Collier, second letter.
[24] Brome, *City Wit*, V, I.
[25] *Love's Labor's Lost*, V, 2, 463.
[26] *Twelfth Night*, I, 5, 96. The critics have usually preferred to

definitely alludes to the Italian mountebank's attend-
ant, "He's like a zany to a tumbler that tries tricks
after him to make men laugh," and again, "The
other gallant is his zany and doth most of these
tricks after him."[27] Marston in the *Malcontent*
(1604) refers to "the French Harlekene," quite
possibly Tristano Martinelli who was making a name
for himself in Paris during the early years of the
century. Day also had evidently seen some Zanni
act, for a page in his *Ile of Gulls* (II, 3) says, "I,
like Harlakene in an Italian comedy, stand making
faces at both their follies." Whether Bottom's
Bergamask dance has anything to do with an Italianate conception of the rustic's rôle is rather doubtful
since Bottom was not a rustic but a "rude mechanical," nor has he any traits in common with the Zanni
from Bergamo, one of whose specialties was awkward dancing.[28]

Such general references—and they might be multiplied—show plainly enough that the Italian actors
were even more familiar to Englishmen than the
scattering notices in official records would lead us

interpret Zany as "an inferior buffoon" without regard to the function of the clown in Italian improvised comedies. Cf. Furness Variorum edition of *Twelfth Night* on this passage, for a summary of
the chief definitions of the term. Florio's, from the *Worlde of
Wordes* (1598) is the best, for he as an Italian knew what he was
talking about: "Zane: Name of John, Also a sillie John, a gull or
noddie. Used also for a simple vice, clowne, foole, or simple fellow
in a playe or comedie."

[27] *Every Man in his Humour*, IV, 1. *Cynthia's Revels*, II, 1. Cf.
Day, *Law Tricks*, I, 10.

[28] *Midsummer Night's Dream*, V. Tiraboschi's *Vocabolario dei
dialetti bergamaschi* defines Bergamasca as "sorta di ballo rusticale."

to suppose. The numerous translations or adaptations of Italian plays offer another kind of proof of the same fact. Some of these versions, like Gascoigne's *Supposes,* set the fashion for many imitations and are doubtless in that way responsible for some of the Italianate features of Elizabethan drama.[19] There is not wanting still more direct evidence of Englishmen's intimate acquaintance with the *commedia dell'arte* in particular. Whetstone refers to the practice of improvisation in saying that the "Comedians of Ravenna" were "not tied to any written discourse" but had "certain grounds or principles of their own" on which to work.[20] A clearer allusion is that in the *Spanish Tragedy* (IV, 1):

> The Italian tragedians were so sharp of wit
> That in one hour's meditation
> They would perform anything in action.

Lorenzo admits the possibility of this kind of playing,

> . . . for I have seen the like·
> In Paris 'mongst the French tragedians.

Hieronimo: In Paris! mass! and well-remembered!
> There's one more thing that rests for us to
>   do . . .
> Each one of us
> Must act his part in unknown languages,
> That it may breed the more variety;
> As you, my lord, in Latin, I in Greek,

---

[19] Cf. J. W. Cunliffe's edition of the *Supposes,* also his articles on Italian-Elizabethan connections, Pub. Mod. Lang. Association, noted below, bibliography. Cf. below, App. B.

[20] *Heptameron of Civil Discourses,* 1582.

> You in Italian, and for because I know
> That Bellimperia hath practised the French,
> In courtly French shall all her phrases be.

Bellimperia had been urged to take a part, for "What's a play without a woman in it?" Again a typical Italian suggestion is Balthazar's,

> It shall be played by princes and courtiers,
> Such as can tell how to speak;
> If, as it is our country manner,
> You will but let us know the argument.

So the tragedy is played from a scenario, though the poet condescends to set it down "in English more largely for the easier understanding of every public reader."[31]

Another description of an improvised play is found in a much later comedy, Middleton and Rowley's *Spanish Gypsy,* acted at court in 1623 or 1624. Roderigo asserts (III, 1),

> . . . the scenical school
> Has been my tutor long in Italy,

and in Act IV, scene 2, Fernando precisely explains the method of that scenical school:

> . . . There is a way
> Which the Italians and the Frenchmen use,

---

[31] Act IV, sc. 4. That the piece was supposed to be played from a scenario is evident from the quoted passages, and still more from the spectator king's, "Here comes Lorenzo: look upon the plot, And tell me, brother, what part plays he?" It has occurred to me that perhaps the arguments prefixed to Scala's plays may have been printed and distributed to the audience, as was done here in the *Spanish Tragedy,* and later at performances in the Comédie Italienne and the Foires in Paris. Cf. below, Chap. VII.

> That is, on a word given, or some slight plot,
> The actors will extempore fashion out
> Scenes neat and witty.

Rôles are then apportioned as in the *Spanish Tragedy,* Fernando directing the assignment as he glances over the plot:

> Let this father be a Don
> Of a brave spirit, . . .
> Play him up high; not like a pantaloon,
> But hotly, nobly, checking this his son,
> Whom make a very rake-hell, a deboshed fellow. . . .

Sancho demands "one of the foolish knaves" for his part, and in the next scene where the play begins he acts very much like a Zanni. In fact the whole of this play-within-a-play is much more nearly in the Italian manner than the tragedy plotted by Hieronimo, although the names and perhaps some of the conceits here are of Spanish inspiration.

Whether Cleopatra's forecast of how "the quick comedians extemporally shall stage us" refers to the Italian practice, is doubtful,[32] yet there is one more unmistakable allusion to it in Brome's *City Wit* (1632): "In that lies the nobility of the device; it should be done after the fashion of Italy, by ourselves, only the plot premeditated to what our aim must tend; marry, the speeches must be extempore."

A much disputed phrase in *Hamlet* can, I think, only point to this same Italian custom of improvisation on a plot. Polonius praises the traveling actors in terms very suitable to the wandering comici (II, 2); for them "Seneca is not too heavy nor

[32] *Antony and Cleopatra,* V, 2.

Plautus too light," they were the only men in the world "for the law of writ and the liberty." Surely Collier's common-sense interpretation of "the law of writ and the liberty" as written and improvised plays is more probable than the explanations of recent critics who would have the expression refer to "regular and romantic plays." The modern distinction would certainly not have occurred to Shakespeare whereas the difference in the two methods of acting fell within his own experience.[33]

It has often been questioned whether or not the English themselves ever learned to improvise in the Italian way from a scenario. The stage "plats" discovered by Malone among Alleyn's property are in form somewhat similar to scenarios though they give much more meager directions. One of them is a synopsis of a fully written play, the *Battle of Alcazar*, and it is quite possible that they all like this one may represent abstracts for use in rehearsal, on the order of those described by De Sommi as aids to his company. All the plats were at one time in the possession of Alleyn's troupe and date from 1592 to 1600.[34] They are little more than lists of entrances and exits with very few suggestions for the action, such as the scenarios give often quite in detail. The only one that bears any resemblance to an Italian improvised comedy is the *Dead Man's Fortune*, a fantastic intrigue with a prolog and musical interludes in the Italian style, in which Pantaloon and his man "pesscode" take a prominent part.

[33] Cf. Furness Variorum edition of *Hamlet* for notes on this passage.
[34] These fragments are printed by Greg, *Henslowe Papers*, 129 f.

If any of the pieces be from a *commedia dell'arte*
is this one, but as the outline will make sufficient
apparent, the difficulties in the way of identifying t.
source are very considerable :[35]

The plotte of the deade mans fortune/
    Enter the prologue/
Enter laertes Eschines and vrganda
Enter pesscode to him his father
Enter Tesephon allgeryus laertes wth.
    atendantes: Darlow :lee : b.samme :to
    them allcyane and statyra
Enter validore & asspida at severall dores
    to them the panteloun

mus
ique   .   .   .   .

Enter carynus and prlior to them
    statyra and allcyane
Enter vrganda laertes Echines: Exit
Eschines and Enter Bell veile
Enter panteloun & his man to them his wife
    Asspida to hir validore

Dar
lee
sam Enter Tesephoun allgerius alcyane & statyra
wth. attendantes to them carynus &
prelyor to them laertes & bell veile
Enter valydore & asspida cuttynge of
    ruffes to them the maide

Enter panteloun whiles he speakes
validore passeth ore the stage disguisde
then Enter pesscode to them asspida to
them the maide wth. pesscodds apparell

musi
que   .   .   .   .

Enter carynus and prlyor == here the
    laydes speakes in prysoun

    [*] Greg, *op. cit.*, 133 f.

Enter laertes & Bell veile to them the
Jayler to them the laydes

Enter Tesephon allgerius at severall dores
disguised wth. meate to them the jayler
Enter panteloun & pesscode = enter asspida
   to hir validore & his man.b. samme to
   them the panteloun & pescode wth. spectakles

· · · · · · · · · musi
                        que
Enter tesephon allgerius wth. attendantes Dar
   & others to them Burbage a messenger
   to them Euphrodore = Robart lee & b samme & tyre
                              man

Enter carynus & prlor to them vrganda
wth. a lookinge glasse acōmpaned wth. satires
plainge on ther Instruments

Enter carynus madde to him prelyor
   (d) madde
Enter asspida & (validore) pescodde to hir
Enters rose
Enters panteloun & pescodde
Enter aspida & validore disguised like rose w^th.
   a flasket of clothes to them rose wth. a
   nother flasket of clothes to them the panteloun to them (to them) pescodde

· · · · · · · · · musique
Enter kinge Egeron allgeryus tesephon   Enter
   wth. lordes the (x) executioner w^th. (is) his Vrganda
   sworde & blocke & officers wth. holberds Alcione
                               Statira
   to them carynus and prlyor then after that Enter
   the musicke plaies & ther Enters 3 an Laertes
                               Eschines
   tique faires dancynge on after a nother Enter
   the first takes the sword from the ex wt. out
   ecutioner and sends him a waye the other disguise

caryes a waie the blocke & the third sends
a waie(s) the offycers & vnbindes allgeryus
& tesephon & as they entered so they departe

Enter to them vrganda laertes and
Eschines leadinge ther laides hand in hand

Enter the(n) panteloun & pescode
Enter validore (and assipida)

Enter asspida to hir rose
Enter the panteloun & causeth the
cheste or truncke to be broughte forth
finis[36]

Since this play was probably acted before 1593 it
can have no connection with the only scenario in
which Urganda figures, an eighteenth century parody
of the lyric tragedy *Amadis*.[37] Moreover the plot is
not definite enough to be traced to a particular
source. It is hard to see how so slight an outline
could have been developed even by actors used to
improvisation, much less by those who never regularly practiced the art. Tarlton indeed was noted
for his "piperly extemporising" in his clown's
rôle[38] and for the ease with which he made a jest off
hand on matters of contemporary interest,[39] and
Wilson and Kemp were probably as expert, yet Eng-

[36] Cf. Creizenach, *Geschichte des neueren Dramas*, IV, 335–6.

[37] Parfaict, *Dict. des théâtres*, I, 178.

[38] Harvey, *Foure Letters*, 1592, second letter.

[39] Nash, *Pierce Penilesse*, 66–7, speaks of a "ridiculous Asse," an
astrologer, on whom "Tarlton at the Theatre made jests." Baker,
Theatrum Redivivum (1662), 27, pays a tribute to the clown's extempore songs and (p. 34) to his powers in pantomine. Cf. Halli-
well, introd. to *Tarlton's Jests*, xxviii, and Meres, *Palladis Tamia*, on
"our witty Wilson."

lish actors as a class seem never to have worked out the flexible method of their foreign rivals. Nash's complaint that the players finished off his *Isle of Dogs*[40] must mean that they wrote up the acts he left incomplete, not that they supplied the dialog on the stage, for the play as published is fully written. Jonson with his delightful explicitness asserts that English plays are not like the Italian "extemporal" but all "premeditated things."[41] There is also Hamlet's invective against the clowns' abuses of their privileges, to prove that the best Elizabethan opinion was unfavorable to the lax Italian custom. This fact of stage history ought, I think, to be decisive for differentiating the English plats from scenarios and for labeling them abstracts of written plays for use in rehearsal.[42]

Among many Italianate plots, many disguise and *lazzi* scenes that in Elizabethan plays may possibly be echoes of *commedie dell'arte*,[43] I have found but one that can with any probability be referred to a

[40] *Lenten Stuffe*, ed. Grosart, 200, note. Nash says that he had himself only finished the "induction and first act" of this piece, "the other five acts, without my consent or the least guessse of my drift or scope by the players were supplied."

[41] *Case is Altered*, II, 4. It ought to be added that Jonson refers to England as Utopia; perhaps a case could be made out on the basis of this to prove that improvisation was common in England and that Jonson looked to Utopia for better conditions. But this seems too far-fetched.

[42] There was occasionally some improvisation in Elizabethan plays; cf. Greene's *James IV*, I, 3, and similar passages in Marlowe's, *Dr. Faustus*, in the comic scenes.

Greene's *Groatsworth of Wit* (1596), 23, speaks of the extempore rimes of the puppet showmen.

[43] Cf. App. B.

scenario source,—the mountebank performance in *Volpone*.[44]   It will be remembered that the villain-hero of the comedy disguises himself as a charlatan in order to prosecute his design on Celia, the virtuous wife of Corvino. Jonson appropriately chooses a retired corner of St. Mark's Place, Venice, for this bit of action, probably because some traveler had told him that here the mountebanks were wont to assemble.[45]   Mosca and Nano, Volpone's parasite and dwarf disguised, build a stage under Corvino's window in the hope that Celia may be drawn out to witness the show.   While the platform is being set up Peregrine and Sir Politick argue about these fellows:

"Per.   Who be these, sir ? . . .
Sir. P.   Fellows, to mount a bank. Did your instructor
          In the dear tongues, never discourse to you
          Of the Italian mountebanks ? . . .
          Here you shall see one.
Per.   They are quacksalvers,
          Fellows that live by vending oils and drugs. . . .
Sir. P.   They are the only knowing men of Europe !
          Great general scholars, excellent physicians, . . .
          The only languaged men of all the world !

[44] II, 1. Koeppel, *Quellen-Studien*, etc., says nothing of this scene nor so far as I know does any other editor notice it particularly.

[45] Although Jonson knew Coryat well he could not have built this scene on the description in the *Crudities*, for *Volpone* was played in 1605 and Coryat was not in Venice till 1608. Italian mountebanks probably performed in London as early as this, though the only specific reference I have found is that in Chalmers' *Supplemental Apology*, 209, note, a quotation from a warrant granted in 1630 to F. Nicolini and his company, "to dance on the ropes, to use interludes and masques, and to sell his powders and balsams." Evidently the "masques" belong to the "interludes," which latter must have been *commedie dell'arte*.

Per.   And I have heard, they are most lewd impostors;
       Made all of terms and shreds, no less beliers
       Of great men's favors than their own vile
           med'cines;
       Which they will utter upon monstrous oaths;
       Selling that drug for twopence, ere they part,
       Which they have valued at twelve crowns before.
Sir. P. Sir, calumnies are answered best with silence.
       Yourself shall judge.—Who is it mounts, my
           friends?
Mosca. Scoto of Mantua, sir.⁴⁶
Sir. P. Is't he? Nay, then,
       I'll proudly promise, sir, you shall behold
       Another man than has been phant'sied to you.
       . . . . . . Here he comes.

(Enter Volpone, disguised as a mountebank Doctor, and
followed by a crowd of people.)

Vol. Mount, zany.   (To Nano),
Most noble gentlemen and my worthy patrons! It may
   seem strange that I, your Scoto Mantuano, who was
   ever wont to fix my bank in the face of the public
   Piazza . . . should now, after eight months' absence
   from this illustrious city of Venice, humbly retire myself into an obscure nook of the Piazza . . . to tell you
   true I cannot endure to see the rabble of these ground
   ciarlatani that spread their cloaks on the pavement
   as if they meant to do feats of activity, and then come
   in lamely, with their mouldy tales, out of Boccaccio,

⁴⁶ Scoto was a real person, an Italian juggler who was in England
about this time, as Gifford notes, ed. of *Volpone*, 204, note 3. Cf.
James I, *Daemonologie* (Workes, etc., London, 1616, Bk. I, 105). "He
will learn them manie juglarie trickes at Cardes, dice, and such like,
to deceiue men's senses thereby: and such innumerable false prac-
ticques; which are prouen by ouer-manie in this age: as they who
are acquainted with that Italian called Scoto, yet living, can report."

like stale Tabarine, the fabulist:[47] some of them dis-
coursing of their travels, and of their tedious captivity
in the Turk's galleys,[48] when indeed were the truth
known, they were Christian's galleys, where very tem-
perately they eat bread and drunk water, as a whole-
some penance . . . for base pilferies. . . . Well let
them go. . . . I have nothing to sell, little or nothing
to sell. . . . I protest, I and my six servants are not
able to make of this precious liquor, so fast as it is
fetched away from my lodging by gentlemen of your
city, . . . blessed unguento, this rare extraction, that
hath only power to disperse all malignant humours,
that proceed either of hot, cold, moist, or windy causes.
. . . 'Twill cost you eight crowns. And—Zan Fritada,
prithee sing a verse extempore in honour of it."[49]

[47] Gifford assumes this Tabarin to have been the French charlatan
of the Pont-Neuf who flourished in Paris some time between 1619–26,
playing in farces which were accessory to selling his wares. Cf. Fournier, *Théâtre français*, etc., I, 498 f. As *Volpone* was acted in 1605
this identification of Gifford's seems improbable. I rather think that
the man alluded to in the text was that other and earlier Italian actor,
Giovanni Tabarin, who had certainly been known to English troupes
in Vienna and Paris, c. 1572. Cf. Rasi, *Comici italiani*, II, 555 f.

[48] Cf. Rasi, *op. cit.*, I, under F. Andreini, for an account of the
adventure of this Capitano among the Turks; he spent several years
in slavery to the Moslem. Andreini was also one of the most notable
"languaged men" among the *comici*.

[49] Garzoni, *Piazza universale*, mentions Zan Fritada more than once.
I quote one passage in Symonds' translation (*Mem. of Count C. Gozzi*,
I, 76). "You will see our swaggering Fortunato and his boon companion Fritata . . . keeping the whole populace agape into the night
with stories, songs, improvisations," etc.

Zan Fritata was as much an historical person as Scoto. He is
mentioned not only by Garzoni but in the *Capitolo in morte di Simone
da Bologna*:

Fritada ch'in virtù te generos
De canta e sona col Fortunat
E sovra al banc a te vitorios. . . .

After Nano's uninspired song, Volpone continues:

"Gentlemen if I had but time to discourse to you the miraculous effects of this my oil, surnamed Oglio del Scoto; with the countless catalogue of those I have cured of the aforesaid and many more diseases; the patents and privileges of all the princes and common-wealths of Christendom! . . . For myself I always from my youth have endeavored to get the rarest secrets, and book them in exchange or for money: I spared nor cost nor labour, where anything was worthy to be learned. . . . I will undertake by virtue of chem-ical art, out of the honourable hat that covers your head, to extract the four elements; that is to say, the fire, air, water and earth, and return you your felt without burn or stain. . . .

You all know I never valued this ampulla or vial at less than eight crowns; but for this time I am content to be deprived of it for six; six crowns is the price, . . . I ask you not the value of the thing for then I should demand of you a thousand crowns, so that the Cardi-nals Montalto, Fernese, the great Duke of Tuscany, my gossip,[50] with divers other princes, have given me; but

Cf. Carrara's reprint of ed. of 1585, p. 17. Carrara notes several poems by Fritata.

It is interesting to compare Volpone's praises of his drug to another paragraph from Garzoni (550 f.) in which is given an idea of the Italian charlatans' speeches on a similar subject. "Charlatans sell powders for indigestion . . . tapers for perpetual lights; the philoso-pher's oil, the fifth essence, to make you rich; oil of *tasso barbasso* for chills; an ungent to give you a good memory; . . . lime paste to kill rats; . . . burning glasses to light fires from the sun; . . . spec-tacles to make you see in the dark."

[50] Gossip, *Comare* or *compare*, was a very common term of address between the best of the *comici* and their patrons, because princes, dukes and even kings and queens, stood sponsor to the children of their protégés. Cf. Jarro, *L'epistolario, passim.*

I despise money. . . . I have neglected the messages
of these princes, mine own officers, framed my journey
hither, only to present you with the fruits of my
travels.—Tune your voices once more to the touch of
your instruments, and give this honourable assembly
some delightful recreation.

Per. What monstrous and most painful circumstance
      Is here, to get some three or four gazettes,[61]
      Some threepence in the whole! for that 'twill
      come to."

Nano's song is more like a Zanni's than the first he
sang:

      " You that would last long, list to my song,
      Make no more coil but buy of this oil," etc.,

just the kind of jingle that could most easily be
improvised.

Volpone next, like the men he is imitating, comes
down again in his demands:

"Well, I am in a humour at this time to make a present of
the small quantity my coffer contains: to the rich in
courtesy, and to the poor for God's sake. . . . Therefore, now, toss your handkerchiefs, cheerfully, cheerfully; and be advertised that the first heroic spirit that
deigns to grace me with a handkerchief, I will give it a
little remembrance of something. . . .

      (Celia, at a window above, throws down her hand-
kerchief.) Lady, I kiss your bounty, and for this
timely grace you have done your poor Scoto of Mantua,

---

[61] Jonson's local color is as usual exact; a gazette is a small Venetian coin, mentioned by Garzoni as the object of the charlatans'
efforts. This correspondence between Jonson and Garzoni, like several
others, makes the hypothesis that the scene in *Volpone* was suggested
by the *Piazza universale*, not improbable. Garzoni had not been translated into English, but Jonson of course read Italian.

I will return you, over and above my oil, a secret of
that high and inestimable nature, shall make you for
ever enamoured on that minute, wherein your eye first
descended on so mean, yet not altogether to be despised, an object. Here is a powder concealed in this
paper, that made Venus a goddess (given her by
Apollo), that kept her perpetually young, cleared her
wrinkles, firmed her gums, filled her skin, coloured her
hair; from her derived to Helen, and at the sack of
Troy unfortunately lost; till now in this our age, it
was happily recovered. . . . The rest of this present,
remains to me, extracted to a quintessence, so that
wherever it but touches in youth it perpetually preserves, in age restores the complexion, seats your teeth,
. . . makes them white as ivory, that were black as—
Corvino. Spite o' the devil, and my shame! come down here;
    Come down—No house but mine to make your
      scene!
    Signor Flaminio, will you down, sir! down!
    What, is my wife your Franciscina, sir!
    No windows on the whole Piazza, here,
    To make your properties, but mine! but mine!
      (Beats away Volpone, Nano, etc.)
    Heart! ere to-morrow I shall be new christened,
    And called the Pantalone di Bisognosi,[52]
    About the town.''

If it were not for the concluding hurly-burly one

[52] Gifford's note on Pantalone is inadequate, ''i. e. the Zany, or fool
of the beggars. Such at least is the vulgar import of the words, but
Jonson probably affixed a more opprobrious sense to them.'' H. B.
Wilkins, editor of a critical edition of *Volpone*, does not understand
any better than Gifford the allusions to Fritata, Pantalone, etc.
Franceschina was of course the *servetta* in Scala's scenarios and perhaps from them was adopted by Marston for the name of his *Dutch
Curtizan;* the connotation of the name was the opposite of maidenly or
wifely virtue. Cf. the Franceschina of Chapman's *May Day* (1601).

14

could rest content in the assumption that Jonson was
only describing from life a street performance he
had witnessed, or perhaps that he vivified a traveler's tale to add color to his comedy. But the closing action, the lady in the balcony, the lover disguised, the jealous husband, the beatings, above
all the names,—Pantalone de 'Bisognosi, Flaminio,
Franceschina,—suggest that Jonson had heard and
was here reproducing part of an improvised farce.
A scene from the first act of Scala's *Fortuna di
Flavio* (Gior. II) furnishes a somewhat similar outline and might easily have been given in London by
some of the Italians who were there in Jonson's life-
time; it was certainly acted in Paris by the Gelosi,
whose character names Jonson puts into Corvino's
mouth:

"Arlecchino the charlatan (he is really the companion to Gratiano, chief charlatan) has the bench
arranged for mounting to sell his wares; then the
servants put on it a seat and a valise, then call the
companions; Gratiano and Turchetto (the latter a
girl disguised as a page) come out of the Inn, all
mount the bench and Turchetto begins to sing and
play; Flaminia stands at the window to see the
charlatans; Burattino comes to listen; then Franceschina comes, stops to look on; then Pantalone
arrives, salutes Orazio and all stay to watch. Gratiano praises his goods, Arlecchino does the same;
Turchetto plays and sings. The Captain seeing
Flaminia at the window suddenly salutes her, Franceschina salutes the slave-boy. The Captain ob-
serves Arlecchino, recognizes him as the man who

holds in governance his lady, and pulls him down off the bench. Pantalone tells Orazio that the Captain is his enemy; Gratiano raises his hand against the Captain, the Captain the same to him; Arlecchino flees, Captain follows, and in the bustle the bench is overturned and everyone runs into his own house."

The parallel is not close enough to press very far. The scene in the scenario is merely one of a kind extremely common in the *commedia dell'arte,* a kind that Jonson must have seen if he knew any improvised plays—and he could hardly escape at least a few in the theatrical world of his day. It is natural to him to minimize the rough-and-tumble action, which was the chief attraction of Scala's farce, and to increase the satirical color by Volpone's monologs and the comments of the bystanders.

Jonson was not entirely individual however in disapproving and satirizing the mountebanks; the Elizabethans in general seem to have had no very good opinion of Italian charlatans. Nash speaks of "a tedious mountebank's oration . . . when in the whole there is nothing praiseworthy,"[53] and elsewhere mentions the "legerdemaine of these juggling mountebanks."[54] The author of *Mucedorus* (I, 1) remarks on an "obscure servile habillament" as appropriate to "a Florentine or a mountebancke," and Chapman makes Monsieur tell Bussy that he is "more vainglorious than any mountebank."[55]

[53] *Pierce Penilesse,* ed. Grosart, 6.
[54] *Ibid.,* 108.
[55] *Bussy d'Ambois,* III, 1.

About 1617 a ridiculous *Antimask of Mountebanks* was given at Gray's Inn,[56] merely a conglomeration of speeches and songs, "musicall charmes, familiar receipts," entirely unlike an improvised play though quite on the order of the Italian street performances that contributed so much to the *commedia dell'arte*. The second song is a jingle that rings as thin as Nano's extempore rime.

> From all diseases that arise
> From ill-disposed crudityes
> From too much study, too much paine,
> From lasines, or from a straine,
> From any humours doing harme
> Be it dry, or moist, or colde or warme,
>   I come to cure whatere you feele
>   Within, without, from head to heele.

After four songs of this kind a mountebank in a "fantasticke" habit recites some of the "familiar receiptes," of which the most quotable is an "approved medicine against melancolicke feminine": "If any lady be sicke of the sullens she knows not where, let her take a handfull of scimples I know not what, and use them I know not how, applying them to the party greeved I know not who, and she shalbe well I know not when."[57]

Arlecchino might have jested in just such terms as

---

[56] Nichols, *Progresses*, etc., of *Q. Elizabeth*, III, 332.

[57] Some of the horrid compounds listed by Wittipol among "Spanish fucuses" (*Devil is an Ass*, IV, 1) remind one of Garzoni's account of the Italian charlatan's pharmacopia; in this case as elsewhere however, it is not safe to stress the international analogy. English medicine was quite as magical and superstitious as Italian. Cf. F. Grendon, *Anglo-Saxon Charms*.

these at the inanities of popular medical ignorance
and its lingo, but so might a French or an English
clown on his own impulse; the expression of such
satire is as universal as the social phenomenon it
ridicules and there is, I think, no need for assuming
a definite and particular Italian model here any
more than in many of the situations and *lazzi* which
recall *commedie dell'arte* in Elizabethan comedies.
Drayton indeed says severely that his countrymen
are the "very apes and zanies . . . of everything
that they doe heare and see,"[58] but I feel sure that
while there was a distinct influence of the Italian on
the English drama it was, as with Molière, more.
general than special, and that there is little to be
gained from forcing into the same category things
essentially so different.[59] Anyone who will take the
trouble to turn to Bartoli's *Onorata fuga di Lucinda*
and compare it to the *Two Gentlemen of Verona,*
or who will read Peacock's abstract of *Gl'ingannati*
with an eye to *Twelfth Night,* can see for himself
certain likenesses of motivation and plot, even
broadly of character, but still more strongly, as has
been said about *Tartuffe* and *Il Pedante,* he must be
struck by vast differences in tone, technic and detail.
So anyone who chooses may set Shakespeare's
Holofernes beside Gratiano and may discover that
they are both tiresome pedants who speak a would-
be learned dialect of their own and make love
absurdly; so Scala's Pantalone may be likened to

[58] *Poets and Poesie,* 1627.
[59] Cf. Feuillerat's admirable discrimination of the spirit of the
Italian pastoral from that of Lyly's pastoral plays, *John Lyly,* Part
II, 321 f.

numerous old fathers on the English stage, but in order to do this, every individual trait must be peeled from the English characters,—Pantalone and Gratiano are of course to begin with little more than skeletons.

If the *commedia dell'arte* is understood at all it must certainly be regarded as a repository of ancient themes and motifs some of which, like Latrocino's tooth-pulling,[60] are often to be found in the English theater,—whether they came thither from the Italian stage or from native tradition. But as the scenarios already quoted have shown, the *commedia dell'arte* was little else than this literary and popular rag-bag, a kind of Harlequin's suit in itself; it was not interested in ideas except very much at second-hand, nor in fine discriminations of character, while the Elizabethan drama at its best cared exceedingly for both. Moreover the Italians were never, as were the Elizabethans even at their worst, bent upon maintaining more than the merest pretence of decency and morality. Such wide divergencies in the way of attitude toward the material treated warn us not to give to the *commedia dell'arte* too promi-

---

* In Middleton's *Widow*, IV, 2.

Another Elizabethan *lazzo* that resembles Zanni's tricks are Biondello's impudence to Vincentio (*Taming of the Shrew*, IV, 4), cf. Scala's Gior. XIII, *Il Dr. disperato*, Act I. In the same Italian play Pantalone is refused admittance to his own house, as is Antipholus of Ephesus, *Comedy of Errors*, III, 1. In Scala's *Travagliata Isabella*, Act III (Gior. XV), the two old men, Dottore and Pantalone, talk of a "buona roba" much in the style of Justice Shallow, *2 Henry IV*, III, 2.

Such instances might be multiplied almost indefinitely if they were significant of anything but common Renaissance fashion.

nent a place among the influences forming the English drama.

On the other hand it will not do to discount entirely the importance of the improvised plays in London. They formed only a small part of the repertory of the actors who presented them and who introduced foreign audiences to many kinds of elaborate entertainments, but in themselves they were so lively and so clever that they would naturally give a great stimulus to students of theatrical technic,—enough has been quoted of definite allusion to show the impression they made on English spectators. As models for imitation they could however offer something less satisfactory than the written plays, because they were in performance so fluid, so changing from day to day in matters of detail. For these reasons it is hard to trace English scenes to Italian; even comedies like Field's which in preponderance of incident, in cut-and-dried characterization and in commonplace expression approximate nearest in effect to filled-out scenarios—even in these there is a difference in spirit between an English hack-writer and an Italian actor. The improvised plays went a step, several steps, beyond such wretched farces in the direction toward which they tend,—toward horse-play and boisterous license. It was not until the Restoration had brought a different tone into the English drama that the *commedia dell'arte* was freely and openly imitated and of that change I shall have something to say in a moment.

CHAPTER VII.

It is all very well to be conservatively judicious in estimating the influence of the puppetlike Masks on foreign stages and cautiously sceptical in refusing to attribute great vogue to any one scenario, yet on the whole there is no denying that Arlecchino, Pulcinella and their comrades did not dance and jest their way into European popularity without provoking a host of envious imitators. After the first quarter of the seventeenth century the machinery of the *commedia dell'arte* was constantly worked by all sorts of actors; its masked characters, broad jokes and improvised fun were introduced into scenes of written plays, into *melodrammi* and comic operas, and, most usually, into pantomimes and marionette shows where such farcical doings legitimately belong. As the public became over-familiar with this kind of thing and cloyed by it, the professional players met the demand for novelty as many of them do to-day, by foisting onto their traditional repertory inventions suggested by their immediate audience and by the special abilities of their troupes.

In Italy *commedie dell'arte* proper persisted side by side with the newer spectacular and musical entertainments; the old-fashioned improvised plays were, however, varied by introducing into their ancient plots a quantity of minor Masks, while in the comic operas emphasis gradually shifted entirely away from plot and *lazzi* to music and scenery.

France soon tired of the regulation *commedie dell'arte*—the best jokes pall in a foreign tongue—and demanded of the Italians something that made a more direct appeal; accordingly about 1625 Giovan-Battista Andreini's example was followed very generally in Paris and spectacular pieces became the most prominent on the Italian stage there. Parody and satire crept in as the result of much competition between rival companies, until with the invention of the pantomime the irregular troupes marked their greatest triumph. Finally from Paris Italian and French amusements made their way to England,—there the Christmas pantomime still pre-serves at least three of the old Masks. Some description of these last resorts of Pantalone and his family must necessarily round out this history and it will be given here in summary fashion for the sake of completeness, not with any idea of tracing a direct line of evolution between the *commedia dell'arte* and products so unlike itself.

It was only in Italy and chiefly on the popular stages that the improvised pieces held their own until the strife between two Venetian theaters brought about important reforms at the close of the eighteenth century. In Italy the improvised jokes of the Masks were understood; what cared the pit how often it saw a familiar intrigue if only the time-worn incidents were shuffled into a combination that seemed fresh and then were painted over with some gay local color? Old men therefore might always be represented as infatuated with pert serving-maids, lovers might eternally plot to abuse their

elders, faithless youths be tirelessly pursued by the
sweetheart they have abandoned, knavish lads perpetually plan the discomfiture of some overconfident
enemy,—all the ancient round of action might go on
by the ancient methods. So in fact it did. Tricks,
practical jokes, disguises, pretended madness and
death were however given force by repetition and
reduplication; where one "pretended lunatic" to a
scenario sufficed Scala, the eighteenth century demanded four at least; where Isabella Andreini chose
one disguise and found it enough throughout one
play, Gherardi's Colombine must needs keep her
audience awake by tormenting Arlequin in a constantly changing personality, now as doctor, now
as lawyer or peddler.[1]

Duplication of plot interest was not the only way
of stimulating interest in the old repertory. A
second and rather more inspired method was by
freshly studied satire on this or that locally noto-
rious individual or class,—of course the most natural
development of the practices of the earlier actors,
those first presenters of Pantalone as Venetian
Magnifico and Arlecchino and Pedrolino as Bergamask peasants. Niccolò Barbieri crystallized the
prosperous rustic of the country near Milan in his
creation of Beltrame.[2] The famous Mask of Stentorello originated in Luigi del Buono's not unkindly
caricature of lower class Florentines and rapidly

[1] Gherardi, *Théâtre italien, Colombine avocat pour et contre,* I,
291 f.

[2] Barbieri was at the head of a company in Paris, 1625–8, and played
in Italy also. Cf. Bartoli, *Scen. ined.,* cxliii, and for Beltrame, the
scenario published by Toldo, Gior. Stor., XLVI, 128 f.

became typical of these cheerful good-for-naughts.[3]
Another north Italian personage was the weari-
somely prolix Desévedo de Mal Albergo of Parma,
a modification of Dottor Gratiano, whose suggestive
name derives from the Latin *Desapidus*.[4]
The southern provinces were even more fertile in
comic characters than was the north of Italy.
Scaramuccia, one of the most notable of this group,
"dressed all in black, his sword on his thigh," was
like most of the Masks born in Naples, "a cowardly
bully."[5] Among his friends are Giangurgolo, a
large-nosed, gluttonous Calabrian ne'er-do-well;[6]
Guappo, or Vappo, a popular Neapolitan parody of
the medieval knight;[7] Rogantino, a cowardly Roman
brute, and his more courageous and cheerful cousin,
Meo Patacca.[8]

[3] Jarro, *Maschera di Stentorello*, describes the character (p. 48) as
"lepido, non scurrile; allegro, non cinico e salace . . . raffigurare
il popolano fiorentino della piu infime . . . classe."

[4] Bartoli, *Scenari ined.*, clxxxii–iii. Desévedo appears in one of the
scenarios in the same volume, *La bellissima commedia in tre persone.*
Cf. also Riccoboni, *Hist. du théâtre italien*, 56.

[5] Croce, *Teatri di Napoli*, 129. The Neapolitan Mask Croce defines
as "a person who spoke a coarse dialect full of awkward provincial-
isms, and who sometimes appeared as a 'gentiluomo di seggio,' was
more often confused with the Captain, sometimes practiced other
trades" (*Pulcinella*, 94). Scaramuccia was the creation of Tiberio
Fiorillo who made a great name for himself in France in the seventeenth century; cf. Rasi, *Comici italiani*, I, under Fiorillo.

[6] The name may be translated Jack-the-Glutton. Cf. Scherillo,
Comm. dell'arte, 108, note 2; Croce, *Pulcinella*, 102, and *Teatri di
Napoli, passim;* Senigaglia, *Cap. Spavento*, 166 f. Riccoboni gives
a picture of Giangurgolo and he appears in two of Bartoli's scenarios,
I quattro pazzi and *I tappeti ovvero Colafronio geloso.*

[7] The name is from the Spanish for "elegant"; cf. Senigaglia, *Cap.
Spavento*, 173 f. and 178 f.

[8] The connection of comic types with different localities cannot be

Pulcinella, one of the oldest southern Masks, became one of the most widely famous and was one of the longest lived. In his later days he has often been noticed by visitors to Italy; Baretti says of him severely, "there is not a single good trait in him; his cunning is very low, he is always outdone when he meets with a person of sense, so that in the end he is generally discovered, imprisoned, whipped and hanged."[9] Goethe, speaking to Eckermann of the Pulcinella he saw in his youth in Naples, gives him a better character and reports some of his doings a little in detail: "One of the chief jokes of this hero of low comedy . . . consisted in seeming sometimes to forget his part as an actor. He pretended to have returned home, talked familiarly with his family, told them about the piece in which he acted and of another in which he was about to act. 'But, my dear husband,' his wife would exclaim, 'you appear to forget the august company in whose presence you are.' 'È vero! È vero!' returned Pulcinella; recollecting himself, he returned to his former part. The theatre of Pulcinella is in such repute that no one in good society boasts of having been there. Ladies . . . never go at all; it is only frequented by men.

quite denied, yet there is no need to go as far as Mercey; he said that "every province" of Italy had its comic Mask, "the personification of the ridiculous elements and moral habits of its people." (Rev. des deux mondes, 15 avril, 1840, 196 f.) There was too much variety in the various presentations of the same Masks to permit calling them the invariable personifications of local traits. Mercey is always the disciple of Schlegel; here he leaves too much out of account the influence of each actor in the creation of the Masks, and emphasizes too much the influence of climate.

[9] *Italy and the Italians*, Chap. I, cited Collier, *Punch and Judy*, 58.

Pulcinella is, in fact, a sort of living newspaper. Everything that has happened in Naples during the day may be heard from him in the evening. However these local allusions, combined with his low popular dialect, make it almost impossible for foreigners to understand him.'"[10]

Evidently the Mask and his name simply gave a kind of external unity to the performances of a versatile entertainer who probably wove his topical allusions into a threadbare plot, much as the Pulcinella of to-day still does in Naples,[11] in the manner of innumerable humble wits in other European *théâtres de quartier.* Most of the characters in these modern pieces are not masked, many of the plays themselves are partly written, yet since a good part of the dialog and songs has to do with matters of recent occurrence and there is therefore need for much improvisation, it is here that the last real *commedie dell'arte* are to be sought.

Here and in the marionette theater the Masks survive because they furnish a convenient machinery, not because they are made to resemble very closely their predecessors on the Cinquecento stage. Collier's ingenious history of Mr. Punch assumes that his hero derives in a direct line from a Roman Mime through Pulcinella, but never was analogy

[10] *Conversations of Goethe with Eckermann,* Bohn's edition, 440, under date of Feb. 14, 1830.

[11] Lyonnet, *Pulcinella et compagnie,* gives an interesting account of the modern theater where the present Pulcinella amuses his audience nightly as his predecessor did in Goethe's experience,—with topical allusions and low farce.

Cf. Mercey, Rev. des deux mondes, XXI and XXII.

harder pressed to the violation of probability. Every age and country of the world, from China centuries ago to Elizabethan England and beyond, has had its own puppet-plays and has put into them old stories of its own. Most of the Italian *burattini* act out, quite seriously, chivalric legends of Charlemagne and his peers; many others present scenes of everyday life in a broadly farcical manner. The particular English play of Punch and Judy recorded in Cruikshank's comic pictures owes something to many sources, chiefly to popular tales and songs, and little or nothing to the *commedia dell'arte*.[12] Rather may its ancestry be vaguely traced perhaps to those "motions" and "puppetry and pied ridiculous antics" inveighed against by Chapman and Johnson in more than one jealous outburst.[13]

The kind of stale or coarse wit, that has now been driven to the lowest genre theaters and to the most farcical marionette booths, prevailed till the mid-eighteenth century on many stages of a better class.

[12] Collier asserts, p. 62, that the puppet-play he reproduces is from the repertory of an Italian showman, but aside from the appearance of Scaramouch there is nothing peculiarly Italian in the piece.

[13] Magnin's *Hist. des marionettes* (1852) still remains of value for the number of facts from various sources it contains. Cf. the more modern studies of Creizenach, *Gesch. des neu. Dramas*, and Warsage, *Au royaume des marionettes*. For the Elizabethan "motion," *Bartholomew Fair*, V, 1 and 3. For the modern Italian puppets, Pitrè, *Studj di poesia popolare*, 11 f., and Toldo, Gior. Stor., LI. 1 f.

The generic name *burattini* for the small wooden actors has been assumed to be derived from the Zanni Mask, Burattino; there exists a play of 1628, *Le disgrazie di Burattino*. It seems quite as likely that the Mask may have got his name and some part of his stupid knavish character from the puppet.

Goldoni in his youth, enemy though he was to the improvised plays, certifies that *commedie dell'arte* were given everywhere and especially in Bologna by "people of merit," and excellently given with applause.[14] He further witnesses to the practice of gentlemen who so loved comedy that they maintained a troupe at their own expense, although the actors had nothing to play but old repertory. The last statement was hardly true even for comedy,—and of new tragedies and musical plays there were more than enough—yet such comedies as pretended to be new were probably written, either fully or in epitome, after traditional patterns.[15] Goldoni himself followed the line of least resistance in his earliest work, and indeed never quite ceased to compose scenarios or to call some of his characters by type names. He was moreover so bound by the old academic conceptions of the nature and technic of the drama and so hampered by the habits of the actors for whom he wrote that it is marvellous his plays remain as fresh and lively as they do. Though tradition and convention held him down he nevertheless pointed the way for theatrical progress and through his own efforts effected a real reform.

He began by criticizing with a keenness born of ardent love the theaters and actors of his Venice. He found "dirty and scandalous intrigues," interpreted by actors who evaded their responsibilities of expression by hiding behind masks, and for a

---

[14] *Memorie* (1788), II, 185.

[15] *Memorie*, I, 206–7. Cf. I, 142, where Goldoni states his wish to see a real comedy "non amando io le arlecchinate."

poet's words substituted the mechanical repetition
of a few hackneyed conceits and the easy commonplaces of daily talk. Very few like Sacchi, the Venetian Arlecchino of the day, worked hard to give
variety and snap to their dialog, imitating their
illustrious predecessors of the Renaissance in the
study of "poets, orators, philosophers, Seneca,
Cicero, Montaigne," and turning all appropriately
to folly.[16] To relieve their general poverty of ideas
Goldoni early in his career set himself definitely to
the task of suppressing the four best known Masks,
and substituting for their tedious stupidities his own
humorous and realistic comedy of character.[17] So
radical a change, he fortunately told himself, must
be slowly entered upon; actors must be handled with
gloves, the public must be stimulated to an interest
that would make it more attentive, more willing to
follow the intricacies of a new plot and the subtleties
of delicate character-drawing than to guffaw from
habit over stale, hackneyed scenes.

At first therefore the reformer wrote scenarios in
which he himself took a part, by example stimulating
others to take the pains he took. His next step was
to outline plots with all but one rôle left to improvisation and that one, the principal, written out
in full.[18] Later he introduced the Masks by their

[16] *Memorie*, I, 304–6.

[17] *Memorie*, II, 185 f. "La mia reforme tendeva alla soppressione
delle quattro maschere della commedia italiana," i. e., Pantalone, Dr.
Gratiano, Brighella and Arlecchino.

Re, Gior. Stor., LVIII, 167 f., shows in detail how much Goldoni
learned from the popular Venetian theater of his day.

[18] *Memorie*, I, 297. Cf. II, 207 f. Goldoni (*Ib.*, II, Chap. 2) mentions the many hundreds of *concetti* he wrote for insertion in improvised plays.

old names into written plays, adapting their func-
tions more or less flexibly to the general conception
of their rôles. Luckily for Goldoni his ideas were
not too far in advance of his times to be immediately
successful; he firmly believed in the academic shib·
boleths,—that comedy should observe the unities,
should deal with middle and low-class life, and
should aim chiefly at the correction of public morals
by "delightful teaching."[19] All these preposses·
sions together with his careful study of public taste
and anxious conciliation of the actors for whom he
wrote made the children of his brain seem not too
unfamiliar to be welcome.[20]

Nevertheless he and his work had at first to en-
counter bitter opposition. The old Masks did not
die without a struggle. Represented by a rival
theater and a satiric playwright they made a last
stand for their lives, or rather for their position in
respectable society, and for a moment they were
again as popular as at the height of their fame.
Carlo Gozzi, the mouthpiece of the conservatives,
gave himself to the battle with all the force of his
bizarre genius and of his personal dislike for Goldoni
and for the actors of the new pieces. This man gives
out, he says of his rival, "that he wishes to do away
with the four worthy and amusing Masks of the old

[19] Cf. prolog to *Terensio* and *Memorie*, I, 199 f. and II *passim.*
[20] Goldoni's account of how he rearranged the plot of Richardson's
Pamela when he dramatized it, shows the care with which he observed
the prejudices of his public; because a Venetian would never understand a noble lord's making a marriage with a serving-maid, Goldoni
has Pamela's father represent himself as a Jacobite earl in disguise,
and Pamela therefore becomes a proper match for "Milord B."

15

Italian theater and with the harmless material of the professional improvised comedy, treating it, wrongly and shamefully, as foolish, immodest and hurtful"; he then goes on with blind injustice to accuse Goldoni's plays of being "one hundred times more suggestive, more immodest and more pernicious to the public" than the scenarios.[21]   Vituperation alone however was too feeble to combat the popularity of this "pernicious" innovation and Gozzi was driven to innovate on his own account. He wrote for certain actor friends of his own a series of curious extravaganzas which he called *Fiabe*— Fables is an inadequate translation—for which he gathered material everywhere.   His idea was to use the old Masks in new plots combining the intrigue of some well-known fairy tale with pungent satire on contemporary events, and not least on Goldoni and his co-workers.   Pantalone, Brighella, Tartaglia, Arlecchino, Truffaldino and his wife Smeraldina, were allowed to improvise large portions of their rôles, introducing *lazzi*, puns and folk-songs as they chose, but the serious persons in the plots—Kings, Queens, ministers and lovers—had most of their speeches written for them by the author of the scenarios, and written often in mock-majestic verse parodying some utterance of the enemy.   Spectacle, music and gorgeous costume helped the ingenious invention and Gozzi was rewarded by a momentary

---

[a] Gozzi, *Memorie*, I, 34.   I pass hurriedly over this eighteenth century struggle because it has been well treated in English by Symonds, *Mem. of Count C. Gozzi*, introduction, and by Vernon Lee in her *Studies of the Eighteenth Century in Italy*.   Cf. also Magrini, *I tempi, la vita e gli scritti di C. Gozzi*, and Masi's edition of the *Fiabe*.

popularity as great as his rival's. Goethe remarks to Eckermann on Gozzi's troupe, "The effect produced by these people was extraordinary."[22]

The world looked, wondered and laughed and fancied it was applauding a resurrection of the "ancient Italian comedy." Yet what it saw was really one more proof that the Masks were being driven into alien territory. Gozzi's *Fiabe* depended for their popularity much more on music, machinery and premeditated, very local satire than on the improvised jokes and *lazzi* of their clowns, and in so far they resembled many of the half-written pieces at the Comédie Italienne in Paris during the seventeenth and eighteenth centuries. Scala's extravaganzas, his *Enchanted Tree*, his *Orseida*, his *Innocent Persian Maid*, his *Rosalba the Witch*, had ministered in their day to the aristocratic craving for elaborate scenic complications of all sorts, and Giovan-Battista Andreini with his theatrical machinists had brought similar magnificence within reach of the populace.

Loret writes in 1658 of the marvels of the Italian stage:

La grande troupe italienne . . .
Font voir de telles raretés
Par le moyen de la machine,
Que de Paris jusqu'à la Chine
On ne peut rien voir maintenant
Si pompeux ni si surprenant.
Des ballets au nombre de quatre,
Douze changements de théâtre,
Des hydres, dragons et démons,

[22] Goethe, *Conversations*, etc., 437 and 439.

Des mers, des fôrets et des monts,
Des décorations brillantes,
Des musiques plus que charmantes,
De superbes habillements. . . .
Ne font que le quart des merveilles.[22]

So much energy seems to have gone into these scenic inventions that there was little left for the creation of new plots. In fact the Fedeli and their successors preserved as repertory many of the old scenarios once given by the Gelosi, and this passing down of actual scenarios together with the training of young actors by their elders, explains the preservation of ancient plots, *lazzi* and Masks and makes certain changes in method and product all the more worth noting.[24]

As to the necessity for these changes Du Bos speaks emphatically: "We have had within these fourscore years two different companies of Italian comedians established at Paris. These comedians have been obliged to speak French, since it is the language of those that pay them, but as the Italian pieces which are not composed in our own manners are incapable of amusing the public, the comedians have found it also necessary to act such pieces as are written in the French manner." He adds that the French require "more probability, regularity

---

[22] Cited Despois, *Théâtre français sous Louis XIV*, 58, note.

[24] The Comédie Italienne was established by royal privilege on a footing of legal equality with the Comédie Française in the seventeenth century; the Italians were allowed to play at the Petit-Bourbon in 1658, at the Hôtel Guenegaud in 1673, after 1680 at the Hôtel de Bourgogne. Cf. Despois, *op. cit.*, 57–63.

and dignity in dramatic poems than is commonly insisted upon on the other side of the Alps.''[25]

Probability and dignity are certainly about the last characteristics that would occur to a reader of the scenes from the Italian repertory published by Gherardi in 1700. Most of his plays are primarily musical comedies with vaudeville features,— songs and choruses, dances and "turns," suited to the trick-performances and rope-walkers who composed the majority of the Italian troupe.[26] A large number of his scenes were written, some in Italian, most in French with a dash of Italian—it is the latter that Gherardi published—and into them is worked a deal of satire on contemporary vices and follies. The Masks did their best to ridicule by parody the serious operas and plays of their rivals at the Opéra and the Comédie Française.[27] Colombine as Venus, Arlequin as Vulcan, Pierrot as Mercury, singing their way through long stanzas of doggerel,[28] must have been absurd enough, and even

[25] Du Bos, *Critical Reflections*, I, 140.

[26] Cf. the *melodrammi giocosi* so popular in Italy at this time and later, many of which are printed by Solerti, *Albori*, etc., *passim*, by Arteaga, *Rivoluzioni*, etc., and in the *Raccolta di melodrammi giocosi*, etc., *passim*.

[27] Bartoli, *Scen. ined.*, xcii f., and Ademollo, *Una famiglia*, etc., introd. For Gherardi cf. Rasi, *Comici italiani* and Parfaict, *Hist. du théâtre italien*, 121. His plays have been studied by Guillemot, Rev. contemporaine, 2e série, LI, 92 f., and by Toldo, *Alcuni scenari*, etc., 461 f., and in Rassegna nationale, 16 aprile, 1897.

[28] *Les adieux des officiers, ou Venus justifiée*, IV, 295 f.

The vogue of parody was started on the French stage by L. du Peschier's *Comédie des comédies*, c. 1629, a piece purporting to be from the Italian but probably original. Printed Fournier, *Théâtre français*, etc., I, 519 f.

more absurd Colombine as Apollo and Arlequin as
Thalia, exchanging repartee and *lazzi* over a donkey
named Pegasus,[29] or *Arlequin-Phaeton* in an elaborate burlesque of Quinault's mythological opera of
that name. *Arlequin Protée* makes fun of *Bérenice*,
and in *Le tombeau de Maistre André* there is not a
little mockery of the high-sounding passions of *Le
Cid*.[30]

Parody of serious dramatic art was not the only
form of satire that Gherardi and his company permitted themselves. *Castigat ridendo mores* was
their motto and they justified it by their wholesale
exposure of social rottenness. The vanity and fri-
volity of women, the money basis beneath pretences
of love, the hollowness of professions of honor, the
corruption of public officials, the charlatanry of the
so-called learned classes and the pedantry of the
Academy, all are unsparingly revealed with a cool
cynicism that is perhaps the best witness to the
truth of the portrayal. Everything in Gherardi's
theater is "to laugh"; we cannot imagine one of his
old men weeping "for tenderness" like Scala's
Pantalone when his lost daughter is restored, or one
of his young lovers like Scala's Flavio, nobly rescu-
ing at the dictates of honor the friend who has be-
trayed him. Every mention of love and honor is
greeted on this later stage with a sarcastic grin;
if a lover is faithful he must be a fool is the assump-

---

[29] *Les Chinois*, IV, 199 f.

[30] Sometimes the satire was very personal; cf. *Arlequin lingère du
Palais*, in which a prominent actress at the Français is ridiculed under
the name of Chimène. A number of plots were taken by Gherardi
from Molière, cf. Toldo, *Molière en Italie*.

C. Gillot.

1673-1722.

tion,—he ought therefore to be thwarted and duped in his attempts to gain back his love. The explanation of this scepticism is perhaps that public interest was beginning to shift away from the individual problems that make Scala's themes now look so narrow and his satire so hackneyed, and that the growing consciousness of larger social relationships was stammeringly coming to expression in many places of which this vaudeville theater was one.

At the end of the seventeenth century unfortunately there was no chance for anything like free speech. In 1697 the Comédie Italienne was closed by the police for some reason not yet quite clear, possibly because, as St. Simon says, their comedy *La fausse prude* had offended Mme. de Maintenon, quite as probably on account of some more subtle criticism of the corrupt authorities.[31] The actors scattered, some to Italy, some to the irregular French companies who gave more or less illegal performances at the Foires. In 1716 many of them were recalled and reestablished in the Palais-Royal as the "Regent's Company" giving as their opening piece an ancient scenario, *La finta pazza*, probably the same that Scala had printed more than a hundred years before.[32]

Under the ambitious leadership of Luigi Riccoboni this Italian company went through various vicissitudes whose history is only pertinent here in

[a] There is a general tendency to accept St.-Simon's statement, although no proof of it in the shape of the offensive comedy or of other documents has come to light. Cf. Despois, *Théâtre français*, 69–70, and Parfaict, *Dict. des Théâtres*, VI, 455.

[b] Parfaict, *Dict. des Théâtres*, II, 607–8.

its bearings on the *commedia dell'arte*. Riccoboni
had already attempted in Italy to forestall Goldoni's
reforms by substituting literary comedy for improvised farces and so doing away with the Masks; he
had translated and played successfully several of
Molière's masterpieces and had studied dramatic
theory and technic and the history of the theater so
thoroughly that he was able to write two treatises,
one in prose and the other in verse, praising his profession and his country's stage.[33] In one of these
little books he characterizes Scala's scenarios as
"très-scandaleux" and points out the great improve-
ments later actors have made both in written and in
improvised plays; impromptu dialog, he goes on to
say, may be very delightful when given by a lively
and well-trained troupe, must be tedious and
wretched when even one member of the band is
mediocre.[34] It is probably he who in a prolog to one
of the plays given by his company in Paris, 1725,
defines his art in terms that Goldoni might have
used: "A comedy . . . should have one aim, to
amuse the mind,—but by enlightening it; to win the
heart, while purifying it; if it does not satisfy

---

[33] Cf. Rasi, *Comici italiani*, II, under Riccoboni; Ademollo, *Una
famiglia, passim;* Albert, *Théâtres de la Foire*, 94 f., and Toldo,
Molière en Italie, 69.

[34] *Hist. du théâtre italien*, 61 f. Cf. Gherardi's Avertissement to
his first volume: "Qui dit bon comédien italien dit un homme qui a
du fond, qui joue plus de l'imagination que de mémoire; qui compose
en jouant, tout ce qu'il dit; qui scait seconder celuy avec qui il se
trouve sur le théâtre; c'est à dire qu'il se marie si bien ses paroles
& ses actions avec celles de son camarade, qu'il entre sur le champ
dans tout le jeu & dans tous les mouvemens que l'autre luy demande."

morality and feeling, it is no comedy but a miserable farce."[85]

With all his learning and good intentions Riccoboni unluckily was without the genius that gave success to Goldoni's not dissimilar theories. Most of the productions at the Italiens on which he spent so much thought were too dull to compete with the Opéra and the Français. The Italian company therefore in 1721 installed itself at the Foire St.-Laurent, gave up all pretence at high art and frankly catered to the paying multitude, who only demanded "new *lazzi* by Arlequin."[86] Their repertory of farces, parodies and musical vaudeville was a continuation of that played by Gherardi's troupe and differed from it rather by its new and up-to-date satire and its somewhat more ridiculous exaggerations than by any vast improvement in method, such as the manager claimed.[87] The Masks lived on, at least the more important did, and carried over their names and some of their peculiarities of costume into the exceedingly popular entertainments of the Foires. By 1751 a critic can say that the Italians have been obliged to give up most of their absurdities, such as the mixture of dialects, and to eke out their poor acting by ballets. He goes further: "The Italian comedy can never be thought anything but foreign to our manners and imper-

[85] Quoted by Albert, *Théâtres de la Foire*, 117. This is of course the old academic definition of comedy, inherited from sixteenth century classicists.

[86] Albert, *op. cit.*, 116 f., and Lanson, *Hommes et Livres*, 267-9.

[87] *Les parodies du nouveau théâtre italien*, 4 volumes. Cf. Lanson, *op. cit.*, 261 f.

fectly played by actors of different provinces of
Italy; it should be viewed critically, for it is very
undisciplined; it should indeed only be regarded as
a kind of supplement to a more useful and better
constructed drama."[38] Such a supplement French
playwrights like Marivaux and Regnard and Beau-
marchais might be said to have made of it; they
took certain ideas of plot and *lazzi* from the Italian
stage, and in their Arlequin and Figaro created
characters that have often been compared to the
Masks,[39]—unconvincingly, for such individual, fully
written comedies, whether sentimental or farcical,
are very unlike *commedie dell'arte*.[40]

When Goldoni reached Paris shortly after the
middle of the century he found the actors for whom
he had come to work quite divided in their wishes;
most were accustomed to improvising some of their
scenes and nearly all were used to vaudeville and
averse to mastering the difficulties of interpretation
offered by good comedy. He was accordingly
hampered in his activity as he had been in Venice,
and neither his scenarios nor his written plays were
at first successful.[41] Even as late as 1772 Grimm
found that the Italian company gave one of Goldoni's
comedies wretchedly "because they are not in the
habit of learning their rôles by heart, still less of

[38] Maillet-Duclairon, *Essai sur la connoissance des théâtres français*, 31.

[39] Cf. Toldo, *Figaro et ses origines*, and Lanson, *op. cit.*, 241 f.

[40] The very high-minded and sentimental hero of Marivaux' *Arlequin
poli par amour*, for example, is absolutely different from Scala's
Arlecchino.

[41] Goldoni, *Memorie*, III, *passim*, especially Chap. III.

learning verse," moreover because they have forgot
their own language for French.[42] Although Goldoni's efforts were still further hindered by the
union of the Opéra Comique with the Comédie
Italienne in 1762, a combination which increased the
vogue of miscellaneous musical extravaganzas,[43] he
nevertheless did slowly progress toward apprecia-
tion and toward his goal, the reform of the stage.
The French liked his plays, his example influenced
French taste and by 1780 the *commedia dell'arte*
had gone as completely out of fashion in Paris as
in Italy.[44]

Meanwhile in the booths of the great Fairs of St.-
Germain and St.-Laurent had been worked up
through force of circumstance a new kind of
amusement, the pantomime, in which the Masks
continued to show their agility. This style of
entertainment did not originate among the Italians but was the answer of lively brains among
the so-called Forains (actors at the Foires),
to pertinaceous attempts made by the privileged
theaters to suppress them. Beginning in a modest
way about 1660 or earlier as mere tricksters in side-
shows, these humble actors had become in a short
time popular enough to draw large crowds.[45] They

[42] Grimm in a letter of 22 Oct., 1772; cited Ademollo, *Una famiglia*,
etc., L, note.
[43] *Memorie*, III, 9–10, and Ademollo, *op. cit.*, xlviii and notes.
Cf. Albert, *op. cit.*, 252.
[44] Rasi, *Comici italiani*, II, 643–4.
[45] Campardon gives 1595 as the earliest date for the establishment
of the Foires, but theatrical performances did not begin there till
c. 1660.

gave outdoors on their long, narrow balconies simple little pieces requiring at most three or four speakers, —farces, called Parades, which like the early Italian *contrasti*, made no pretence to elaborate plot or to refined wit; they show superlatively well the tendency of true popular entertainment to revert to quarrelsome horse-play and to the coarsest indecency.[46] The dialog—in French—was partly improvised and partly learned by characters who bore stock names and dressed in a stereotyped manner. Among the performers, especially after the closure of the Comédie Italienne in 1697, were a few Italians, and to their influence was due the appearance of Scaramouche, Trivelin, Arlequin and Isabelle in the Parades.[47]

Such brief pieces made no painful demands on the attention, the acting was of the liveliest, and consequently the public flocked in such numbers to the Foires that the dignified Comédie Française and the Italiens before its suppression, suffered a serious falling-off of patronage. The privileged theaters were powerful enough to obtain injunctions against their rivals, prohibiting one after another dialogs, parodies, monologs, songs and ballets. The Forains answered each decree by the most ingenious eva-

[46] Cf. the collection of Parades published in 1756, *Théâtre des Boulevards*, etc. The editor describes the pieces as "farces de tête sur des plans qu'ils (i. e. the actors) en avoient conservés par tradition, ou qu'ils avoient eux-mêmes composés." In manner of composition therefore, as well as in style of wit, the Parades resemble simple *commedie dell'arte*.

[47] The two best studies of these very interesting irregular theatres are Campardon's *Les spectacles de la Foire*, and Albert's *Les théâtres de la Foire*.

sions of its spirit in pieces that never failed to keep the letter of the law. When all speech was forbidden them they went on acting silently, enlightening the audience the while as to the progress of the fable by *écriteaux*—scrolls of explanatory verses let down from the ceiling of the stage. When this in turn was forbidden they passed about among the spectators a printed outline of the plot with the songs fully written out, and when the orchestra played the air the house was encouraged to sing the gay words on the programs.[46] So through one curious innovation and another the buoyant Forains maintained their popularity to such a degree that their respectable competitors saw the folly of trying to repress natural instincts by legislation and ceased to prosecute brains too clever and individuals too courageous to be intimidated.

Meanwhile the pantomime had come to stay. It was found a convenient form for the representation of extravaganzas even after the immediate necessity for doing without speech had passed away. The favorite personages introduced into it from the Italian stage were the Pantaloon—sometimes under other names—Arlequin, Scaramouche and Colombine. Yet it is chiefly by their names, their agile dances and their comic *lazzi* that they resemble the Italian types. Arlequin did indeed retain a costume of many colors and a black half-mask like those of ancient days, but the others were modishly tricked out in the fashion of the hour, and moreover had

---

[46] For a fuller description of these devices with illustrative cuts, cf. Albert, *op. cit.*, 44 f.

their wits as much bettered as their garb by the Parisian atmosphere.

Early in the eighteenth century, as I have already said, the pantomime crossed the Channel and became very popular in London. The way had been prepared for it by a tolerably long process of familiarizing the English public with the Italian stage, a process begun perhaps by Drusiano in 1577–8. In 1658 was printed by Sir Aston Cokayn, *Trappolin suppos'd a Prince,* which according to the author's account seems possibly to have been from an improvised original:

> Gallants, be't known, as yet we cannot say,
> To whom we are beholding for this play:
> But this our poet hath licensed us to tell,
> Ingenious Italy hath liked it well.
> Yet it is no translation; for he ne'er
> But twice in Venice did it ever hear.[49]

In 1661 was published a versified piece of satire in which Mounsier Pantaloon took a part[50]—an indication that English acquaintance with the Masks was carried on after the Jacobean expressions of it referred to in the last chapter.

[49] *A Dialogue between two other Giants, Mounsier Pantaloon and Signor Sancho: with a cue of Jack Phanatick concerning the late conflict between them on Tower Hill.*

[50] Cf. Scott, Pub. Mod. Lang. Assoc., XI, 442–3. Miss Scott calls the play "an adaptation of an Italian tragi-comedy in prose and verse entitled *Trappolino creduto principe,* as the Prologue explains." There was an old scenario among those in Biancolelli's collection (mid-seventeenth century) called *Arlecchino creduto principe,* played in Paris 1716 and 1740 (Parfaict, *Dict.,* etc., I, 222) which may have had something to do with Sir Aston's play. The theme is a favorite in the *commedia dell'arte,* cf. Brouwer, *Ancora una raccolta,* 396, for an account of a seventeenth century scenario, *Il creduto principe.*

Evidently Rymer a little later considered Italian example familiar enough to be dangerous to the solidity of British taste, for in his essay on the *Tragedies of the Last Age* (1678) he criticizes the quarrel of Melantius and Amintor in the *Maid's Tragedy* thus: "Harlequin and Scaramouttio might do these things. Tragedy suffers 'em not; here is no place for cowards, nor for giddy fellows & Bullies with their squabbles."[51] The same serious-minded critic in another essay calls the great scene in *Othello* effective because of the "Mops & the Mows, the Grimaces, the Grins & Gesticulations." Such scenes as this (he adds) "have made all the World run after Harlequin & Scaramouche."[52] Probably Rymer had seen the Italians act, perhaps when a company of them visited London in 1673, the same described in one of Dryden's prologs:

> The Harlequin merry-andrews took their place,
> And quite debauched the stage with lewd grimace;
> Instead of wit & humours, your delight
> Was there to see two hobby-horses fight;
> Stout Scaramouche with rush lance rode in
> And rode a tilt at Centaur Arlequin.[53]

If Harlequin and Scaramouche were disapproved by literary censors there is evidence of their popularity with the uncritical multitude. The public taste for parody and rude fun, whetted by such exhibitions as Dryden contemns, demanded from

[51] Spingarn, *Critical Essays of the Seventeenth Century*, II, 204.
[52] *A Short View of Tragedy* (1693), ed. Spingarn, *op. cit.*, II, 239.
[53] Prolog to the *Silent Woman*, 1673. From the allusion to Centaur Arlequin I infer that the play was one of Gherardi's collection, probably going back to G.-B. Andreini's *Centaura*.

this time on increasing recognition and satisfaction in the theater. Perhaps it was the Italians who spurred John Wright to parody a version of Seneca's *Thyestes* in English heroic couplets, by a *Mock Thyestes*, "A Farce in Burlesque Verse," performed with applause the same year as its model.[54] Certainly it is Italian example that accounts for Mr. Mountford's *Life and Death of Dr. Faustus made into a farce. . . . With the Humours of Harlequin and Scaramouche,*[55] a piece full of *commedia dell'arte* reminiscences. Scaramouche takes the rôle of Wagner—very blasphemously too—and Harlequin is brought in chiefly for the sake of his *lazzi* and to fight with Scaramouche. He describes himself, this shade of Arlecchino, as "poor Harlequin: by the Learned I am called Zane, by the Vulgar Jack Pudding. I was late fool to a Mountebank; last night in the mistaking the Pipkin I eat up a Pot of Bolus instead of Hasty Pudding; and devoured three yards of Diaculum Plaister instead of Pancake, for which my Master has turned me out of Doors instead of Wages." In farcical scenes the two clowns bind themselves to the devil, try to conjure out of a primer and are frightened by various enchantments which disappear whenever in

[54] In 1674. Cf. Langbaine, *Account of the Drama*, 514.

[55] The original was printed in London, 1697; it has been republished by Francke, 1886. Cf. Dieblers, *Faust-und-Wagner pantomimen in England*, Anglia, VII. There are of course reminiscences of Marlowe quite as patent as of the *commedia dell'arte*.

Cf. Ravenscroft's *Scaramouche a Philosopher, Harlequin a Schoolboy, Bravo, Merchant & Magician, a comedy after the Italian manner* (London, 1677), a farce based in part on Molière's *Fourberies de Scapin*, and through that going back to an Italian original.

their swearing they mention the name of God. Such nonsense apparently was just what the British audience liked, for the play had a tolerably long run and set the fashion for other farces, one of which at least was directly modeled on it[56] and others taken from Gherardi's collection.

In 1718 a French company presented at Lincoln's-Inn-Fields *The Two Harlequins*, "A Farce of Three Acts, written by Mr. Noble and Acted by the King's Italian Comedians at Paris," according to the title-page of the French and English edition published in London the same year. A comparison with *Les deux Arlequins* in Gherardi's third volume[57] shows it to be identical with the French text printed on alternate pages of the English book; the translation is literal, even stupidly so, for the author reproduces an entirely irrelevant note of "Mr. Noble's" on Baron, "the never-too-much regretted French comedian," who had had a part in the original production of the play. The comedy is one of the few that Gherardi prints almost in full; there are but two improvised scenes, the first and second of the second act. These bits of extemporized fun are thus described in the English version:

"In this Italian Scene, which begins the second Act, Harlequin appears as pursued by Marinetta,

[56] This was a Drury Lane pantomime, *Harlequin Dr. Faustus*, by J. Thurmond.

[57] *Les deux Arlequins, comédie en trois actes mise au théâtre par M. Noble, & représentée pour la première fois, . . . le 26 de Septembre, 1691.* Gherardi, *Théâtre italien*, III, 311–380.

Another translation from Gherardi was E. B.'s *Foire at St.-Germain*, London (1718?), from *Théâtre italien*, VI, 203 f., Regnard's *La Foire St.-Germain*, pl. 1695.

16

whose Love and Passion he had slighted. This
Scene contains what she says to him to endeavor to
raise his Love; he scornfully refuses, and gives her
to understand he loves only Colombine, which dec-
laration inspires Marinetta with Sentiments of Rage
and Jealousy, and Harlequin goes off rallying and
laughing at her." In the next scene "Marinetta
transported with Rage and Jealousy, swears to be
reveng'd of Harlequin, threatens to kill him, and at
the Time she is in the Height of her Passion and
taking for the other, says these words with a great
deal of warmth . . ." and there follows a written
speech beginning "Perfidious, ungrateful Traitor,
too hateful object, . . ." But the details of Marinetta's tragical mirth need concern us here no more
than the intricacies of the tedious brief plot, an
intrigue of the *Menaechmi* type. *Lazzi* abound,
with all the mistakes, the disguises, the falls and the
beatings that could be desired; one scene (II, 10)
contains a parody on *Le Cid;* at the close of the
play "the Bottom of the Stage opens with grotesque
Musicke, and four little Harlequins dance with
Scaramouche. . . . Between the Musicke and the
Dance a Voice sings two Couplets in Praise of old
Age." In short the farce is an excellent example of
an old scenario expanded to suit the taste of a later
age.

About the time this was being played in London
Addison saw Arlecchino in Italy and was pleased
with him: "Harlequin's part is made up of blunders
and absurdities; he is to mistake one person for another, to stumble over queens and to run his head

against every post that comes in his way. This is all attended with something so comical in the voice and gestures, that a man . . . can hardly forbear being pleased with it.''[58] It is hardly conceivable that if Dryden and Rymer had seen Arlecchino in his own Italian environment they would have given so mildly apologetic a portrait of him, and yet had they lived a little longer both the old critics might have modified their judgments—though probably toward greater severity—after seeing frequent performances of Italian comedies in London by their proper actors.

The French troupe which gave to English audiences *The Two Harlequins* was followed across the Channel in 1724 by an Italian company, perhaps by more than one, a few of whose plays have left printed records, text and translation having been apparently popular enough to warrant publication. The title of one reads, *Arlecchino Principe in sogno* . . . *or Harlequin Prince in a Dream, German baron, flying phisitian, & pretty Marget; a comedy* (*or pantomime in five acts*) *as it was acted* . . . *in the Haymarket by the Company of Italian Comedians.*[59] The rage for pantomimes seems to have been in full swing[60] and in the way to be satisfied by

* *Remarks on Italy*, ed. of 1718, 77.

* Printed London, 1724. The piece seems to be a compound of *Arlecchino finto principe*, an old scenario played in Paris, 1716 (Parfaict, *Dict.*, I, 222), *Il medico volante*, and either *Arl. Baron allemand, ou le Triomphe de la Folie* (played in Paris, 1712) or *Arl. barone tedesco*, probably the same as the above except that it was in Italian, played in Paris, 1716 (Parfaict, *Dict.*, I, 203 and 241). Of course other plot elements entered into the composite.

* John Rich, who became the English Harlequin, had much to do

the most ridiculously conglomerate entertainments, made up often from half a dozen old scenarios, as this is.

Three plays from the repertory of these visiting Italians are all that the British Museum preserves;[61] how many others may have been printed and lost, or have been given and not thought worth keeping, must be a matter of conjecture. That Riccoboni was in London in 1727 with a troupe and that he published two of his treatises there[62] proves the liveliness of British interest in the strangers and their work. Even more convincing as to the vogue of the farces and of their influence on the English theater is the vast amount of imitative material that survives. To-day it is hardly possible to think of a Drury Lane pantomime without Harlequin and Colombine, their burlesque love affairs and their

with setting the fashion; one of his earliest pantomimes was built on an Italian French plot, *The Cheats of Scapin or the Tavern-Bilkers*, "an entertainment of dancing, action and motion only," 1702. Cf. Wyndham, *Annals of Covent-Garden*, I, 12.

[62] *Le disgratie d'Arlecchino, vis. Harlequin's misfortunes; or his marriage interrupted by Brighella's cunning*, perhaps identical with the *Disgratie d'Arlecchino*, played in Paris, 1716 (Bartoli, *Scen. ined.*, xli), or with the *opéra comique* of the same name, sung at the Foire St.-Germain in 1721 and characterized by Parfaict as "du dernier misérable." (*Dict.*, II, 319; the abstract makes this piece appear a poor copy of *Les deux Arlequins*.)

Le furbarie per vendetta or Brighella's revenge . . . with Harlequin's transformation, etc., possibly a version of the ever-popular *Fourberies de Scapin*, or perhaps an enlarged and pantomimic rendering of the *Fourberies d'Arlequin*, given in Paris, 1722 (Parfaict, *Dict.*, II, 634), which the editor calls "a tissue of scenes from the ancient Italian theater."

[62] Ademollo, *Una famiglia*, etc., 22. Riccoboni's poem, *Dell'arte rappresentativa*, was dedicated to Lord Chesterfield.

fantastic ill-luck, yet in the early years of the eighteenth century imitation of the Italians was not confined to giving free versions of the Masks; there were many allegorical-mythological pantomimes, forerunners of certain operas that we know.[63] Our concern is not with these last but with the Harlequinades proper, those gay absurdities for which the general formula is an elopement and a pursuit.

Harlequin or Scaramouche is nearly always the hero of the piece, Colombine the heroine; they may in the first acts be dressed and disguised in any number of ways, just as they were for some of the Franco-Italian performances in Paris;[64] they may belong to any country and to any rank of life from imperial to peasant, but they are always faithful lovers persecuted by a cruel father, who rush away from his tyranny into dangers they have not foreseen and who are forced to assume disguises beneath their dignity. At the end they are sure to be happily reconciled to their parent in the time-honored manner and to pose for the audience in their typical costumes and names. The reason for this almost

[63] Such as the *Mars and Venus* presented at Drury Lane, 1717. Wyndham, *Annals*, etc., I, 12.

[64] Of the musical and pantomimic pieces listed by Parfaict of which Arlequin was the hero and of their settings, a few titles will show the variety. *Arl. dans le Château enchanté* (I, 222); *dans les îles, triomphe ameriquain* (Ib.) *dans l'île de Ceylon* (I, 222–4); *Empereur dans la lune*, from one of Gherardi's comedies (I, 229); *Arl. Endymion* (I, 230); *Arl. et Scapin magiciens par hasard* (I, 232); *Arl. finto astrologo, bambino, statua e perrequetto* (I, 240); *Arl. Grand-Mogul* (I, 247); *Arl. formé par magie et domestique par intrigue* (Ib.). All these and many more as extraordinary were played in the first half of the eighteenth century.

unvarying plot outline is that it furnishes an admirable pretext for the rapid transformations and spectacular changes of scene which gave its true charm to the pantomime.

A "prospectus" of one of these extravaganzas is like the scenario of a *commedia dell'arte* except that it gives more detailed directions as to comic business and that it reproduces in full the songs and choruses. Occasionally there is some versified dialog printed but ordinarily such speech as is allowed is in prose. As to the details of style and incident it is useless to generalize; each outline mixes in varying proportions, instrumental and vocal music, dances of different kinds, gesture and brief monologs or conversations. The most startlingly various elements in the spectacle were the transformations either in an individual actor or in the whole scene. One of Rich's successes was *Harlequin Sorcerer*,[65] in which the protagonist is hatched from an egg by the heat of the sun, and an eye-witness says, "from the first chirping in the egg, his receiving motion, his feeling of the ground, standing upright, to his quick trip around the empty shell, through the whole progression, every limb had its own tongue and every motion a voice."[66]

Nearly a century later the very elaborate pantomime of *The Silver Arrow or Harlequin and the Fairy Pari Banon* shows the hero in a more normal

---

[65] *A dramatick entertainment call'd Harlequin a Sorcerer; with the Loves of Pluto and Proserpine.* (One act in verse, by L. Theobald, London, 1729.)

[66] Quoted by Wyndham, *Annals*, etc., I, 6, from Jackson's *Hist. of the Scottish Stage*.

rôle, while it is his environment that changes with
lightning rapidity from "a terrific representation
of the Fire-King's abode," to "a rich Persian
Chamber" and that again to "a Range of Bed-
Rooms in the King's Arms," an old-fashioned English Inn.[67]   Into this last scene is introduced a *lazzo*
as unconnected with the plot as much of the comic
business in the *commedia dell'arte:* "At the opening
of the scene," the prospectus tells us, "a numerous
group of various characters are ushered into their
sleeping-rooms. Harlequin appears and determines
on having some fun, to which end he knocks at all the
doors, producing a ludicrous effect, the different
characters appearing half undressed; others in their
Night-Gowns, &c.; this furnishes the Clown with an
idea; no sooner do the characters return than he
dresses the warming-pan grotesquely and then
alarms the Inn. A dreadful bustle then takes
place." Harlequin's "ideas" are after all not his
own but merely slight variations on ancient ways of
appealing to simple wits by surprise, awkwardness
and indecorum.[68]

Perhaps the best general conception of the pantomime in its first flush of success is to be gained from
a satiric poem, *Harlequin-Horace, or the Art of*

[67] *Airs, Choruses & Business . . . in a new pantomime of the Silver
Arrow; or Harlequin & the Fairy Pari Banon . . .* Theatre Royal,
Drury Lane. (London, 1819.)

[68] The English pantomime is worthy of a volume to itself. Such
titles as I have collected will be found in App. B; here my purpose
is only to suggest a few possible analogies between the pantomime
and the *commedia dell'arte*. Cf. further, Wyndham, *Annals*, etc.,
I, 8–10.

Modern Poetry, a virulent assault on the British stage of 1731 and on John Rich in particular as responsible for the prevalent "joint-mixture of Trick and Buffoonery."[69] Like the moralists of the sixteenth century the clerical author, Mr. James Miller, accuses Harlequin of having by a single wave of his hand conjured "the whole Town every Night into your Circle; where like a true Cunning-Man, you amuse 'em with a few Puppy's Tricks while you juggle 'em of their pelf"; the women in the audience, he adds, "are now (thanks to your Instructions, Sir) as impenetrable Proof to anything that tends to put them out of Countenance . . . as . . . yourself." In the poem the means to these ends are described with some minuteness:

> . . . . 'tis *Aegri Somnia* now must please,
> Things without Head, or Tail, or Form, or Grace,
> A wild, forc'd, glaring, unconnected Mass. . . .[70]
> In one Scene make your Hero cant and whine,
> Then roar out *Liberty* in every Line;
> Vary one Thing a thousand pleasant Ways,
> Shew *Whales* in *Woods* and *Dragons* in the *Seas*. . . .[71]
> Begin with *Bluster* and with *Bawdry* end. . . .[72]
> The Feats of *Faustus* and the Pranks of *Jove*
> Chang'd to a *Bull* to carry off his Love;
> The *swimming Monster* and the *flying Steed*,
> *Medusa's Cavern* and her Serpent Breed,
> *Domes* voluntary rising from the Ground,

[69] Printed anonymously, London, 1731, but since ascribed to the Rev. James Miller; dedicated in a heavily abusive letter to "J..n R..h, Esq.," of course John Rich.

[70] *Harlequin Horace*, p. 2.

[71] *Ib.*, p. 6.

[72] *Ib.*, p. 8.

And *Yahoo Rich* transformed into a *Hound,*
All acted with a Show of Truth deceive
Which if related we should ne'er believe. . . .
The number of your Acts we never mind,
For modern Poets scorn to be confin'd. . . .
Be sure to introduce a *Ghost* or—*God,*
Make *Monsters, Fiends, Heav'n, Hell,* at once engage,
For all are pleas'd to see a *well-filled* Stage;
The antient Chorus justly's laid aside,
And all its office by a Song supply'd. . . .[73]

The reason for such lawless doings is once more, as
of old, laid at the door of the multitude, undiscrimi-
nating and coarse:

Long labour'd Rich, by Tragick Verse to gain
The Town's Applause—but labour'd long in vain;
At length he wisely to his Aid call'd in,
The active *Mime* and *checker'd Harlequin.*
Nor ruled by Reason, nor by Law restrain'd,
In all his Shows, Smut and Prophaneness reign'd.[74]

Alas for the Reverend Mr. James Miller and his
fulminations! In 1814 a better-natured satire witnesses how popular during all these years had been
the pantomime, how delightful it still was. This
piece is itself a farce, *Harlequin Hoax,*[75] and an excellent example of the very absurdities it ridicules.
The plot "proposed" for the pantomime—the little

[73] *Ib.,* p. 25 f.
[74] *Ib.,* p. 30 f.
[75] *Or a Pantomime Proposed,* by T. Dibdin, played at the Theatre
Royal, Lyceum, and printed in London, 1814. Two other satires of
the same general character are *The British Stage; or the Exploits of
Harlequin, a farce,* . . . London, 1724, and *Harlequin Student; or the
Fall of Pantomime, with the Restoration of the Drama,* . . . London,
1741.

farce deals with a set of theatrical people planning a new entertainment—is thus outlined: ''Harlequin is carried up on the tail of a kite, and when at the top of the theater, drops through a trap at the bottom, and returns enveloped in flames, as if shot from the crater of a volcano; then thrown into a cascade of real water with sufficient force to let the splash he makes convince the audience that the element is genuine. . . . To meet Columbine at the street-door Harlequin throws himself out of a three pair of stairs window, and is caught with his head in a lamp-iron; the lamp-lighter pours a gallon of oil down his throat . . . and sticks a lighted wick in his mouth and a set of drunken bucks, having no better business on earth than to break lamps, knock his nob to shivers and all go to the watch-house together.'' Among the directions for Harlequin's *lazzi* are, ''Cut a mug at the clown, come the sly, queer the old one and brush off with a roley-poley,'' obligingly interpreted by Harlequin's running around the stage, making faces at Liston, giving him a hard slap, pulling away Raymond's chair just as he is about to sit down, falling, jumping up and running off.[76] A spectacular conclusion,—a Temple of Concord with fireworks—rounds out the perform- ance in the conventional manner and must have served to blunt yet further the already dull points of the satiric dialog.

This lively production was hardly of course ex- pected to stop the vogue for pantomime in England and certainly had not that effect. Harlequin, Co-

[76] *Harl. Hoax*, p. 10.

lumbine and Pantaloon danced and stumbled and joked on, as in fact they still do in London at Christmas time, keeping only their names and a hint in their costumes to remind the audience of their Italian forebears. The names indeed as in the case of so many traditional titles, soon began to have a kind of significant personality of their own; each came to stand for some leading trait of the character that bore it. Robert Harley, Earl of Oxford, was satirized in 1705 as "Harlequin le Grand,"[77] and in 1750 the Wesleyan preachers were ridiculed in the guise of Harlequins dressed as old women.[78] Pantaloon and Harlequin are the favorites among the Masks when it comes to using their names as convenient proverbial tags; if Gratiano, Brighella and the rest figure in the same useful way, it is only in Italy where they were best known.[79]

Occasionally into modern experience comes some further reminder of the *commedia dell'arte*. Brighella has a part in Wagner's youthful opera, *Lie-*

[77] *A Dialogue between Louis le Petite* (sic) *and Harlequin le Grand* . . . (London, 1705?). Cf. *Harl. Hydaspes, or the Greshamite* . . . (London, 1719), and *The Harlequins, A Comedy after the manner of the Théâtre Italien* (a political satire on affairs in Ireland), London, 1753. There is nothing Italianate about this last but the names of two or three characters.

[78] *Harlequin Methodist. To the tune of An Old Woman cloathed in Gray* . . . (London, 1750?).

[79] Alexander VIII for instance was popularly christened Papa Pantalone, 1690; cf. Ademollo, *Teatri di Roma*, 173 and 184. Cf. above, chap. V, for earlier examples of the satirical use of the Mask names. In Italy there were many political songs like *Pantalon, Amigo de la Verità. Canzonetta sopra la Guerra seguia* (sic) *nel Cremonese l'Anno 1647 e 48* . . . (Milano, 1650?). The British Museum contains several Dutch Harlequinades which seem to prove that the custom of such satire spread to Holland.

besverbot,[80] another Zanni in Lothar's *Arlecchino
Re*, a band of traveling actors in Ganne's *Saltimbanchi* and Leoncavallo's *Pagliacci*. M. Moland
was so impressed with the dramatic quality of
Scala's plots that he translated and amplified several
of them into short stories.[81] Maurice Sand with
the aid of several clever friends tried successfully
to practice the art of improvising dialog on his
private stage at Nohant.[82] Later another French
enthusiast published an earnest plea for reviving the
ancient Italian custom in a new Parisian theater.[83]
Beside all these artificial and more or less sentimental attempts to revivify the *commedia dell'arte*,
there remain those actual relics of its habits and
its types on the popular Italian stages already
described.

Whether or not improvised comedy will ever live
again as a serious art such as it undoubtedly was
in the sixteenth century, might be debated at some
length, though for the most part inconclusively and
on the rather unsteady ground of theory. Looking
back into the Cinquecento and recalling how the
custom of improvising dialog from a scenario grew
up in response to a particular situation too complicated ever to recur again, it seems as though the
peculiar union of individual initiative and coopera-
tion required for such extempore art, would not be

[80] Wagner was influenced by Gozzi in his two early operas *Die Feen*
and *Liebesverbot*. Cf. his autobiography, *My Life* (N. Y., 1911), I,
87 and 140.

[81] Moland, *Les méprises, comédies de la Renaissance racontées.*

[82] Sand, *Masques et Bouffons*, introduction.

[83] Marazin, *Le théâtre des Boulevards et la comédie improvisée.*

possible in different circumstances. On the other hand the blasé and unthinking public to which the *commedia dell'arte* all through its history has chiefly appealed, is always with us, ever ready to regale its bourgeois taste by laughing, as its kind laughed three centuries ago, at progressive ideas and at the victims of the social majority—the weak, the stupid, the deformed, the aged—by watching physical distortions and by listening to tawdry music and to vulgar innuendo. Our cheaper theaters—by cheaper I do not mean necessarily low-priced—still present *ad nauseam* the stale old devices that the Italians made so effective in regular plots. According to a rough classificaiton all the kinds of material that went into the *commedia dell'arte* are still flourishing among us, and are likely to flourish for as long as human nature finds amusement in old stories, blows and quarrels, indecorum, surprises and the sight of the "biter bit."

This sort of entertainment exists frankly for mercenary purposes, of which the least disreputable is to give the multitude what they like. It has nothing to say, no "problem" interests ever get into it except as matter for ridicule; the suffragette, for example, is appearing at this moment on numerous vaudeville stages, tricked out and shouting like the absurdest strong-minded female who ever loomed large and threatening in an old-fashioned imagination. Just so the Ibsenesque new woman was pilloried a generation ago in travesties that now seem tame as well as meaningless; just in this spirit the *commedia dell'arte* in its prime "took off" the intel-

lectual problems of the sixteenth century, those
earnestly debated questions of individual relationships that if not to-day supplanted have been at
least freshly restated in the light of more complex
social analyses. Farce of this kind always expresses the habitual reactions of the plain man to
situations that the serious dramatist regards as offering food for painful attention and opportunity for
reconstruction. The finer issues that absorb keen,
observant, far-sighted leaders, touch the commonplace majority of course, only to a vaguely uncom-
fortable fear and distrust that must relieve itself in
boisterous laughter until it grows so alarmingly
conscious that it calls for organization and perhaps
opposing warfare.

If this point of view is justifiable the *commedia
dell'arte* will be seen to belong to the class of drama
that has contributed nothing to the spiritual advance
of mankind. Gherardi and his collaborators indeed
now and then glimpsed an interesting fresh idea
and tried to make something telling of it, but in
general the machinery of the improvised plays
crushed the individual innovator. If one member
of a troupe were more critical, more intellectually
alive than the others, he was much more likely to
be drawn into the easy mass judgments and habits
of his fellows than he was to raise his comrades to
his level. So the professional comedy moved along,
well in the rear of progress, scattering amusement
more or less questionable on its way, and remarkable
chiefly for the brilliance of its technic.

What its perfect execution must have done to im·

prove dramatic methods is easier to imagine than to estimate very exactly. The spontaneous dialog, even though it was interrupted by set speeches, may well have helped to break up, by force of example, the ponderous tedium of rhetorical academic attempts at play-writing. The need for padding thin plots must have stimulated the invention of stage machinery, ballets and variety features. Still more the necessity of the most flexible adaptability among the actors must inevitably have brought about an improvement in theatrical training. In such ways as these the professional comedies in their best period attained to a delightfulness that covered their poverty with splendid show, that spurred on Molière's genius and left not even Shakespeare untouched.

APPENDIX A.

The following is a list of the chief printed and manuscript collections of scenarios and the principal plays that have been published singly so far as I have been able to trace them. The oldest known scenario that can be certainly dated is the one I quote at length above, Chapter IV, republished by Stoppato from:

Un discorso degli trionfi, Giostre, Apparati, e delle cose più notabile nelle sontuose Nozze dell'Illustrissimo et Eccellentissimo Signor Duca Guglielmo, Primo Genito del Generosissimo Alberto Quinto, Conte Palatino del Reno e Duca di Baviera alta e bassa nell'anno 1568, a 22 de Febraro, ecc., ecc., di Massimo Trojano da Napoli, Musico dell'Illus. ed Ecc. Signor Duca di Baviera. In Monaco . . . MDLXVIII.

Alessandro Piccolomini who died in 1578 is said to have written thirteen scenarios, work which Rossi conjectures would belong to his youth;[1] this would put the recognition of the improvised comedy before 1568. Still, as the scenarios of Piccolomini have not survived if they ever existed, the play at the Bavarian court must stand as the first of its kind.

The most important collection of outline plots, the oldest and one of the largest, is that of fifty pieces

---

[1] Rossi, *Lettere di M. A. Calmo*, lxxx, note I.

made by Flaminio Scala[2] from which several examples are given above, Chapter IV. It undoubtedly contains a number of plots many years older than the date of publication of the book, for the Gelosi, Scala's troupe, began to play at least as early as 1570; moreover no *capocomico* of those days would print outlines of pieces that were new and might be stolen by rival companies.

It is impossible to date exactly the other scenarios in collections that have survived. A. Bartoli has printed a volume made up of twenty-two outlines from a MS. in the Magliabecchiana, written in the eighteenth century but containing older pieces.[3] There are eighteen comedies, one tragedy, one "opera tragica," one tragi-comedy and one "opera mista." At least one of the comedies is taken from a large collection made by Domenico Biancolelli which exists in manuscript in Paris.[4] Another large manuscript collection (one hundred and three pieces) is that of Basilio Locatelli, to be found to-day in the Casanatense in Rome and in an abbreviated form in the Corsiniana.[5] The latter has been

---

[2] *Il teatro delle favole rappresentative overo la ricreatione comica, boscareccia e tragica, divisa in cinquanta giornate composte da Flaminio Scala detto Flavio, comico del serenissimo signor duca di Mantova.* In Venetia . . . 1611.

[3] A. Bartoli, *Scenari inediti della commedia dell'arte* . . . (Firenze, 1880), a volume of the *Raccolta di opere inedite o rare di ogni secolo della letteratura italiana.*

[4] The titles of Scala's, Biancolelli's and Locatelli's scenarios, as well as those of later date scattered in various records of the stage are printed by Bartoli, *Scen. inediti,* xxviii f.

[5] Valeri, *Gli scenari inediti di Basilio Locatelli* (Roma, 1894), has shown that the two volumes in the Casanatense are the originals from which the Cardinal Maurice of Savoy had the two volumes in the Cor-

17

described as a handsome manuscript of the seventeenth century in two volumes, containing the outlines of sixty-six comedies, ten tragi-comedies, ten pastorals, two "opere turchesche," one "opera reale" (*La gran pazzia d'Orlando*) and one tragedy. Brouwer has shown that Locatelli's scenarios were not all his own, for the two examples this modern scholar prints, *La Turchetta* and *La Tavernaria*, nearly resemble Porta's comedies, *La Turca* and *La Tabernia*. The Masks in the collection, this editor points out, are similar to those in Scala's plays and in the plots published by Bartoli, except that Pulcinella does not appear in them at all.

Pulcinella is however a leading figure in the large Neapolitan collection rediscovered in recent years by Croce.[6] These two thick manuscript volumes belong to the end of the Seicento and contain in all one hundred and eighty-three scenarios. The first volume is entitled: *Gibaldone di Soggetti da recitare all'impronto. Alcuni proprij, e gl'altri da diversi. Raccolti di D. Annibale Sersale Conte di Casamarciano.* It is a quarto of 479 pages. The second volume is called: *Gibaldone comico di varij suggetti di Commedie ed opere Bellissime copiate da me Antonio Passante detto Oratio il Calabrese, per commando dell'Ecc. mo signor Conte di Casamarciano.*

siniana compiled. For a description of the shorter collection cf. F. de Simone Brouwer, *Due scenari inediti del secolo XVII*, Gior. Stor., XVIII (1891), 277 f. Cf. also Croce's review of Valeri's book, Gior. Stor., XXIX, 212.

[6] B. Croce, *Una nuova raccolta di scenari*, Gior. Stor., XXIX (1897), 211 f. P. Toldo, *Di alcuni scenari inediti della commedia dell'arte*, etc., R. Accademia di scienze, Atti XLII (1907, 460 f.) examines in detail several pieces from this collection, dating them c. 1676–1700.

1700. The titles given by Croce show nothing startlingly different from those of other collections
except that as I have said Pulcinella takes a very
prominent place in them; he seems to be the sub-
stitute for Arlecchino and appears in the titles as
"burlato," "innamorato," "pazzo per forza,"
"dama gelosa," etc. One play, *I quattro Pulcinelli*,
must be a *reductio ad absurdum* of the *Menaechmi*
theme.

Two more collections in manuscript that await
further investigation are those discovered respectively by De Simone Brouwer in the Casanatense in
Rome (forty-eight scenarios), and by V. Rossi in the
Correr Museum at Venice (fifty-one pieces), of
which the discoverer has printed a description and
two examples.[7]

A number of eighteenth century volumes published
in Paris are important for the later history of the
commedia dell'arte, of which the chief are the *Dictionaire des théâtres de Paris* and the *Histoire de*

[7] *a.* F. De Simone Brouwer, *Ancora una raccolta di scenari*, in Rendiconto della reale accademia dei Lincei, classe di scienze morali,
storiche e filologiche, Ser. V, vol. X (Roma, 1901), 391 f.

This collection belongs to the end of the seventeenth century,
though a number of the titles of the separate plays listed seem to go
back as far as 1642; of these the most interesting is a version of
Calderon's *Medego de su honra*. There is also a version of *La regina
d'Inghilterra*, for which cf. above, Chap. IV.

b. V. Rossi, *I Suppositi dell'Ariosto ridotto a scenario di commedia
improvvisa* (Bergamo, per nozze Flamini-Fanelli, 1895). This scenario is from the same seventeenth century collection as the one published by Rossi in *G. B. della Porta ed un nuovo scenario, L'astrologo*,
in Rend. del reale istit. lombardo (1896), Ser II, vol. XXIX, 14 f.
Rossi thinks Porta himself was not the author of this scenario of his
play.

*l'ancien théâtre italien depuis son origine en France
jusqu'à sa suppression en l'année 1697,* by the
brothers Parfaict.[8] The two Italian actors who
were most prominent in the rôle of Arlequin in
France at this period each got out a collection of
plans on the order of *commedie dell'arte,* P. F. Biancolelli, "dit Dominique," *Le nouveau théâtre italien*
(Anvers, 1713), and E. Gherardi, *Le théâtre italien
de Gherardi* (Paris, 1700 and after). The six
volumes of the latter contain only the French and
French-and-Italian written scenes of the partly improvised plays of all sorts given by Gherardi and his
Italian company.

A number of single scenarios have been published
in recent years of which I note those that I have
been able to examine myself.

BROUWER, F. DE SIMONE, *Due scenari inediti del
secolo XVII,* Gior. Stor., XVIII (1891), 277.

CORBONI, P., *Cristoforo Colombo nel teatro* (Milano,
1892), 196 f., a scenario on Columbus played at
Genoa, 1708.

GOZZI, C., *Il contratto rotto,* an eighteenth century
scenario, in his *Opere,* IV, 35.

MADDALENA, E., *Uno scenario inedito,* from the Bibl.
Palatina in Vienna; pub. in Sitzungsberichte der
kaisl. Akademie der Wissenschaften, Wien,
phil.-hist. Klasse, CXLIII (1901), part 16, 1 f.

MARTUCCI, G., *Uno scenario inedito della commedia
dell'arte; Flaminio disperato,* from an early

---

[8] Cf. bibliography for full titles of these books. Bartoli lists the
most important titles of scenarios from these sources, *Scen. ined.,*
xxvii f.

seventeenth century MS.; pub. in Nuova Antologia, Ser. II, vol. LI (1885), 219 f.

NERI, A., *Una commedia dell'arte*, a description of a
comedy written up from an improvised play, apparently the source of Molière's *Médecin
volant;* the Italian play is dated Milano 1673.
Gior. Stor., I (1883), 75 f. Cf. Toldo, *Alcuni
scenari*, etc., 462, for a discussion of this
scenario.

RE, E., *Scenari modenesi*, from the Bibl. Estense in
Modena, two scenarios apparently of the six-
teenth century, showing some resemblances to
Scala's plays. Gior. Stor., LV (1910), 325 f.

SCHERILLO, M., *La commedia dell'arte in Italia*
(Torino, 1884), chap. VI, *Un scenario di G. B.
della Porta: La Trapolaria.*

STOPPATO, L., *La commedia popolare in Italia*
(Padova, 1887), chap. VI, *Uno scenario inedito,*
from the Museo Correr in Venice, a seventeenth
century MS. Also the scenario cited above,
Trojano's.

TOLDO, P., *Un scenario inedito della commedia
dell'arte,* of the seventeenth century, apparently
an influence on Molière's *M. de Pourceaugnac.*
Gior. Stor., XLVI, 128.

BARTOLOMEI, G., *Didascalia, cioè dottrina comica*
(Firenze, 1658), contains six scenarios or
sketches of the *commedia di mezzo* which the
author wished to introduce to the attention of
academies. They were a kind of compromise
between the professional and literary plays.

APPENDIX B.

THE INFLUENCE OF ITALIAN COMEDY IN ENGLAND.

I wish to call attention here to a triple influence of
Italian on English drama; first, to the known trans-
lations and adaptations of Italian plays into Eng-
lish; second, to possible traces of Italianate taste in
English comedies; third, to the vogue of the Italian-
French pantomime in England.

I. Italian models have been traced for the following plays:

BUGBEARS, c. 1561; from A.-F. Grazzini, *La spiritata.*
Cf. Archiv für das Studium der neueren
Sprachen, XCVIII, 1897, XCIX, C.

CHAPMAN, G., *May Day,* pr. 1611; from A. Piccolomini, *Alessandro.* Cf. Stiefel in Shakespeare Jahrbuch, XXXV, 1899, 180 f.

CHEEKE, H., *A certayne Tragedie written first in
Italian by F. N. B., entituled Freewyl* . . . pr.
c. 1589; from F. Negri Bassanese, *Libro Arbi-
trio.* Cf. M. A. Scott, Pub. Mod. Lang. Assoc.,
XI, 1896, 435.

DYMOCK, C., *Il Pastor Fido, or the Faithfull Shep-
heard,* 1607; from B. Guarini, *Il pastor fido.*
Cf. Scott, *loc. cit.*

GASCOIGNE, G., *The Supposes,* 1566, from L. Ariosto,
I suppositi. Ed. J. W. Cunliffe (Boston, 1906).

Gismond of Salerne, 1567/8; from L. Dolce, *Dido*
(and other sources). Cf. J. W. Cunliffe, Pub.
Mod. Lang. Assoc., XXI, 1906.

JONSON, B., *Alchemist*, 1610, largely influenced by Bruno, *Il candelaio*. Cf. paper before the Mod. Lang. Assoc. of America by C. G. Child, 1905.

KINWELWERSH, F., and GASCOIGNE, G., *Jocasta*, 1566, from L. Dolce, *Giocasta*. Ed. J. W. Cunliffe (Boston, 1906).

Laelia, a Latin university play, 1590, a translation of *Gl'ingannati*, by a member of the academy of the Intronati at Siena. Schelling, *Elizabethan Drama*, I, 196–7, erroneously attributes *Gl'ingannati* to G. B. della Porta; the authorship has been much disputed, but the probable authors have been narrowed to two, A. Piccolomini and L. Castelvetro; cf. G. Cavvazzuti, Gior. Stor., XL, 1902, 343 f. Schelling, *op. cit.*, I, 196 f., and II, 77–8, lists a number of other Italian plays translated into Latin at the English universities. One of these, Ruggle's *Ignoramus*, taken from Porta's *La Trapolaria* (pl. 1615), was translated into English by Coddington and printed in 1662.

MARSTON, J., *What You Will*, pr. 1607, is a free version of Sforza degli Oddi's *I morti vivi*; cf. Holthausen's examination of the relation in Shakespeare Jahrbuch, XLI, 1905, 186 f.

MUNDAY, A., *Fidele and Fortunio, the deceiptes in love Discoursed in a Commedie of ij Italyan Gent(lemen)* . . . by A. M. . . . 1584. Cf. the Malone Society reprint, 1909. From L. Pasqualigo's *Il Fedele*, a comedy translated into French by Larivey in 1611. An English Latin version of *Il fedele* also exists, *Victoria*.

[?REYNOLDS, H.] *Tasso's Aminta*, 1628. Cf. Scott, *loc. cit.*

SHAKESPEARE, W., *Twelfth Night*, c. 1600, a very free adaptation of *Gl'ingannati*. The Italian play in an abbreviated translation is given in the appendix to the Variorum edition of *Twelfth Night*, ed. H. H. Furness, from T. L. Peacock's *Works* (London, 1875), 276 f. Cf. W. W. Greg, Mod. Lang. Rev., 1900, 189.

TOMKIS, *Albumazar*, 1615; from Porta, *L'astrologo*. Cf. W. König, Shakespeare Jahrbuch, IX, 1874, 209.

In addition to these satisfactory attributions I note a few suggestions which are interesting though inadequately proved.

CREIZENACH, W. M. A., *Geschichte des neueren Dramas*, IV, 247, remarks on parellels between Jonson's *Epicoene* and Aretino's *Marescalco*. Ibid., a suggestion of the Italianate character of *The Wit of a Woman* (pr. 1604) and of Middleton's *No Wit, No Help like a Woman's*.

KLEIN, J. L., *Geschichte des Dramas*, IV, 548 f., compares Shakespeare's *All's Well that Ends Well* to B. Accolti's *Verginia*, a connection that a careful reading of the two plays does not confirm.

Ibid., IV, 786 f., likens the *Two Gentlemen of Verona* to Parabosco's *Il viluppo* and *Twelfth Night* to N. Secchi's *Gl'inganni*, as well as to *Gl'ingannati*. Cf. Ulrici's criticism, Shakespeare Jahrbuch, VI, 1871, 351.

Ibid., V, 385 f., compares *Othello* to Dolce's *Marianna* and *Romeo and Juliet* to Groto's *Hadriana*, not convincingly.

WARD, A. W. A., *Hist. of English Dramatic Literature*, 1899, I, 247, compares Heywood's *Play of Love* (c. 1530) to an Italian *frottola*, but without suggesting a definite Italian origin for it.

II. A few of the minor plays of the period which seem to me most decidedly Italianate in tone and theme are:

ANON.: *Fair Em*, pl. c. 1593, has a hero "innamorato per fama," a theme of love versus friendship, disguises, a pretence on the part of the heroine that she is blind and deaf. The last comic device is similar to Isabella's frequent pretence of madness in Scala's scenarios.

Misognus, c. 1570?, may possibly be of Italian derivation; the kind of plot and characters suggest such an origin.

Mucedorus, pr. 1598, is a romantic extravaganza with a hero "innamorato per fama," like Scala's Trineo. Cf. *L'Orseida*, above, Chap. IV. The tone of Mucedorus is however on the whole that of medieval romance and Italian court pastoral rather than that of the usual *commedia dell'arte*.

The Rare Triumphs of Love and Fortune, pl. c. 1582, is a characteristic court entertainment suitable for acting by either Italian or English players.

CHAPMAN's comedies are all similar to Italian plays

but only one has been traced to a definite source (cf. above). *All Fools* contains a particularly good example of the Pantaloonlike old father in Gostanzo (cf. especially IV, 1) of the Gratiano in *Dr. Pock* (cf. III, 1), and the deceiving young lovers and their servants, much as they appear in the *commedia dell'arte*. The sub-plot is moreover built on jealousy and centers in a group of low-class characters, like the Brighella or Burattino sub-plots of some of Scala's scenarios.

DAY, J., *Humor out of Breath,* pr. 1608, is an intrigue comedy of the Italianate order.

Law Tricks, pr. 1608, is one of several plays indebted to *How a Man may choose a Good Wife from a Bad,* and through that may possibly go back to a novella of Cintio (cf. Baskerville, Pub. Mod. Lang. Assoc., XXIV, 1909, 726) or it may be based on an Italian comedy derived from Cintio.

LYLY, J., *Mother Bombie,* pr. 1594, has a duplicate plot interest, which makes me think it may be from an Italian original rather than from a play by Terence. Cf. however Bond, ed. of Lyly's *Works,* II, 473, note on the *Italian Influence on Lyly,* and Feuillerat, *John Lyly,* 320 f.

FIELD, N., *A Woman is a Weathercock,* pl. 1609, and *Amends for Ladies,* c. 1612, are especially full of the hackneyed *commedia dell'arte* tricks, disguises, *concetti,* etc.

MARSTON, J., *Parisitaster,* pr. 1606, has been traced to the *Decameron,* III, 3, but may be from an

Italian comedy on the same novella. For the connection with Boccaccio, cf. Koeppel, *Quellen-Studien*, 27.

MIDDLETON, J., *The Widow*, c. 1608–9, is a play that has been accounted for from the *Decameron*, III, 3, and II, 2; cf. Baumann, *Middleton's Lustspiel The Widow u. Boccaccio's Il Decameron*, etc. (Halle, 1904). The disguises in this play, together with the window flirtations and the charlatanlike performances of Latrocino (IV, 2), are *commedia dell'arte* features. So too are the scenes in which Martia in a shirt is mistaken for a lad.

III. The following titles of typical farces and pantomimes show a *commedia dell'arte* influence after the Restoration:

A Collection of the most esteemed Farces and Entertainments performed on the British Stage. . . . Edinburgh, n. d. (mid-eighteenth century?).

Harlequin Hydaspes; or the Greshamite, a mock opera (in prose and verse). London, 1719.

The British Stage; or the Exploits of Harlequin, a farce (a satire on the public taste for pantomime). London, 1724.

A dramatick entertainment call'd Harlequin a Sorcerer; with the Loves of Pluto and Proserpine. London, 1725.

Harlequin Student; or the Fall of Pantomime, with the Restoration of the Drama, an entertainment, etc. London, 1741.

Harlequin Incendiary or Colombine Cameron. A musical pantomime. London, 1746.

Harlequin Mungo; or a Peep into the Tower; a new pantomimical entertainment. . . . London (1750?).

Harlequin Premier; a farce. . . . (Brentford) 1769.

The Witches; or Harlequin's Trip to Naples (verses illustrated by a series of plates cut to form different combinations). London, 1772.

The Choice of Harlequin; or the Indian Chief; a pantomimical entertainment, in two parts. London, 1782.

An exact account of the favorite pantomime called Harlequin's Chaplet. London, 1790.

The History and comical adventures of Harlequin and his pleasing companion Columbine. Holborn (1790?).

Sketch of the Story, etc., with the songs and recitatives in the . . . Entertainment of the Talisman; or Harlequin made happy, etc. . . . (London) 1792.

The Savages; or Harlequin Wanderer. An Entertainment of song, dance and comic spectacle, etc. (London) 1792.

A correct account of the celebrated pantomime entertainment of Harlequin's Museum or Mother Shipton Triumphant, etc. London, 1793.

The Witch of the Lakes; or Harlequin in the Hebrides, as performed at Sadler's Wells. (London) 1797.

Airs, duets and choruses in a new pantomime called

Harlequin and Quixote; or the Magic Arm. (By J. C. Cross.) London, 1797.

Sketch of the Mountain of Miseries; or Harlequin Tormentor, a comic entertainment. . . . (London) 1797.

Songs, Choruses, etc., in the new pantomime of Harlequin's Tour, or the Dominion of Fancy, as performed at the Theatre-Royal, Covent-Royal, etc. London, 1800.

Harlequin's Amulet, or the Magick of Mona. The songs, choruses, etc., with a description of the pantomime. London (1801?).

Dibdin, T., Harlequin Hoax; or a Pantomime Proposed. A comic extravaganza. . . . London, 1814.

Songs, Duets, Choruses, etc., in the new grand pantomime called Harlequin Whittington, or Lord Mayor of London. . . . The Whole arranged by Mr. Farley. London . . . 1814.

The new pantomime of Harlequin and Fortunio; or the Shing-Moo and Thum-Ton, with a sketch of the story, etc. London, 1815.

Airs, choruses and business with a description of the scenery in the new pantomime of Harlequin and the Dandy-Club; or 1818. (London) 1818.

Choruses, recitative and Dialogue with a short description of the Business of each Scene of the new pantomime called Harlequin Munchausen or the Fountain of Love, in which those real facts recorded by that Caleb Traveller, Baron Munchausen, have been varied and expanded according to the admitted privilege of Pantomime. . . . London . . . 1818.

rs, Choruses and Business . . . in a new pantomime of the Silver Arrow; or Harlequin and
the Fairy Pari Banon. . . . (London) 1819.

ırlequin and O'Donoghue, or the White Horse
of Killarney. An . . . equestrian . . . pantomime. . . . (1850.)

ıod-night, Signor Pantaloon. A comic opera in
one act. Adapted from the French. . . .
(1850?)

BIBLIOGRAPHY.

I list here the principal works that I have used exclusive of the scenarios and English and Italian plays catalogued in Appendices A and B. I give the titles, place and date of publication in each case, but sometimes, especially in the case of old books, abbreviate a little by the omission of inessentials.

ACCOLTI, B.: Verginia, comedia . . . recitata nelle solenne noze del magnifico Antonio Spannochi nella inclyta cipta di Siena. Firenze, . . . 1513.

ADEMOLLO, A.: Alessandro VI, Giulio II e Leone X nel Carnevale di Roma. Documenti inediti. (1499-1520.) Firenze, 1886.

Una famiglia di comici italiani nel secolo decimottavo. Firenze, 1885.

Intorno al teatro drammatico italiano dal 1550 in poi. Nuova Antologia, I marzo, 1881, 50 f.

Teatri di Roma nel secolo decimosettimo. Roma, 1888.

ALBERT, M.: Les théâtres de la Foire. (1660-1789.) Paris, 1900. Illustrated.

ALLACCI, L.: Drammaturgia . . . accresciuta. . . . Venezia, . . . 1755.

ALLEN, P. S.: The Medieval Mimus, Modern Philology, VIII, Jan. and July, 1910.

AMICIS, V. DE: La commedia popolare latina e la commedia dell'arte. Napoli, 1882.

L'imitazione latina nella commedia italiana del
secolo XVI. Firenze, 1897.

ANCONA, A. D': Due farse del secolo XVI. Bologna,
1882. (Scelta di curiosità letterarie, No. 187.)

I dodici mesi dell'anno nella tradizione popolare.
Archivio per lo studio delle tradizioni popolari,
II, 1883, 239 f.

Lettere di comici italiani del secolo XVII. Per
le nozze Martini-Benzoni. Pisa, 1893.

Origini del teatro italiano; libri tre; con due
appendici sulla rappresentazione drammatica
del contado toscano e sul teatro mantovano nel
secolo XVI. Torino, 1891, 2d ed., 2 vols.

La poesia popolare italiano. . . . Livorno, 1878.

Sacre Rappresentazioni dei secoli XIV, XV e
XVI. Firenze, 1872, 3 vols.

Studj sulla letteratura italiana dei primi secoli.
Ancona, 1884.

Varietà storiche e letterarie. Milano, 1885. 2
vols.

E COMPARETTI, D. (ed.) : Canti e racconti del popolo
italiano. Torino, 1870–1891. 9 vols.

ANDREINI, F.: Le bravure del Capitano Spavento,
divise in molte ragionamenti in forma di Dia-
logo di F. A. da Pistoia Comico geloso. . . .
Venetia, 1615. (First ed., 1607.)

Nuova aggiunta alle Bravure del Capitano Spavento, di Francesco Andreini. . . . Venetia,
1614.

ANDREINI, G. B.: Lo Specchio, composizione sacra e
poetica; nella quale si rappresenta al vivo
l'Imagine della Comedia, quanto vago, e de-

forme sia alhor che da Comici virtuosi, e viziosi rappresentata viene. . . . Parigi, 1625.

Teatro celeste, nel quale si rappresenta come la Divina bontà habbia chiamato algrado di Beatitudine, e di Santità Comici Penitenti, e martiri. . . . Parigi, 1624.

ANDREINI, ISABELLA: Lettere d'Isabella Andreini Comica gelosa, et academica intenta nominata l'Accesa. . . . Venetia, 1607.

Fragmenti di alcune scritture. . . . Venetia, 1627.

Mirtilla, pastorale. . . . Verona, 1588.

ARISTOTLE: Theory of Poetry and Fine Art, ed. S. H. Butcher. London, 1907. 4th ed.

ARGTEAGA, E.: Le rivoluzioni del teatro musicale italiano dalla sua origini fino al presente. . . . Venezia, 1785. 3 vols.

BANKS, J.: The Unhappy Favorite, or the Earl of Essex. . . . London, 1685.

BAPST, G.: Essai sur l'histoire du théâtre, la mise-en-scène, le décor, le costume, l'éclairage, l'hygiène. Paris, 1893.

BARBIERI, N.: La Supplica, ricoretta ed ampliata. Discorso famigliare di Niccolò Barbieri, detto Beltrame, diretto a quelli che scrivendo o parlando trattano de'Comici, trascurendo i meriti delle azzioni virtuose. . . . Venetia, 1634.

BARTOLI, A.: Scenari inediti della commedia del l'arte, contributo alla storia del teatro popolare italiano. Firenze, 1880. (In Raccolta di opere inedite o rare di ogni secolo della letteratura italiana.)

18

BARTOLI, F.: Notizie istoriche de'comici italiani che fiorirono intorno all'anno MDL fino a'giorni presenti. . . . Padova, 1781. 2 vols.

BASCHET, A.: Les comédiens italiens à la cour de France sous Charles IX, Henri III, Henri IV et Louis XIII. Paris, 1882.

BATES, E. S.: Touring in 1600. Boston and New York, 1911. Illustrated.

BEAUVOIR, R. DE: Il Pulcinella et l'homme des madones. Paris, 1834.

BELANDO, V.: Gl'Amorosi Inganni, comedia . . . di V. B. detto Cataldo Siciliano. . . . Paris, 1609.

BEOLCO, A.: Tutte le opere di Messer Angelo Beolcho. . . . Vicenza, 1584.

BEVILACQUA, E.: Giambattista Andreini e la compagnia dei Fedeli. Giornale Storico della Letteratura Italiana, XXIII, 1894, 76 f., and XXIV, 82 f.

(BIANCHI, L. DE): Le cento e dodici conclusioni in ottava Rima del plusquamperfetto Dottor Gratiano, Partesana da Francolino, comico geloso. . . . Verona, e ristampato in Mantua, n. d. (1585?).

BIANCOLELLI, P. F.: dit Dominique, Nouveau théâtre italien. . . . Anvers, 1713.

E ROMAGNESI: L'Isle du Divorce. . . . La Haye, 1733.

BIRCK, P.: Literarische Anspielungen in den Werken Ben Jonsons. Strasburg, 1908.

BOCCACCIO, G.: Opere volgari. . . . Firenze, 1827–1839. 17 vols.

BOCCHINI, B.: Raccolta di tutte le opere di Bartolomeo Bocchini, detto Zan Muzzina. . . . Modena, n. d. (1665?). Contains La corona Maccheronica. Bologna, 1660.

BOHM, A.: Fonti plautine del Ruzzante. Gior. Stor., XXIX, 1897, 101 f.

BOHN, E.: Orlandus de Lassus als Komponist weltlicher deutscher Lieder. Jahrbuch für münschener Geschichte, I, 1887, 184 f.

BONFIGLI, L.: Un capitolo in morte di Simone da Bologna, comico geloso. Riprodotto da stampa del 1585. . . . Arezzo, per le nozze Carrara-Bernaroli, 1907.

BREWER, J. S., and J. GAIRDNER, ed.: Calendar of Letters and Papers Foreign and Domestic of the Reign of Henry VIII. London, 1880 f., 16 vols.

BROME, R.: Dramatic Works, containing fifteen comedies now first collected. London, 1873. 3 vols.

BROUCHARD, C.: Les origines du théâtre de Lyon. Lyon, 1865.

BROWNE, R., BENTINCK, G. C., and BROWN, H. F., ed.: Calendar of State Papers and MSS. relating to English affairs in the Archives of Venice. London, 1864–1909. 16 vols.

BRUNI, D.: Fatiche comiche. . . . Parigi, 1623. Prologhi. . . . Parigi, 1623. (From ed. of Torino, 1621.)

BURCKHARDT, J.: Civilization of the Renaissance in Italy. Translated by S. G. C. Middlemore. London, 1878.

CAMERINI, E.: Nuovi profili letterari. Milano, 1875. 4 vols.

I precursori del Goldoni. Milano, 1872.

CAMPARDON, E.: Les Spectacles de la Foire. Théâtres, acteurs, sauteurs et danseurs de corde, monstres, géants, nains, animaux curieux ou savants, marionettes, automates, figures de cire et jeux méchaniques des Foires St.-Germain et St.-Laurent, des Boulevards et du Palais-Royal, depuis 1595 jusqu'à 1791. Paris, 1877. 2 vols.

CARDUCCI, G.: Cantilene e ballate, strambotti e madrigali, nei secoli XIII e XIV. Pisa, 1871.

CARRARA, E.: La poesia pastorale. (Storia dei generi letterari italiani, Milano, n. d. (1909), vol. 3.)

CECCHI, G.-M.: Gl'Incantesimi, Comedia. . . . Venetia, 1550.

La Romanesca, commedia, ed. D. Bonamici. Firenze, 1874.

CECCHINI, P.-M.: Breve discorso intorno alle commedie, commedianti et spettatori. . . . Vicenza, 1614.

Frutti delle moderne commedie et avisi a chi le recita. . . . Padova, 1628.

CHALMERS, G.: A Supplemental Apology for the Believers in the Shakespeare Papers. London, 1799.

CHAMBERS, E. K.: Court Performances under Elizabeth. Modern Language Review, II, 1906, October.

Court Performances under James the First. Mod. Lang. Rev., IV, 1909, January.

The Medieval Stage. Oxford, 1904. 2 vols.

CHASLES, P.: Etudes sur l'Espagne et sur les influences de la littérature espagnole en France et en Italie. Paris, 1847.

CHIESA, F. A. DELLA: Teatro delle donne letterate con un breve discorso della preeminenza e perfettione del sesso donnesco. Mondovi, 1620.

CHURCHILL, G. B., and KELLER, W.: Die lateinischen Universitäts-Dramen in der Zeit der Königen Elisabeth. Shakespeare Jahrbuch, XXXIV, 220 f.

CIAMPI, I.: Le Rappresentazioni sacre del medio evo in Italia considerate nella parte comica. Roma, 1865. ·

COHN, A.: Shakespeare in Germany in the sixteenth and seventeenth centuries. . . . London, 1865.

COLLIER, J. P., ed.: Five old plays. London, 1857. (Roxburghe Club, Vol. 69.)

Miscellaneous Tracts. (London) 1870. 5 vols.

History of English Dramatic Poetry to the Time of Shakespeare and Annals of the Stage to the Restoration. London, 1831. 3 vols.

(COLLIER, J. P., ed.): Punch and Judy. With twenty-four illustrations designed and engraved by George Cruikshank and other plates, accompanied by the dialogue of the puppet-show, an account of its origin and of the puppet-plays in England. London, 5th ed., 1870.

CONSTANTINI, A.: La Vie de Scaramouche. Réim-. pression de l'édition originale (1665) avec une introduction et des notes par L. Moland. Paris, 1876.

CORBIN, J.: The Elizabethan Hamlet. London and New York, 1895.

CORNEILLE, P.: Oeuvres . . . ed C. Marty-Laveaux.
. . . Paris, 1862–8, 12 vols.

CORYAT, T.: Coryats Crudities. . . . London, 1776
(from ed. of 1611), 3 vols.

CRANE, T. F.: Italian Popular Tales. Boston and
New York, 1885.

CREIZENACH, W. M. A.: Geschichte des neueren
Dramas. Halle a. S., 1893–1909, 4 vols.

CRESCIMBENI, G.-M. DE': L'istoria della volgar
poesia. . . . Venetia, 1731.   (From   ed.   of
Roma, 1698.)

CROCE, B.: Pulcinella e il personaggio del Napole-
tano in commedia. Roma, 1899.

Un repertorio della commedia dell'arte.   Gior.
Stor., XXXI, 1893, 458 f.

I teatri di Napoli, secolo XV–XVIII. Archivio
per le provincie napoletane, XIV f., and Napoli,
1891.

CUNLIFFE, J. W.: The Influence of Italian on English
Drama. Modern Philology, IV, 1907, No. 4.

Italian Prototypes of the Masque and Dumb-
Show. Publications of the Modern Language
Association of America, XXII, 1907, 140 f.

ed.: Supposes and Jocasta. Two plays translated from the Italian, the first by Geo. Gascoigne, the second by Geo. Gascoigne and F.
Kinwelmersh. . . . Boston and London, 1906.

CUNNINGHAM, P.: Extracts from the Accounts of
the Revels at Court in the Reigns of Queen
Elizabeth and King James I. London, Shakespeare Society, 1842.

DASENT, J. R., ed.: Acts of the Privy Council of England. . . . 1552–1591. London, 1890–1900. 20 vols.

DECOMBE, L.: Les comédiens italiens à Rennes au XVIIIᵉ siecle. Rennes, 1900.

(DESBOULMIERS, J. A. J.): Histoire anecdotique et raisonné du théâtre italien depuis son établissement en France jusqu'à l'année 1769, contenant les analyses des principales pièces et un catalogue de toutes celles tant italiennes que françaises données sur ce théâtre, avec les anecdotes les plus curieuses de la vie et des talens des acteurs et actrices. . . . Paris, 1769, 7 vols.

DESPOIS, E.: Le théâtre français sous Louis XIV. Paris, 1894, 4th ed.

DIEBLERS, A.: Faust-und-Wagner-Pantomimen in England. Anglia, VII, 1884, 341 f.

A Dialogue between Louis le Petit and Harlequin le Grand. London (1705?).

DIETERICH, A.: Pulcinella, pompejanische Wandbilder und römische Satyrspiele. Leipzig, 1897.

DOSSON, S.: Les sujets et les personages de la comédie nationale à Rome. Paris, 1891.

DRIESSEN, O.: Der Ursprung des Harlekin; ein culturgeschichtliches Problem. Berlin, 1904.

DU BOS, J. B.: Critical Reflections on Poetry, Painting and Music. Translated into English by T. Nugent. London, 1748, 5th ed., 3 vols.

EINSTEIN, L.: The Italian Renaissance in England. New York, 1902.

FABIANI, G.: Memoria sopra l'Origine ed instituzioni delle principali Academie della Città de Siena, detti gl'Intronati, dei Rozzi e dei Fisiocritici. . . . Venezia, 1757.

FAINELLI, V.: Chi era Pulcinella? Gior. Stor., LIV, 1909, 59 f.

FALCONI, C.: Le quattro principali maschere italiane nella commedia dell'arte e nel teatro del Goldoni. Roma, 1896.

FERRETTI, E.: Le maschere italiane nella commedia dell'arte e nel teatro di Goldoni. Roma, 1904.

FEST, O.: Der Miles Gloriosus in der französischen Komödie. Erlangen u. Leipzig, 1897.

FEUILLERAT, A., ed.: Documents relating to the Office of the Revels in the time of Queen Elizabeth. . . . London, 1908. (Materialen zur Kunde des älteren englischen Dramas, vol. 21.)
John Lyly. Cambridge (England), 1910.

FEUILLET, O.: Vie de Polichinelle et ses nombreuses aventures. Paris, n. d.

FLAMINI, F.: Il Cinquecento. Milano, n. d. (1898–1900.) (Storia letteraria d'Italia scritta di una Società di Professori, vol. 6.)

FLEAY, F. G.: A Chronicle History of the London Stage, 1559–1642. London, 1890.

FLECHSIG, W. E.: Die Dekorationen der modernen Bühne in Italien von den Anfängen bis zum Schluss des XVIten Jahrhunderts. Dresden, 1894.

FONT, A.: Essai sur Favart et les origines de la comédie mêlée de chant. Toulouse, 1894.

FOURNIER, E., ed.: Le théâtre français au XVI* et XVII* siècles. . . . Paris, n. d., 2 vols. (Collection of comedies.) Illustrated.

FRANCIA, L. DI: Alcune novelle del Decameron illustrate nelle fonti. Gior. Stor., XLIX, 1907, 201 f.

FRESCO, U.: Una tradizione novellistica nella commedia del secolo XVI. Camerino, 1903.

GARZONI, T.: La Piazza universale di tutte le professioni del mondo. . . . Venezia, 1587, and 1616.

GASCOIGNE, G.: Complete Works, ed. J. W. Cunliffe. Cambridge, 1907-10, 2 vols.

GASPARY, A.: Storia della letteratura italiana, tradotta del tedesco da Nicòla Zingarelli. . . . Torino, 1887-91, 2 vols. in 3.

GHERARDI, E.: Le théâtre italien de Gherardi, ou le Recueil Général de toutes les comédies et scènes françaises jouées par les Comédiens Italiens du Roy pendant tout le temps qu'ils ont été au service. . . . Paris, 1738 (from ed. of 1700), 6 vols. Illustrated.

GHILINI, G.: Teatro d' uomini letterati. . . . Venetia, 1647.

GIANNINI, G.: Teatro popolare lucchese. Torino-Palermo, 1895.

    ed.: Canti popolari della montagna lucchese. Torino, 1889.

GILDERSLEEVE, V. C.: Government Regulation of the Elizabethan Drama. New York, 1908.

GIUDICI, E.: Storia del teatro italiano. Milano, 1860.

GOETHE, J. W. VON: Conversations with Eckermann, Translated by J. Oxenford, Bohn's Library. London, 1909.

GOLDONI, C.: Memorie. Venetia, 1788, 3 vols.
    Opere teatrali. Venezia, 1788-1792, 22 vols.

GONZAGA, C.: Gl'Incantesimi, comedia. . . . Venetia, 1592.

Gozzi, C.: Le Fiabe, a cura di E. Masi. Bologna, 1884, 2 vols.

Memoirs of Count Carlo Gozzi, translated into English by J. A. Symonds . . . with Essays on Italian Impromptu Comedy, Gozzi's Life, the Dramatic Fables and Pietro Longhi, by the Translator. London, 1890, 2 vols. Illustrated.

Graf, A.: Attraverso il Cinquecento. Torino, 1888.

Graf, H.: Der Miles Gloriosus im englischen Drama. . . . Rostock, 1891.

Grazzini, A.-F.: Commedie di A.-F. Grazzini, detto Il Lasca, riscontrate sui migliori codici . . . da P. Fanfani. Firenze, 1859.

Greene, R.: Life and complete Works in prose and verse . . . ed. A. B. Grosart. London, 1881–86. (Huth Library.)

Greg, W. W., ed.: Henslowe's Diary, 1591–1609. London, 1904–8.

ed.: Henslowe Papers, being documents supplementary to Henslowe's Diary. London, 1907.

Grendon, F.: The Anglo-Saxon Charms. New York, 1909.

Grysar, C. G.: Der römische Mimus. Sitzungsberichte der kais. Akademie, Wien. Phil-hist. Klasse, XII, 1854, 237 f.

Guillemot, J.: La comédie dans le vaudeville. Revue contemporaine, 2e série, LI, 1866, 92 f. and 713 f.

Halliwell-Phillips, J. O.: Dictionary of archaic and provincial Words, obsolete phrases, proverbs and ancient customs from the 14th century. London, 1881, 10th ed., 2 vols.

ed.: Tarlton's Jests and News out of Purgatory. London, 1844. (Shakespeare Society.)

.... The Harlequins. A Comedy after the Manner of the Théâtre italien, in one act and in prose. ... London, 1753.

HAZLITT-DODSLEY: A Select Collection of Old Plays by R. Dodsley. Chronologically arranged, revised and enlarged by W. C. Hazlitt. London, 1874–6, 4th ed., 15 vols.

.... Harlequin Methodist, To the Tune of An Old Woman cloathed in Gray. ... London (1759?).

HEYWOOD, T.: Apology for Actors, in three books. (From ed. of 1612.) London, 1841. (Shakespeare Society Publications.)
Dramatic Works. ... London, 1874, 6 vols.

HUNTER, J.: Popular Romances of the West of England. London, 1865.

INGEGNERI, A.: De la poesia rappresentativa e del modo di rappresentare le favole sceniche. Ferrara, 1598.

... La Descrittione del nuovo riaprimento dell'-Accademia Intronata. L'Oratione in lode di quella e l'imprese di suoi Accademici. ... Siena, n. d. (1603?).

JAMES I.: Workes of the most high and mightie prince, James, ... London, 1616.

JARRO, cf. Piccini.

JONSON, B.: Works, with notes critical and explanatory and a biographical memoir by W. Gifford, with introduction and appendices by Lieut.-Col. Cunningham. London, 1816, 9 vols.
Staple of News, ed. De Winter. New York, 1905. (Yale Studies in English.)

Volpone, ed. H. B. Wilkins. Paris, 1906. (Dissertation.)

JUSSERAND, J. J.: Shakespeare en France sous l'ancien régime. Paris, 1898.

KLEIN, J. L.: Geschichte des italienischen Dramas. Leipzig, 1866-9, 4 vols. in 5.

KLINGLER, O.: Die Comédie Italienne nach der Sammlung von Gherardi. Strasburg, 1902.

KOEPPEL, E.: Quellen-Studien zu den Dramen Ben Jonsons, John Marstons u. Beaumont u. Fletchers. Erlangen, 1895. (Münchener Beiträge zur romanischen u. englischen Philologie, vol. 11.)

Quellen-Studien zu den Dramen G. Chapmans, Ph. Massingers, u. J. Fords. Strasburg, 1897. (Quellen u. Forschungen zur Sprach- u. Culturgeschichte der Germanischen Völker, No. 82.)

KYD, T.: Works, ed. F. S. Boas. Oxford, 1901.

LANSON, G.: Hommes et Livres; études morales et littéraires. Paris, 1895.

LANGBAIN, G.: An Account of the English Dramatick Poets. . . . Oxford, 1691.

LEE, VERNON, cf. Paget.

LEMERCIER DE NEUVILLE: Histoire anecdotique des marionettes modernes. Paris, 1892.

LOEHNER, E. VON: Carlo Goldoni e le sue Memoire. Frammenti. Archivio veneto, XXIII, part I, 45 f.

LOMBARDO, G.-D.: Nuovo Prato di Prologhi. . . . Venetia, 1628.

LOVARINI, E.: Notizie sui parenti e sulla vita del Ruzzante. Gior. Stor., XI, 1888, 177 f.

LYONNET, H.: Pulcinella et compagnie. . . . Paris, 1901.

MAGNIN, C.: Histoire des marionettes en Europe depuis l'antiquité jusqu'à nos jours. Paris, 1862, 2d ed.

Les commencements de la comédie italienne en France. Revue des deux mondes, XX, 1847, 1090 f.

MAGRINI, A.: Il teatro olimpico, nuovamente descritto ed illustrato. Padova, 1847.

MAGRINI, G. B.: I tempi, la vita e gli scritti di Carlo Gozzi. Benevento, 1883.

MAILLET-DUCLAIRON, A.: Essai sur la connoissance des théâtres français. . . . Paris, 1751.

MALONE, E.: An Historical Account of the English Stage. London, 1805. (In Chalmers ed. of Shakespeare's Plays, vol. I.)

MANNINGHAM, J.: Diary, 1602-3, ed. J. Bruce. Westminster, 1868. (Pub. Camden Society, XCIX.)

MANZONI, L.: Libro di Carnevale dei secoli XV e XVI. Bologna, 1881. (Scelta di curiosità letterarie, CLXXXII.)

MARAZIN, J.: Le théâtre des boulevards et la comédie improvisée. Limoges, 1886.

MARSTON, J.: Works, ed. A. H. Bullen. London, 1887, 3 vols.

(MARTINELLI, T.): Compositions de Rhetorique de M. Don Arlequin. . . . (Paris, c. 1599?) Unique copy in the Bibliothèque Nationale, Paris, Y2-922.

MARTUCCI, G.: Un comico dell'arte. Nuova Antologia, Ser. II, XLVIII, 1884, 618 f.

MAZZI, C.: La congrega dei Rozzi di Siena nel secolo XVI, con appendice di documenti, bibliografia e illustrazioni concernenti quella ed altre accademie e congreghe senesi. Firenze, 1882, 2 vols.
Le feste senesi per la Madonna d'Agosto nel 1546. Nuova Ant., Ser. II, XXVIII, 577 f.

MEISSNER, J.: Die englischen Komödianten zur Zeit Shakespeares in Osterreich. Wien, 1884.

MERCEY, F.: Le théâtre en Italie: Stentorello. Revue des deux mondes, XXI, 1840.
Les quatre Masques du théâtre italien. Ib., XXIII, 703 f.

MERES, F.: Five Sections of "Palladis Tamia" . . . in C. M. Ingleby's Shakespeare Allusion Books, 1874. (Pub. New Shaks. Soc., Ser. 4, No. 1.)

MERLINI, D.: Saggio di recerche sulla satira contro il villano. Torino, 1894.

MEZIÈRES, A. J. F.: Prédecesseurs et contemporains de Shakespeare. Paris, 1894.

MIDDLETON, J.: Works, ed. A. H. Bullen. London, 1885–6, 8 vols.

(MILLER, J.): Harlequin-Horace or the Art of Modern Poetry. . . . London, 1791.

MINTURNO, A. S.: L'arte poetica, nella quale si contengono i precetti eroici, tragici, comici. . . . Napoli, 1725. (From ed. 1564.)

MOLAND, L.: Les Méprises, comédies de la Renaissance racontées. Paris, 1869.
Molière et la comédie italienne. Paris, 1867.

MOLIÈRE (J. B. Poquelin): Oeuvres . . . ed. E. Despois and P. Mesnard. Paris, 1873–93, 13 vols.
Oeuvres complètes. . . . Ed. L. Moland. Paris, 1881, 12 vols.

MONTAIGNE, M. DE: Voyage en Italie, 1581. Ed. A. d'Ancona, Città di Castello, 1895.
Essays translated by John Florio. London, Temple Classics, 6 vols.

MONNIER, P.: Le Quattrocento. Paris, 1908, 2 vols.

MOTTA, E.: Rappresentazioni sceniche in Venezia nel 1493 in occasione della venuta di Beatrice d'Este. Gior. Stor., VII, 1886, 386 f.

MOUNTFORD: The Life and Death of Dr. Faustus made into a farce by Mr. Mountford, with the Humours of Harlequin and Scaramouche. London, 1697. Reprinted and edited by O. Francke, Heilbronn, 1886.

MURRAY, J. R.: The Influence of Italian upon English Literature during the 16th and 17th centuries. Cambridge, 1886.

MURRAY, J. T.: English Dramatic Companies, 1558–1642. . . . London, 1910, 2 vols.

(MUNDAY, A.): Memoir of A. M., ed. J. P. Collier, London, 1851. (Pub. Shaks. Soc.)

NASH, T.: Complete Works, ed. A. B. Grosart. London, 6 vols. (Huth Library.)
Works, ed. . . . R. B. McKerrow. London, 1904–10, 5 vols.

NICHOLS, J.: Progresses and Public Processions of Queen Elizabeth. London, 1823, new ed., 3 vols.
Progresses, Processions and Magnificent Festivities of King James I. London, 1828, 4 vols.

OTTONELLI: Della Christiana Moderatione del theatro libro, detto l'Instanza per supplicare a'signori superiori che si moderi Christianamente il theatro dall'oscenità e da ogni altro eccesso nel recitare, secondo la dottrina di S. Tomaso e d'altri Theologi. . . . Firenze, 1652.

PAGET, V. (Vernon Lee): Studies of the Eighteenth Century in Italy. Chicago, 1908, 2d ed.

PARFAICT, C., and PARFAICT, F.: Dictionaire des théâtres de Paris contenant . . . extraits de celles (pièces) qui ont été jouées par les Comédiens Italiens depuis leur rétablissement en 1716. . . . Paris, 1756, 7 vols.

Histoire de l'ancien théâtre italien depuis son origine en France jusqu'à sa suppression en l'année 1697. Suivie des extraits ou canevas des meilleures Pièces Italiennes qui n'ont jamais été imprimées. Paris, 1767.

Histoire du théâtre français. . . . Paris, 1745–9. 15 vols.

. . . . Les Parodies du nouveau théâtre italien ou recueil des parodies représentées sur le théâtre de l'Hôtel de Bourgogne par les comédiens italiens ordinaires du Roy. . . . Paris, 1738, 4 vols.

PELLIZARO, G. B.: La commedia del secolo XVI e la novellistica anteriora e contemporanea in Italia. Vicenza, 1901.

PERRUCCI, A.: Dell'arte rappresentativa premeditata ed all'improvvisa. . . . Napoli, 1699.

PETRAI, G.: Maschere e Burattini. Roma, 1885.

Lo spirito delle maschere. Torino-Roma, 1901.

PIANGIANI, O.: Vocabolario etimologico della lingua italiana. Roma-Milano, 1907, 2 vols.

PICCINI, G., (Jarro): L'epistolario d'Arlecchino (Tristano Martinelli, 1556–1631). Firenze, 1896.

L'origine della Maschera di Stentorello. (Luigi del Buono, 1751–1832.) Firenze, 1898.

PICCOLOMINI, A.: L'Amor Costante, comedia. . . . Venetia, 1540.

PICOT, E.: Le monologue dramatique dans l'ancien théâtre français. Romania, XVI, 1887, 438 f.

PITRÈ, G. L.: Fiabe, novelle e racconti popolari siciliani. Palermo, 1875, 4 vols.

Studj di poesia popolare. Palermo, 1872.

Usi e costumi, credenze e prejudizi del popolo Siciliano. Palermo, 1889, 4 vols.

QUADRIO, F. S.: Della storia e ragione d'ogni poesia. Bologna e Milano, 1739–49, 4 vols. in 6.

Raccolta di Melodrammi giocosi scritti nel Secolo XVIII. . . . Milano, 1826, 3 vols. (Società tipografia de'classici italiani, Vol. 345.)

RAO, C.: L'argute e facete lettere. . . . Pavia, 1573.

RASI, L.: I comici italiani; biografia, bibliografia, iconografia. Firenze, 1897, 2 vols.

RAYNAUD, G.: La Mesnie Hellequin. Paris, 1891, 51 f., in Études romanes dédiées à Gaston Paris.

RE, E.: La commedia veneziana e il Goldoni. Gior. Stor., LVIII, 1911, 367 f.

REINHARDTSTOETTNER, K. VON: Die plautinischen Lustspiele in spätere Bearbeitungen. Leipzig, 1880.

Über die Beziehungen der italienischen Litteratur zum bayrischen Hofe und ihre Pflege am demselben. Jahrbuch f. mün. Geschichte, I, 1887, 93 f.

RENIER, R.: Appunti sul contrasto fra la madre e la

figliuola bramosa di marito. In Miscellanea nuziale Rossi-Teiss. Trento, 1897.

Arlecchino. Fanfulla di domenica, Anno XXVI, 1904, No. 12.

BENNERT, H. A.: The Spanish Stage in the Time of Lope de Vega. New York, 1909.

RIBBECK, O.: Agroikos; eine ethologische Studie. Leipzig, 1885.

Alazon; ein Beitrag zur antiken Ethologie und zur Kenntniss der griechisch-römischen Komödie nebst Übersetzung des Plautinischen Miles Gloriosus. Leipzig, 1882.

RICCI, C.: I teatri di Bologna nei secoli XVII e XVII, storia annedotica. Bologna, 1888.

RICCOBONI, L.: Histoire de l'ancien théâtre italien depuis la décadence de la comédie latine, avec un catalogue des tragédies et comédies italiennes imprimées depuis l'an 1500 jusqu'à l'an 1650. . . . Paris, 1728.

An Historical and Critical Account of the Theatres in Europe, viz., the Italian, Spanish, French, English, Dutch, Flemish and German theatres, in which is contained a Review of the Manners, Persons and Characters of the Actors; intermixed with many curious dissertations upon the Drama. . . . London, 1741.

Dell'arte rappresentativa. . . . Londra, 1728.

RIGAL, E.: Alexandre Hardy et le théâtre français à la fin du XVI* et au commencement du XVII* siècles. Paris, 1890.

Molière. Paris, 1908, 2 vols.

Le théâtre français avant la période classique, fin

du XVI° et commencement du XVII° siècles. Paris, 1901.

Le théâtre de la Renaissance. (In Petit de Julleville, Histoire de la langue et de la litérature française, III, 267 f.)

(RODET, J. B.) Colombine philosophe soi-disant, comédie . . . mêlée de vaudevilles. Paris, 1803.

ROEDIGER, F.: Contrasti antichi; Cristo e Satana. Firenze, 1887.

ROMANO, E.: I Contrasti fra Carnevale e Quaresima nella letteratura italiana. Pavia, 1907.

ROSA, S.: Satire, odi e lettere, illustrate di G. Carducci. Firenze, 1860.

ROSSI, N.: Discorsi sulla commedia. . . . Vicenza, 1589.

ROSSI, V.: Le lettere di Messer Andrea Calmo . . . con introduzione ed illustrazioni di V. Rossi. Torino, 1880.

Il Quattrocento. Milano, 1897–8. (Storia letteraria d'Italia scritta da una Società di Professori, vol. V.)

RUBIERI, E.: Storia della poesia popolare italiana. Firenze, 1877.

RYE, W. B.: England as seen by Foreigners in the days of Elizabeth and James I. London, 1865.

SALZA, ABD-EL-KADER: Un dramma pastorale inedito del Cinquecento. (L'Irifile di L. de Sommi.) Gior. Stor., LIV, 1909, 103 f.

SAND, M.: Masques et Bouffons. Paris, 1860, 3 vols. Illustrated.

Le théâtre des marionettes. . . . Paris, 1890.

SARTI, C. I.: Il teatro dialettale bolognese. Bologna, 1895.

SAVIOTTI, A.: Feste carnevalesche in Pesaro nel 1527. Pisa, per nozze Braggio-Guerrini, n. d.

Feste e spettacoli nel seicento. Gior. Stor., XLI, 1903, 42 f.

SCHELLING, F.: Elizabethan Drama, 1558–1642. . . . Boston and New York, 1908, 2 vols.

SCHERILLO, M.: La commedia dell'arte in Italia, studj e profilj. Torino, 1884.

La commedia dell'arte, in La vita italiana nel seicento. Firenze, 1897.

La prima commedia musicale a Venezia. Gior. Stor., I, 1883, 230 f.

Storia letteraria dell'opera buffa napoletana. Napoli, 1883.

SCHLAGER, J. E.: Uber das alte Wiener Hof-Theater. Sitzungsberiche der kais. Akademie, Wien. Phil.-hist.-Klasse, VI, 147 f.

SCHLEGEL, A. W.: Lectures on Dramatic Art and Literature. Trans. J. Black. Bohn's Library. London, 1904.

SCHMIDT, A.: Shakespeare Lexicon. Berlin, 1874–5, 2 vols.

SCHÜCKING, L. L.: Studien über die stoffliche Beziehungen der englischen Komödie zur italienischen bis Lilly. Halle a. S., 1901. (Studien zur englischen Philologie, Vol. 9.)

SCOTT, M. A.: Elizabethan Translations from the Italian. Pub. Mod. Lang. Assoc. of America, X, 249 f.; XI, 377 f.; XIII, 42 f.; XIV, 465 f. Baltimore, 1895–9.

SENIGAGLIA, G.: Capitan Spavento. Firenze, 1899.

SHAKESPEARE, W.: Works, ed. W. A. Neilson, Cambridge, Mass., 1906.

New Variorum ed. H. H. Furness. Twelfth
Night, Hamlet, et al. Philadelphia, 1871 f.

SHARPLEY, H.: A Realist of the Aegean. (Translation of the Mimes of Herodas.) London, 1906.

SIDNEY, P.: Defense of Poetry, ed. A. S. Cook.
Boston, 1898.

SOLERTI, A.: Gl'albori del melodrama. Milano-
Palermo-Napoli, 1904, 3 vols.

FERRARA: la corte estense nella seconda metà del
secolo XVI. Città di Castello, 1899. 2d ed.

La rappresentazione della Calandra a Lione nel
1548. P. 693 f. in Raccolta di studj critici dedi-
cata ad Alessandro d'Ancona. . . . Firenze,
1901.

E D. LANZA: Il teatro ferrarese nella seconda metà
del secolo XVI. Gior. Stor., XVIII, 1891, 148 f.

SOMMI, L. DE': Le nozze di Mercurio e di Philologia
(1584), ed. A. Neri. Gior. Stor., XI, 413 f.

SPERRHAKE, W.: Ben Jonsons The Case is Altered
und seine Quellen. Halle, 1905.

SPINGARN, J. E., ed.: Critical Essays of the Seventeenth Century. Oxford, 1908–9, 3 vols.

History of Literary Criticism in the Renaissance.
New York, 1908, 2d ed.

STEVENSON, J., and CROSBY, A. J., ed.: Calendar of
State Papers of the Reign of Elizabeth, 1558–82.
London, 1863–1910, 16 vols.

STIEFEL, A. L.: G. Chapman und das italienischen
Drama. Shakespeare Jahrbuch, XXXV, 1899.

Lope de Rueda und das italienischen Lustspiel.
Zeitschrift für romanische Philologie, XV, 1897,
183 f. and 318 f.

Zur Quellen-Frage von J. Fletchers *Monsieur Thomas*. Englische Studien, XXXVI, 1906, 238 f.

STIER, M.: Chapmans *All Fools* mit besondere Berücksichtigung seiner Quellen. Halle, 1904.

STOPPATO, L.: La commedia popolare in Italia. Padova, 1887.

STUART, D. C.: Honor in the Spanish Drama. Romanic Review, I, 1910, 247 f.

Théâtre des Boulevards ou Recueil des Parades. Mahon, 1756, 3 vols.

Teatro comico fiorentino, contenente 20 delle più rare commedie citate da' signori accademici della Crusca. Firenze, 1750, 4 vols.

Teatro italiano antico. . . . Milano, 1808, 10 vols.

THORNDIKE, A. H.: The pastoral element in English drama before 1605. Modern Language Notes, XIV, 1899, No. 4.

Tragedy. Boston and New York, 1908.

TIRABOSCHI, A.: Vocabolario dei dialetti bergamaschi antichi e moderni. Bergamo, 1873, 2d ed.

TOLDO, P.: Di alcuni scenari inediti della commedia dell'arte et della loro relazione col teatro di Molière. R. Accademia di scienze di Torino, Atti, XLII, 1907, 460 f.

Etudes sur le théâtre de Regnard. Revue d'histoire littéraire de la France, X, 1.

Figaro et ses origines. Milan, 1893.

Molière en Italie, . . . Journal of Comparative Literature, I, 1903, 66 f., 229 f., 366 f.

Nella baracca dei burattini. Gior. Stor., LI, 1908, 1 f.

TORRACA, F.: Il teatro italiano nei secoli XIII, XIV, XV. Firenze, 1885.

TRAUTMANN, K.: Italienische Schauspieler am bayrischen Hofe. Jahrbuch für münschener Geschichte, I, 193 f.

TURRI, V.: Dizionario storico manuele della letteratura italiano. Roma, 1900, 2 vols., 2d ed.

Tutti i Trionfi, carri, mascherati o canti carnascialeschi andati per Firenze dal Tempo del Magnifico Lorenzo de'Medici fino all'Anno 1559. Cosmopoli, 1750, 2 vols., 2d ed.

VALENTINI, F.: Abhandlung über die Komödie aus dem Stegreif und die italienischen Masken. (German and Italian texts.)   Berlin, 1826.

VOLLHARDT, K.: Die Quelle von Molières *Tartuffe*. Archiv für das Studium der neueren Sprachen u. Litteraturen, XCI, No. 1.

WARD, A. W.: History of English Dramatic Literature. London, 1899, 3 vols.

WESSELOFSKY, A.: Alichino e Aredodesa.   Gior. Stor., XI, 325 f.

WHETSTONE, G.: The . . . Historye of Promos and Cassandra, divided into two commical Discourses. In Hazlitt's Shakespeare's Library, London, 1875, Vol. VI.

WYNDHAM, H. S.: Annals of Covent Garden Theatre from 1732 to 1897. London, 1906, 2 vols.

ZANETTI, Z.: La medicina delle nostre donne, studio folk-lorico. Città di Castello, 1892.

INDEX.

Printed in the United Kingdom by
Lightning Source UK Ltd., Milton Keynes
142231UK00001B/3/A

9 781103 120246